Critical Thinking in Psychology

Social Psychology

Critical Thinking in Psychology series – titles in the series

Critical Thinking in Psychology

Social Psychology

Jane Callaghan

and

Lisa Lazard

Series Editor: Dominic Upton

First published in 2011 by Learning Matters Ltd

British Library Cataloguing in Publication Data
A CIP record for this book is available from the British Library

ISBN 978 0 8725 280 7

This book is also available in the following ebook formats:

Adobe ebook   ISBN 978 0 85725 282 1
ePUB ebook   ISBN 978 0 85725 281 4
Kindle   ISBN 978 0 85725 283 8

Cover and text design by Toucan Design
Project management by Diana Chambers
Typeset by Kelly Winter
Printed and bound in Great Britain by Short Run Press Ltd, Exeter, Devon

Learning Matters Ltd
20 Cathedral Yard
Exeter EX1 1HB
Tel: 01392 215560
E-mail: info@learningmatters.co.uk
www.learningmatters.co.uk

Contents

Acknowledgements

We would like to jointly thank series editor, Dominic Upton, and Julia Morris and Kate Lodge of Learning Matters for their helpful comments on draft chapters and support during the writing of this book.

Jane Callaghan would like to thank Tim Simmons for his help in slaying the referencing demon, and for his endless support. She would also like to thank her lovely daughter Tara for being so patient and tolerant of the mother-in-front-of-computer phenomenon. And thanks too to Zebedee, wherever we may find him. She dedicates this book to her mother and father, Moira and Bernard Callaghan.

Lisa Lazard would like to thank her colleagues for sharing their own perspectives on criticality, which have, over the years, informed her own thinking. She would also like to acknowledge Dexter Pearce-Lazard for adding an interesting layer to the experience of writing this book and Darren Pearce-Lazard who undoubtedly made it easier.

Series editor's introduction

Studying psychology at degree level

Being a student of psychology is an exciting experience – the study of mind and behaviour is a fascinating and sprawling journey of discovery. Yet, studying psychology at degree level brings with it new experiences, skills and knowledge. This book, one in a comprehensive new series, brings you this psychological knowledge, but importantly it also brings with it directions and guidance on the skills and experiences you should also be developing during your studies.

Psychology is a growing discipline – in scope, breadth and numbers. It is one of the fastest growing subjects to study at GCSE and A level, and the number of students studying the subject at university has grown considerably over the past decade. Indeed, psychology is now one of the most popular subjects in UK higher education, with the most recent data suggesting that there are some 45,000 full-time students currently enrolled on such programmes (compiled from Higher Education Statistics Agency (HESA); statistics available at www.hesa.ac.uk) and it is likely that this number has not yet peaked.

The popularity of psychology is related to a number of reasons, not the least of which is its scope and breadth – psychology is a sprawling discipline that seeks to analyse the human mind and behaviour, which is fascinating in its own right. Furthermore, psychology aims to develop other skills – numeracy, communication and critical analysis to name but a few. For these reasons, many employers seek out psychology graduates – they bring a whole host of skills to the workplace and any activities in which they may be involved. This book brings together the knowledge base associated with psychology along with these critical skills. By reading this book, and engaging with the exercises, you will develop these skills and, in this way, will do two things: excel in your studies and your assessments, and put yourself at the front of the queue of psychology graduates when it comes to demonstrating these skills to potential employers.

Developing higher-level skills

Only about 15 to 20 per cent of psychology graduates end up working as professional psychologists. The subject is a useful platform for many other careers because of the skills it helps you to develop. It is useful to employers because of its subject-specific skills – knowing how people act is pertinent in almost any job and is particularly relevant to those that involve working directly with people. Psychology also develops a number of generic and transferable skills that are both essential to effective undergraduate study and valuable to employers. These include higher-level intellectual skills, such as critical and creative thinking, reflection, evaluation and analysis, and other skills such as communication, problem solving, understanding and using data, decision making, organisational skills, teamworking and IT skills.

The Quality Assurance Agency in Higher Education (QAA) subject benchmarks for psychology, which set out the expectations of a psychology degree programme, highlight the sorts of skills with which your degree should equip you. The British Psychological Society (BPS), which accredits your degree course, acknowledges that graduate employability is an important area of focus for universities and expects that opportunities for skills development should be well embedded within your programme of study. Indeed, this is a major focus of your study – interesting as psychology is, you will need and want employment at the end of your degree.

The activities in this book have been designed to help you build the underpinning skills that you need in order to become an independent and lifelong learner, and to meet the relevant requirements of your programme of study, the QAA benchmarks and the needs of both you and your potential employer.

Many students find it a challenge to develop these skills, often learning them out of context of their study of the core knowledge domains of psychology. The activities in this book aim to help you to learn these skills at the same time as developing your core psychology knowledge, giving you opportunities continuously to practise skills so that they become second nature to you. The tasks provide guidance on what the skill is, how to develop basic competence in it and how to progress to further expertise. At the same time, development of these skills will enable you to better understand and retain the core content of your course – being able to evaluate, analyse and interpret content is the key to deepening understanding.

The skills that the activities in this book will help you to develop are as presented in Table 0.1.

Table 0.1: Skills developed in this book

Intellectual skills	Other skills
• Critical and creative thinking	• Communication: oral, visual and written
• Reflection	• Problem solving
• Analysing and evaluating	• Understanding and using data
	• Decision making
	• Organisational skill
	• Teamwork
	• Information technology
	• Independent learning

In addition to review and essay questions, each chapter in this book will contain novel learning activities. Your responses will be guided through these activities and you will then be able to apply these skills within the context of developmental psychology.

Features in this book

At the start of each chapter there is a list of **learning outcomes**. These are a set of bullet points that highlight the outcomes you should achieve – both skills and knowledge – if you read and engage with the chapter. This will mean at the outset of the chapter that we try to orientate you, the reader, and demonstrate the relevance of the topic.

We have also included learning features throughout the individual chapters in order to demonstrate key points and promote your learning.

- **Bulleted lists** are used within the chapter to convey key content messages.

- **Case studies** are included as part of a critical thinking activity.

- **Tasks** are a series of short review questions on the topic that will help you assess yourself and your current level of knowledge – use these to see if you can move on or whether you need to reread and review the material.

- **Critical thinking activities** allow for the review of the text by encouraging key critical and creative thinking about the psychology material presented, and provide development of the generic skills. Each of these activities is followed by a **Critical thinking review** which unpicks the activity for you, showing how it should have been tackled, the main skill it develops and other skills you may have used in completing the activity.

- **Skill builder activities** use the psychology material presented in the text but focus on one particular transferable skill as outlined in Table 0.1. Each of these activities is followed by a **Skill builder review** which may provide further hints and which makes explicit the skills it helps to develop and the benefits of completing the activity.

At the end of the chapter there will also be some pedagogic features that you will find useful in developing your abilities.

- **Assignments** assess your awareness and understanding of the topic through a series of questions for you to discuss and debate with your colleagues. You can also use these questions as revision materials.

- **Summary: what you have learned** appears at the end of each chapter as a series of bullet points. We hope that these summaries will match the learning outcomes presented at the outset of the chapter.

- **Further reading** includes items that will provide additional information – some of these are in journals and some are full texts. For each we have provided the rationale for suggesting the additional reading and we hope that these will direct you accordingly.

- **Glossary** entries are highlighted in bold in the text on their first appearance.

- Finally, there is a full set of **references** to support all of the material presented in this text.

We hope you enjoy this text, which is part of a series of textbooks covering the complete knowledge base of psychology.

Professor Dominic Upton
September 2011

Introduction

This book is primarily concerned with understanding human beings as *social* beings. In common with many people who study psychology, as undergraduates we were interested in understanding why people do the things they do and why they are the people they are. Like most undergraduates we were interested in the question, 'What makes people tick?' Imagine our disappointment, then, when we first encountered the formal study of psychology in our first year of university. We were suddenly confronted with descriptions of people as machines, as processors, as biological entities. In short, these were descriptions that were completely alien to us, and did not resonate with our original interest in psychology at all. Where was the human element? Where was the theorisation of people's experiences and interactions? Were we really just very elegant human computers?

Social psychology potentially offers engagement with the questions we find more interesting about human life. But even here, we have encountered many disappointments. Too often we were met with highly cognitive accounts of complex social problems, theoretical ideas that seemed too obvious to be useful, and experimental studies that seemed to be so out of touch with the world that they attempted to explain that generalising their findings to everyday life seemed a step too far. Yet, in among all this, we spotted some really useful ideas too, about being human, about being social, about living in our fast-paced, contradictory and often bemusing world. It is these moments of resonance, and some of the excitement of social psychology, that we hope to share with you.

In this book, we attempt to explore some of the key ideas that characterise both traditional and critical social psychology. In each chapter, we seek to trace a path through a particular 'topic' in social psychology – attitudes, gender, race, etc. We explore in each chapter what is useful and exciting, what we can learn from the mistakes of the past, and how we might build a social psychology that can make sense of the complexity of human social experience.

In Chapter 1, *Attitudes*, we explore the central focus on *attitudes* in psychological research. We consider popular questions often asked by psychologists such as: What are attitudes? How do they work? Do attitudes predict behaviour? We start off by looking at how these questions have been tackled by famous theories such as the theory of reasoned action and the theory of planned behaviour. Threaded through this discussion is a critical questioning of individualistic understandings of attitudes and human behaviour, which leads to a consideration of alternative understandings of attitudes that have been developed in discursive psychological work.

Chapter 2, *Attributions*, is interested in how and why people come up with causal explanations of various aspects of their social lives. We review key developments in attribution theory and core concepts such as sources of bias in attribution. We suggest that in predominant social cognitive explanations of attribution there is a tendency to view people as information processors, and we consider the limitations of thinking about human behaviour in this mechanistic way. We apply some ideas around attribution to the everyday practice of making excuses, using applied examples of offender treatment.

In Chapter 3, *Stereotypes, prejudice and racism,* we explore how social psychological work has explained the social phenomena of racism, racial prejudice and discrimination. We consider accounts like realistic conflict theory, which looks at conflict between social groups as a result of competition, and social cognitive accounts, like stereotyping and social identity theory, which suggest that phenomena like prejudice and racism emerge as a consequence of the human tendency to categorise. We discuss Tajfel and Turner's influential notion of the minimal group, critiquing its individualist assumptions, and unpacking the ideological consequences of under-standing political phenomena like race and racism in terms of cognitive distortions. We go on to examine alternative conceptualisations of racism, drawing on discursive accounts of these phenomena, and explore the notion of 'the other' in an explanation of racism.

Chapter 4, *Social influence: persuasion*, explores how we might be influenced by direct and implicit appeals from other people to change our attitudes (and sometimes consequently our behaviours). We look at how social psychological research has considered persuasion, focusing on the effective-ness of persuasive communication, and how models like cognitive dissonance understand the way that our self-perceptions intersect with persuasive communication to produce attitude and behaviour change. We explore the limitations of these models, questioning the degree to which they can really be understood as *social* psychological theories. We conclude the chapter with a consideration of discursive approaches to persuasion, exploring whether these take better account of the social aspects of influence in persuasive communications.

In Chapter 5, *Social influence: conformity, compliance and group processes*, we explore the issue of social influence from a different perspective. How does the behaviour or influence of other people impact on our own behaviour? We look at compliance (acceding to the instructions of another person, often an authority figure), considering the work of Adorno et al. on authoritarianism and Milgram on compliance. We look at the social processes that produce conformity, looking at Zimbardo's study on social roles, Asch's experiments and more contemporary extensions of these ideas. We develop a critique of the linear operation of power in these approaches and consider the manner in which they deal with ideas of individual autonomy and agency. We explore how social psychological theories have conceptualised social influence as a function of individual and interpersonal processes (social influence as cognitive or perceptual distortion, or as a result of individuals' personal characteristics and social roles). In the second half of the chapter, we consider work that is more 'socially' oriented in its explanations of group processes. This offers us the opportunity to consider the notions of reductionism, determinism and agency, exploring group influence in terms of phenomena like 'mob rule', 'group think' and more nuanced social accounts like minority influence. We take a critical look at the often unexamined constructs that thread through these kinds of conceptualisations, like normalisation, regulation and resistance.

In Chapter 6, *Prosocial behaviour*, we explore the question of how and when people behave in ways that are helpful to others. We consider critically the evolutionary viewpoint that altruistic behaviour is not strictly possible – that even behaviour that appears altruistic is selfish when understood in an evolutionary context, as such behaviour is always oriented to survival of the individual's genetic endowment. We explore social psychological approaches that depict this idea of human behaviour as essentially selfish, looking at models like social exchange theory and research around bystander intervention. We also consider research that suggests that human beings can be prosocial, that helpful behaviour is mediated by our sense of empathy. We also look critically at the theoretical presumptions of selfishness that underpin much research on prosocial behaviour, suggesting that perhaps the theoretical (and other) positioning of researchers in this area has tended to predispose them to a view that people do not help each other, obscuring the range of conditions and contexts under which people engage in prosocial and altruistic behaviour.

In Chapter 7, *Gender and social psychology*, we discuss psychology's focus on gender and question why psychology as a discipline is so interested in people as gendered. We start off by exploring distinctions made between the biological and social basis of gender. This provides the backdrop for discussions of social psychological accounts of gender, which include social learning theory of gender development and gender schema theory. The second half of the chapter draws attention to the important contributions made by feminist social psychology in understanding gender. We draw attention to how feminist work has crucially flagged up the importance of power when researching gender and gendered relationships and how this has often gone unarticulated in mainstream theories of gender. We explore how gender works as a power relationship that has disadvantaged women in various ways across history. We explore feminist challenges to unequal treatment and what this might mean when exploring gender in psychological research.

Chapter 8, *Close relationships*, explores the various social psychological models that purport to explain the phenomenon of love. Social psychological accounts of love and personal relationships presume a universality to the construct of love itself, generally assuming that, while there might be some cultural variation in the expression and experience of love, there is nonetheless an essence to love and romantic attraction that transcends cultural context. Theoretical accounts focus on phenomena such as cognitive prototypes of love, schematic 'love stories', love 'styles', and love as a form of interpersonal communication. In this chapter we argue that these approaches to love and romantic relationships reduce complex social phenomena to simple cognitive processes and neglect the gendered and erotic nature of romantic love. Much research ignores almost entirely the role of sexuality and gender in close relationships, and as such functions to reproduce heteronormative and reproductive notions of gender and sexuality. This chapter builds on earlier concepts about power and regulation, and the manner in which they are produced and repro-duced in close relationships.

The *Methodologies* chapter (Chapter 9) pulls together key strands underpinning both mainstream and critical psychological research reviewed in previous chapters by focusing on the philosophical assumptions that inform social psychological research. We explore the philosophical bases for much social psychological knowledge, critiquing the notion of psychology as 'science' and querying the ontological, epistemological and methodological foundations of the discipline. This sets the backdrop to an articulation of an alternative, more critically oriented paradigm, and to a consideration of qualitative methodologies in social psychology (we focus specifically on IPA and discourse analysis).

Chapter 10 closes the book with a consideration of the key themes that emerge across the previous chapters and the core arguments we have made. We have demonstrated that identities are produced, not as a feature of individual social cognitive processes, nor as a function of purely social processes. Rather our subjectivities – our sense of who we are – are constituted within complex socio-political, discursive and narrative webs.

Chapter 1

Attitudes

Learning outcomes

By the end of this chapter you should:

- *have developed a detailed understanding of key research on attitudes;*

- *understand the core limitations of mainstream research on attitudes;*

- *demonstrate a critical understanding of social representations as a more 'social' alternative to individual attitudinal research;*

- *demonstrate an understanding of alternative trends in studies on this topic, including discursive approaches;*

- *have an understanding of how to analyse a piece of text for its attitudinal content, and have a basic understanding of how to design an attitudinal questionnaire, offering you the opportunity to develop your skills in creative and critical thinking.*

Introduction

The word **attitude** is a familiar part of our vocabulary and routinely creeps into our everyday conversations. We may use the notion of attitudes when trying to figure out what others think or feel about objects, individuals or events. We may also draw on the concept when evaluating the behaviour of others. For instance, it is not uncommon to talk of people 'having' a healthy attitude, a realistic attitude or even an attitude problem! We assume that once we know someone's attitude towards an object, person or event we can, to a greater or lesser extent, know how they will behave towards it. Our pervasive use of 'attitude' in daily life is reflected in the way we often take it for granted that people simply 'have' attitudes. That is to say, 'attitudes' are often treated as though they are a fundamental characteristic of being human. Given that these everyday ideas about attitudes seem intuitively to be true, it may come as a surprise that these taken-for-granted assumptions have been contested within psychological research. In this chapter, we will explore how psychology has attempted to define, measure and explain the notion of attitudes. We will look at common questions asked by psychologists in this field, including: How can attitudes be measured? How do attitudes relate to behaviour? We attempt to show the limitations of traditional research by examining alternative understandings of this topic.

The place of attitudes in psychology

The importance attributed to the notion 'attitude' in social psychology is succinctly captured by Allport (1935) who describes the concept as *indispensable* (p798). Allport was not alone in this view. Other researchers have since claimed that attitudes remain a crucial concept in social psychology (for example, Petty et al., 1997; Conner and Sparks, 2002; Gawronski, 2007). So why are attitudes so important? In early psychological work, it was generally thought that attitudes were the key for understanding human behaviour. The pervasiveness of this view is reflected in early definitions of the field of social psychology itself as the scientific study of attitudes (Thomas and Znaniecki, 1918; Watson, 1925; see also Ajzen and Fishbein, 2005). While recent definitions of social psychology rarely focus on attitudes to this degree, this does not mean to say that the concept has lessened in importance for some researchers. This can be seen in Petty and Wegener's (1998) claim that:

> Attitudes remain important . . . [in] the 21st century because of the fundamental role that individual attitudes . . . play in the critical choices people make regarding their own health and security as well as those of their families, friends and nations. From purchase decisions provoked by liking the product to wars spurred by ethnic prejudices, attitudes help to determine a wide variety of potentially consequential outcomes.

(Petty and Wegener, 1998, p323)

In Petty and Wegener's description, it would seem that attitudes have a powerful impact on our day-to-day activities. This quote suggests that our attitudes shape the things that we do and exert considerable influence on a myriad of our mundane as well as more critical choices and experiences throughout our lives. For some researchers then, the job of unpacking the nature of attitudes is a crucial step in understanding human action. At this point it would not be unreasonable to ask: But what exactly are these things called attitudes? How and why are they influential on our behaviour? We will turn to these questions in the following sections.

Defining attitudes

As we saw above, mainstream psychological interest in the topic of attitudes has a very long history. Given that attitudes have been the central focus of much research produced in social psychology, we might expect that researchers are by now pretty confident about what constitutes an attitude and that there would be a fair degree of consistency and consensus about what definition(s) we could and should use in psychology. Interestingly, this is not the case. There has been considerable disagreement as to how to define 'attitude' and what components make up this construct. This is aptly illustrated by Fishbein and Ajzen (1972). In their review of attitude research, they identified over 500 operational definitions of the construct!

In early research on the topic, there was a general tendency for researchers to use very broad definitions of what attitudes are. An example of this is Allport's (1935) famous definition, which described an attitude as *a mental and neural state of readiness, organised through experience, exerting a directive or dynamic influence on the individual's response to all objects and situations with which it is related* (p810).

For Allport, then, an attitude is a feature of our internal world (or something in our heads) that is acquired and shaped by our experiences and which actively and directly influences what we do and how we behave towards the 'thing' our attitude is about. For example, Bert has a positive attitude towards his boss – in fact, he thinks she's great! He has lots of positive experiences of her – she praises his work when he does well, doesn't make him feel bad when he gets something wrong and she is good at managing her team. His attitude is reflected in his behaviour at work – he speaks highly of his boss and tries to do the best he can to please her. It seems, then, that Bert's attitude can explain his behaviour in the workplace. If we extended this to look at all Bert's attitudes it would seem, on face value, that we could reasonably predict and account for how Bert behaves towards the range of 'attitude objects' or things he comes across in his life.

At first glance, Allport's definition might ring true. However, things are rarely that simple. Let's look a little more closely at Allport's definition. We could argue that this broad definition is a little vague if we start unpicking the definition further and asking questions like: What exactly is a 'mental and neural state of readiness'? We could argue that saying that an attitude is some sort of internal feature of individuals that induces them to act in certain ways does not move us very far in understanding what an attitude is. As Krosnick et al. (2005) point out: *It is hardly surprising that attitudes were seen as the central construct of social psychology, for they were whatever internal sets or predispositions motivated behaviour* (p22).

Broad definitions favoured in early research gave way to some extent to the tripartite model of attitudes developed by the 'Communication and Attitude Change program' at Yale University in the 1950s and 1960s. Underpinning this model was the understanding of attitudes as *predispositions to respond to certain classes of stimuli with certain classes of response* (Rosenberg and Hovland, 1960, p3). In other words, attitudes can be thought of as our immediate inclination to respond in certain ways to the thing or object we have an attitude about. In the tripartite model, the kinds of response we have to the object of our attitude are made up of three major components.

- Cognitive component – the knowledge or beliefs we have about the attitude object.

- Affective (or evaluative) component – how we feel about the attitude object (for example: Do we like it? Do we dislike it?).

- Behavioural (or conative) component – how we intend or think we ought to behave towards the attitude object.

Each of the three components involves evaluating the attitude object in a specific way, but crucially the evaluations produced by each component may differ substantially. For example, Bert is up for promotion at work but hates being interviewed (negative affective component). That said, he understands that job interviews are a good way to assess someone's work competencies and provide him with an opportunity to demonstrate his skills (positive cognitive component). He therefore accepts the offer of an interview for the promotion (favourable behavioural or conative component).

It is reasonably easy to think of examples from our own experiences where what a person says they think about an attitude object doesn't match their behaviour or vice versa. The fact that the model allows for some inconsistency in responses from the three components could be seen as an attempt to account for the complexity of everyday behaviour. An examination of these three components was undertaken by Breckler (1984), who asked university students to fill out an attitude questionnaire in the presence of a real caged snake. The cognitive component was assessed by asking students whether they agreed or disagreed with knowledge-based statements (for example, 'Snakes control the rodent population'). They were also asked about how they felt about the snake (I feel happy; I feel anxious), which was designed to tap into the affective component. The behavioural component was measured by asking students what they thought their responses to the snake might be (I'll scream; I'd like to pick it up), as well as observations of the students' behaviour with the actual snake. Breckler argued that this study showed that the three different responses (cognitive, affective and behavioural) could be seen as three components of an attitude. Breckler also argued that correlations among the three components were high – our thoughts, feelings and behaviours are related to each other.

Breckler's study gives the impression that it is reasonably easy to separate out the three components of an attitude. This, however, has certainly not been the case in other studies using the tripartite model. Indeed, there has been some confusion and disagreement about how to distinguish between components. For example, Ajzen (2005) argues that measures used in some studies that are intended to measure the cognitive component have been used in other studies to measure the affective component. This may well reflect the difficulties of conceptually separating aspects of the cognitive and the affective. This is perhaps best highlighted by a substantial claim in the field that people can display large inconsistencies in their cognitive, affective and behavioural component responses to an attitude object (for example, Eagly and Chaiken, 1993). Importantly, this has implications for what has been one of the major questions in mainstream psychological research: Do attitudes predict behaviour? It could be argued that it is not necessarily the case that if we know something about the other component responses we can predict the behavioural component response.

The relationship between attitudes and behaviour in the tripartite model can be considered straightforward on one level – behaviour is one component that makes up a part of the attitude construct. However, if we want to tackle the question of whether attitudes predict behaviour using this model, then the situation becomes a little more challenging. The relationship between attitudes and behaviour becomes a matter of definition in this model – attitudes must impact behaviour because behaviour itself is part of an attitude! It becomes very difficult then to ask common questions such as 'Do attitudes predict behaviour?' because in this model, behaviour is not and cannot be separated from the attitude itself. It can thus be argued that this model skims over the complexities of the relationship between internal processes and overt action. It is issues such as this that have led to the tripartite model's decline in popularity.

An assumption underpinning the use of the tripartite model (and many other definitions used in attitudinal research) is that attitudes are relatively enduring and so do not change significantly over long periods of time. While it is acknowledged that attitudes might change if we encounter new experiences or new ways of understanding the attitude object, a large body of mainstream research generally sees attitudes as fixed. The idea that attitudes are reasonably stable can be problematic because it throws a question mark over the possibility of individual (as well as broader social) change. One definition that avoids this problem can be found in the work of McGuire (1985) who described an attitude as *responses that locate 'objects of thought' on 'dimensions of judgement'* (p239). What this means is that when we consider an issue, idea or topic (for example, an object of thought), we respond to it by evaluating it, which involves placing 'the object of thought' in a hierarchy (dimensions of judgement). For example, Bert is asked which of his colleagues – Ann, Bob or Sally – is best at their job. To answer this question, he makes a mental list of their good and bad points and, on the basis of that, places them in an evaluative hierarchy – Sally is best because she is good at all aspects of the job, Bob is second best because he is excellent with customers, Ann comes third because she is always late for meetings. Unlike the tripartite model, McGuire's definition does not assume that attitudes are stable – it allows for responses to vary in the degree of their permanence. In this sense, McGuire's definition is much more flexible in terms of allowing for individual (and social) change than other definitions we have discussed.

Task

- Write down five of your own attitudes.

- Does each of these attitudes have an affective, cognitive and behavioural component?

- Think through some of the limitations of this model. For example, are we always emotionally tied to our attitudes?

What do attitudes do?

So far in this chapter we have seen that a number of researchers have argued that attitudes are very important indeed and play a critical role in our daily lives. Why are they important? What exactly do they do? Allport (1935) suggested that attitudes are a means of making sense of our social world – they provide a means to evaluate the things around us. When we have an attitude about something, we have a fairly stable means of knowing how to respond to it. For example, if Bert has a positive attitude about giving work presentations, then he knows he will probably want to put himself forward for this job role. In this sense, attitudes can be seen to save us time and effort. As Allport says:

> Without guiding attitudes, the individual is confused and baffled . . . attitudes determine for each individual what they will see and hear, what he will think or do. To borrow a phrase from William James, they 'engender meaning on the world' . . . they are our methods for finding our way about in an ambiguous universe.

(Allport, 1935, p809)

The idea that attitudes provide a means of getting a handle on and sizing up our environment has been called the object appraisal function of attitudes. For Fazio (2000), the object appraisal function can be considered the most important function of attitudes for individuals.

This isn't, however, the only function of attitudes. One early and very influential piece of work on the purpose of attitudes was developed by Katz (1960), who identified four main attitude functions.

- The knowledge function – this is similar to the idea of the object appraisal function in the sense that attitudes provide us with a means of knowing and understanding our social world.

- The utilitarian function – this function revolves around maximising reward and minimising punishment/cost. For example, Bert's positive attitude towards his boss is likely to serve a utilitarian function because his boss might give him 'nicer' jobs (reward) than ones that he does not like (punishment). This function highlights the social nature of attitudes and points to the ways in which attitudes may alter depending on the context. We will return to this idea later in the chapter (see page 15, 'Putting the "social" back into attitude research').

- The value-expressive function – attitudes play a role in self-expression. For example, the value-expression function may be working in the graffiti we see (Liberate!), the T-shirt slogans we choose to wear ('I speak fluent Geek', 'Teachers are weapons of mass destruction'), the choice to fly the national flag during the football season, the car stickers we choose ('Dad's Taxi'). These kinds of public displays, according to Katz, are about the need to express one's primary values and sense of self. For Katz, this function is rooted in the individual's need for self-actualisation – a term developed by Maslow in his humanist theory of human development – which basically means that all individuals are driven by the urge to be the best that they can be. Self-expression is part of this self-actualisation process.

- The ego-defensive function – this function has a distinctly Freudian flavour and is concerned with those attitudes that work to protect the individual and help them cope with internal unconscious conflicts. The most typical example given to illustrate this function is an individual who espouses homophobic attitudes. If the ego-defensive function is at work it might be the case that this individual constructs gay men and lesbian women as the out-group because they themselves are unconsciously conflicted about their own sexuality.

For Katz, it is important to remember that an attitude might function to serve multiple functions at any given time. It is quite possible for a single attitude to serve all four functions: knowledge, utilitarian, value-expressive and ego-defensive. It is also possible from Katz's perspective that an attitude might be used for different purposes in different contexts. Katz's work on attitude function is generally considered in the field to have been seminal. However, at the time, Katz's work was not examined further by many other researchers, mainly because the functions proposed were considered difficult to measure empirically (Maio and Olsen, 2000). What you may notice here is that the examination of function is based solely at the individual level – it is concerned with what attitudes do for individual people. There is no real explanation of how attitudes function in the broader social world, how they shape and impact our relationships with others and our social networks.

Do attitudes predict behaviour?

We start this section with a task to get you thinking about whether attitudes predict behaviour.

Task — Identify an attitude you may have towards any issue you like (e.g. politics, religion, marriage, sexuality).

Think about the situations when you have and have not expressed it.

Would you discuss this particular attitude with friends, relatives, colleagues, casual acquaintances? If so, why? If not, why not?

It is often not the case that we are consistent with expressing and acting on our attitudes in different public contexts. In other words, what we say and how we act is not always the same as our internal or private attitudes. Our public expressions and our private attitudes are not necessarily consistent across different times and situations. This is well illustrated in La Piere's (1934) classic study, which broadly looked at attitudes towards Chinese people in America. It is important to note that in the 1930s there was widespread anti-Chinese sentiment in the USA. La Piere travelled around the USA with a Chinese couple. During this trip, they visited a number of establishments, including 184 restaurants. Only one restaurant out of 184 refused to serve them. At this point, one might think that perhaps negative, prejudicial attitudes were not as widespread in America at the time as initially seemed to be the case. This is certainly a reasonable conclusion if the answer to the question 'Do attitudes predict behaviour?' is 'yes'. However, there is a twist in this study. Six months after visiting these restaurants, La Piere sent out a questionnaire to each of the restaurants he and the couple had visited, asking whether they would be prepared to accept Chinese customers. A staggering 92 per cent of the 184 restaurants said that they would refuse Chinese clientele! There is a very clear discrepancy illustrated here – attitudes and behaviour do not always match.

What might account for the outcomes of La Piere's study? We know how the restaurant staff said they would treat the Chinese couple (refuse to serve them) in the postal questionnaire and what they actually did at the time (served them). The postal questionnaire asked a question about whether they would serve Chinese clientele – this is a rather general question referring to a general attitude about Chinese individuals in an abstract way. This is very different from the concrete reality of being faced with a Chinese couple in a restaurant. What could be crucial here is the specific instance where we know they served the Chinese couple. This couple appeared cultured, were dressed smartly and were accompanied by a white man. What we are looking at here is a specific attitude towards specific people. It might well be that the couple did not match the negative image the restaurant staff had of Chinese people. The problem then is trying to work out specific instances from general ones (for example, see Ajzen and Albarracin, 2007).

Another way to explain the outcomes of La Piere's study is that the restaurant staff lied on the questionnaire. To get around the possibility that people might tell untruths when asked what their attitudes are, Jones and Sigall (1971) developed the **bogus pipeline**, which is a means of duping participants into thinking that the researcher knows when they are lying or telling the truth. Participants are hooked up to something that looks like a lie detector – the original machine was made up of electrodes, flashing lights and a pointer that moved from 'agree' to 'disagree'. The machine, however, was bogus: it did not actually measure anything! Jones and Sigall created the impression that the machine 'worked' by asking participants to answer questions truthfully about attitudes that the researchers already knew the answers to. (They had managed to get these answers covertly when participants had taken part in a previous study.) As you may well imagine, participants connected to this machine would probably feel that there was very little point in lying or at least telling a glossy, socially desirable version of what they really thought.

More recently the bogus pipeline technique was used by Gannon (2006; Gannon et al., 2007) to explore offence-supportive attitudes among child sex offenders, i.e. attitudes that defended or excused child sex offenders. In 2006, they asked 32 low-risk child sex offenders to fill out an offence belief questionnaire twice, with a few days between each. The second time the participants were asked to fill out the questionnaire, they were effectively split: one group was asked to fill out the questionnaire in the same conditions they had before (i.e. they were a control group where they could, if they so chose, provide less honest answers to the questions), but the second group were asked to fill it out while attached to a bogus lie detector (i.e. they were put in the bogus pipeline condition). What we might expect, based on our discussion of Jones and Sigall's (1971) work, is that the participants in the bogus pipeline condition would reveal more offence-supportive attitudes. It assumes that under normal conditions some people might be more inclined to lie and/or give more socially desirable answers to the questionnaire. In this study, this was not the case. Child sex offenders in the bogus pipeline condition did not express more offence-supportive attitudes than they had done when asked to fill out the questionnaire the first time around. Their answers also did not differ in any meaningful way from the control group.

What can we conclude from Gannon's study? It might well be the case that the participants had answered honestly the first time around. However, it could also be the case that the bogus pipeline does not really encourage more truthful answers. To explore this, Gannon et al. (2007) critically examined the way they had designed the first experiment. They noticed a number of possible flaws in the research design of the 2006 study, and suggested the following changes.

1. Lengthening the time period between readministering the questionnaire – it could well be that participants simply remembered how they had filled it out the first time and duplicated this on the second round.

2. Changing the questionnaire they used for one that was more psychometrically sound.

3. Providing participants with a more thorough demonstration of how the bogus pipeline 'worked'.

4. Using high-risk child sex offenders in their participant sample. The logic for this change is that the high-risk population are more likely to have offence-supportive beliefs. In the 2007 study, the bogus pipeline 'worked' in the sense that participants revealed far more offence-supportive attitudes when filling out the questionnaire than they had done when they had not been attached to the bogus lie detector.

Taken at face value, then, the bogus pipeline seems to provide a reasonably foolproof way of finding out what people's true attitudes are. However, there are some problems with the bogus pipeline. One is that it can be considered to be unethical. Studies that use the bogus pipeline use deception, which is a very important ethical consideration that researchers must take into account when designing and running psychological studies (see BPS Ethical Code of Conduct, 2009). The coercive nature of the bogus pipeline should not be underestimated, particularly when working with participants who are vulnerable. For example, Cross and Saxe (2001) argue that the coerciveness of the bogus pipeline might put so much pressure on prisoners that they end up giving false confessions. This is illustrated in Kokish et al.'s (2005) study, which involved asking sex offenders to fill in a survey about offences while hooked up to a lie detector. A number of these participants confessed to crimes that they had not committed. So it seems that the bogus pipeline can, in and of itself, produce 'untruths' and significant ones at that – ones that could have serious implications for the offenders.

An assumption operating in the bogus pipeline studies is that people's true attitude might well predict their behaviour. The problem for researchers is accessing what their true attitudes are. Are things always this simple? In the Task on page 7 you made a list of attitudes you felt you held and wrote down when you do and don't express them. Have a look at this list again. Sometimes you might not express an attitude because it might not be appropriate to do so with the person you are expressing it to (for example, a friend, family member, colleague, and so on) or because of the place you are in (for example, at home, the pub, at work, and so on). It might well be that the attitude can be expressed in different ways, or that it might vary with the point you are making in different conversations and contexts. What this shows is that there are often more complex social reasons for expressing particular attitudes that we hold in particular ways. Some of these issues are explored in the theory of reasoned action and theory of planned behaviour (Fishbein and Ajzen, 1974; Ajzen and Fishbein, 1980; Ajzen, 1988). We will look at these theories in turn in the following sections.

The theory of reasoned action (TRA)

The **theory of reasoned action** is concerned with causal factors or antecedents that guide our choices to behave in particular ways. Simply put, before an individual performs a certain action or behaviour, they consider the potential consequences and implications of their actions. As Ajzen (1988) notes: *The theory of reasoned action is based on the assumption that human beings usually behave in a sensible manner, that they take into account available information and implicitly or explicitly consider the implications of their actions* (p117).

- Crucial to this theory is the notion of intention – it is intention that immediately determines whether you do or don't do a particular action. Our intentions to perform an action or not are, in turn, determined by two main components.

- Attitude to behaviour – we weigh up the benefits and costs of performing the action. If we think the behaviour is likely to have a positive outcome, then we hold a favourable attitude to the behaviour (Bentler and Speckart, 1979). If we think the behaviour is likely to result in a negative outcome, then we hold an unfavourable attitude to that behaviour (Fishbein and Ajzen, 1975).

- Subjective norm – we consider and factor in how specific individuals or groups will judge the action we are considering doing as positive or negative.

To make this clear, consider this example. Bert has the opportunity to go for a promotion at work. He really wants to go for it (intention). Bert's intention will be impacted by a cost/benefit analysis involving his attitude to the behaviour of going for promotion – on one hand, a promotion means more money as well as kudos (which he really wants!), but on the other hand, he will have to work longer hours. Intention is also impacted by subjective norms – what will other people think about the possibility of promotion. Bert thinks that his mum and his friends would be really happy for him, but that his partner would be resentful of him working long hours. In the end, Bert is very concerned about working long hours (attitude to behaviour) and the upset that this might cause his partner (subjective norm), so he decides not to act on his intention to go for the promotion.

The theory of reasoned action offers an explanation of the link between attitude and behaviour based on the idea that humans are rational beings. This approach has enjoyed a fair degree of success in explaining the relationship between attitudes and behaviour. For example, intention mediated by attitude to behaviour and subjective norms seemed to predict behaviours such as dieting behaviour in adolescent girls (Race Mackey and La Greca, 2008) and when adolescents decided to have sex (Gillmore et al., 2002). However, a key criticism of the theory is that it focuses on behavioural intention, which is presumed to influence behaviour. These behavioural intentions do not necessarily produce consonant behaviours – sometimes we behave in ways that are at odds with our intentions.

The theory of planned behaviour (TPB)

The theory of reasoned action is concerned explicitly with how attitudes impact volitional action – that is, behaviour that people feel they have conscious control over. What about behaviour that we feel we do not completely control? To address this question, Ajzen (1988) developed the **theory of planned behaviour**, which added the component of perceived behavioural control (the degree to which people perceive the action they are considering doing as in their control) to the relationship between intentions, attitudes and behaviour described in the TRA.

To make this clear, the theory of planned behaviour suggests that intention determines behaviour, but our intention is determined by weighing up the costs/benefits of performing the action (attitude to behaviour), of considering whether the people around us will approve/disapprove of the action (subjective norm) and the degree to which we perceive the behaviour as being easy or difficult for us to perform (perceived behavioural control).

We can apply this theory to the example used earlier of Bert going for a promotion at work. He really wants to go for the promotion (intention) and weighs up the pros/cons of the action of applying for it – it means more money but he will have to work longer hours (attitude to behaviour). He considers what other people might think about him going for promotion. His mum would be very proud, but his partner would be resentful of him working longer hours (subjective norm). He is also not convinced he'll get the promotion as there are a lot of people with more experience who are applying for it (perceived behavioural control). Bert decides not to act on his intention to go for the promotion.

As for the TRA, some studies in the field provide support for this theory. For example, Conner and McMillan (1999) used the TPB to explore undergraduate students' intentions to use cannabis and the frequency with which they used it. To capture the students' intentions and usage of cannabis, they gave them a questionnaire that measured a number of components, including intentions, attitudes to behaviour, subjective norms and perceived behavioural control. Analysis of the data suggested that intentions were predicted by attitude to behaviour, norms and perceived behavioural control. Interestingly, students' cannabis use seemed to be predicted by intentions but not perceived behavioural control. Conner and McMillan explain this by the fact that cannabis use is a socially undesirable behaviour. Students who felt they had greater control and choice as to when they used cannabis chose to use it less often, hence escaping social disapproval to some extent. Conner and McMillan take the results as lending support to the TPB. Similarly, other researchers have argued that the TPB can predict, for example, binge drinking in undergraduate students (Norman et al., 2007), physical activity in young smokers (Everson et al., 2007) and the degree of safe sex behaviour among drug users (Mausbach et al., 2009). On the basis of this, then, we might conclude that both the TRA and TPB have a high degree of explanatory weight. However, these theories are not without criticisms, which we will explore next.

Issues and considerations: TRA and TPB

So far we have looked at examples and studies that support both the TRA and the TPB. There are also a number of studies that have not found support for these theories (for example, Darker et al., 2010; Darker and French, 2009; Rise et al., 2008). This begs the question of why studies using these theories have yielded inconsistent, mixed outcomes.

A number of researchers have highlighted problems within the theories that might well account for the inconsistency in 'successes' across studies. For example, neither theory really explains how intention to do an action is actually translated into the actual doing of the action. We can see examples of this in everyday life – we might intend to take up an exercise class, or paint our houses or give up smoking, but never quite get round to it. Schwarzer (1992) argues that the TRA focuses on the intention/motivational stage of decision-making without really saying much about the action phase. The same criticism could be levelled at the TPB. However, there is a clear gap in the theory in terms of how we move from behavioural intention to the behaviour itself. To move from making a decision to doing something to actually doing it, it is fair to say you probably need to have some sort of plan to make it happen. For example, if a smoker in the first year of university says they will give up at the end of their third-year exams, this might not happen unless they have a plan about how they are going to go about doing it. Both theories highlight the importance of planning for future intended actions. But, as Warshaw and Davis (1985) have argued, the theories need to distinguish between intentions and *self-predictions* – our sense of how likely it is that we will actually perform the intended action.

Models like the TRA and TPB are appealing, with their slightly seductive suggestion that human behaviour can be understood through a simple mathematical equation:

> TRA: intention + positive attitude to behaviour + positive subjective norm = accurate prediction of behaviour

TPB: intention + positive attitude to behaviour + positive subjective norm + perceived behavioural control = accurate prediction of behaviour

These theoretical approaches suggest that basic mathematical equations can enable us to work out with relative consistency what people will do. Unfortunately (or perhaps fortunately!), human behaviour is rarely this simple. Consider, for instance, Mulholland and van Wersch's (2007) qualitative study of young people's decision to attend a GUM (genital urinary medicine) clinic for treatment of a sexually transmitted infection (STI). The authors applied the TPB to young people's decision making in relation to attending the clinic. They found that most of the young people intended to go to the clinic but had a negative attitude to the action of going. They also tended to report negative subjective norms about attendance and perceived going to the clinic as a difficult action to perform. Based on the interaction of these factors, the TPB would predict that the action would not be performed and that these young people would not attend the clinic. However, in Mulholland and van Wersch's study all the young people did! Mulholland and van Wersch argue that the application of the TPB does not actually tell us much about how these young people negotiated the decision of visiting a GUM clinic, or why they went, despite being so negatively disposed to this action. Interviews with these young people identified that the decision-making process was complex, with participants negotiating social stigma and isolation but feeling compelled to 'get rid of' the STI (p28). It would seem, then, that the relationship between what we think and our behaviour is much more complex than the TRA and TPB suggest. There is a significant gap between our behavioural intention and our actual behaviour. We would argue that the assumption embodied in this theory – that humans are rational information processors who always act in reasoned and planned ways – skims over the complexity of how people work in the social context they find themselves in.

Given the mixed outcomes of studies testing or using the TRA and the TPB, the predictive capabilities of these theories are questionable. We can question their ability to make predictions further by examining the qualities of the theories themselves and how they are tested. The use of equations makes theories look very impressive and we can easily be lured into thinking that the scientific 'look' of theories must mean that they hold some weight. However, what is it that these equations are actually saying? How are they put to the test? One answer is sufficiently captured in the following quote.

> If you ask people to express what they intend to do in certain carefully defined situations, carefully limit the range of possible responses they can make and carry out some clever calculations with the data, you can sometimes get a reasonable 'fit' between what they say they intend to do and what they 'actually do'.

> (Stainton Rogers et al., 1995, p128)

In addition to Stainton Rogers et al.'s concern about the squeezing of the data to the model, we can also look at the apparent predictive power of these models in another way. We would suggest that the research that underpins the theories of reasoned action and planned behaviour primes participants to behave in particular ways. If we ask people before they perform an action whether it would be a good thing to do, whether it is easy to do and if they think others will approve, then it is not that surprising that many people will end up doing it! Similarly, if you ask them if it is a bad thing to do, it is hard to do, and if they think that others will disapprove, then perhaps it not that astonishing that many people will avoid doing it. It seems quite likely that the research activities that participants engage with crystallise thought processes, and encourage participants to be more planned and predictable in their behaviour. This makes participants more self-conscious. When you consider the degree to which the research itself primes participants to behave in a way that is consistent with the models proposed, the supposed predictive ability of these theories starts to lose some credence.

Task — Think about a decision that you made recently. For example, how did you decide what to have for lunch, or what film to watch when you last went to the cinema?

Did the way you came to this decision look like the structures proposed in the TRA or TPB? Write down what was similar and what was different about it.

Did your decision making resemble a rational information processor? If not, why not?

Asking different questions: alternative understandings of attitudes

Up to this point in the chapter, we have focused on mainstream research and theories about attitudes. We have explored some typical questions asked in this body of research, such as: What are the functions of attitudes? Do attitudes predict behaviour? Throughout the work we have discussed, there appears to exist an assumption that attitudes exist. This might seem like a very odd thing to say, but think about it. Have you ever seen an attitude? Have you read about any research that has? The answer to both these questions is no. This is because an attitude is a hypothetical construct, which basically means it is a useful concept for explaining everyday phenomena. Hypothetical constructs are a means of explaining the behaviour we see. For example, if Tom sees Bertha kick a cat, he might infer that Bertha has a negative attitude towards cats. Notice that he has not directly seen Bertha's attitude, only her behaviour. Similarly, psychological researchers cannot directly access a person's attitude; they infer them from their participants' behaviour, from self-reports and from questionnaires. While researchers are obviously aware that attitudes are hypothetical constructs, there is a tendency to reify them or treat them as if they were real entities. This tendency to describe abstract hypothetical constructs as if they are tangible objects can work to distract from the fact that the concept is only a useful way of understanding and explaining a set of behaviours.

The logical implication of hypothetical constructs is that when they cease to be useful in explaining phenomena, then they won't be used any more, or at least used with much less frequency. A world where people do not use the construct of attitude, or where at least they place less importance on it, might seem to be unimaginable given the frequency of the use of this expression in Western cultures. However, across history, there have been times when the construct of individual attitudes has been more important and less unimportant (see, for example, McGuire, 1985).

What this means, then, is that the construct of 'individual attitude' is not necessarily the only way of understanding the behaviour it seeks to explain. It can also mean that we do not necessarily have to ask questions that focus on cause–effect and prediction (for example, do attitudes predict behaviour?); alternative questions might arise from alternative understandings and explanations. It is these issues that we will explore in the following sections.

Putting the 'social' back into attitude research: social representations

Take a moment to think about the theories we have looked at so far in this chapter. These theories are located in social psychological research, but what exactly have they had to say about social behaviour? The classic ideas and theories we have reviewed focus on individual attitudes – for example, what is Bert's attitude towards an issue? How might Bert's attitude impact his behaviour? Some theories have mentioned subjective norms or what other people think about Bert's behaviour, but this consideration of the social is taken as one aspect that might impact a whole host of more individualised processes. Indeed, subjective norms are often represented in, for example, the TRA and TPB as things that are considered but can be ignored. The social aspects of attitudes in much of this work could be seen as an 'add on' to the more individualised processes that have been the focus of much mainstream research. We would argue that attitudes seem to be much more 'social' than this. We share attitudes with others, with the social groups in which we are located. Indeed, some of our so-called 'individual' attitudes seem to be created through discussing issues with others. To ask questions about this, it would seem that we need to locate attitudes in the social, not just the individual.

Moscovici's extensive work (for example, 1976; 1981; 1984; 1993; 1998; 2001) on the theory of **social representations** is a crucial contribution to efforts to locate attitudes in the social. We do not claim to review Moscovici's work in detail here because the body of work he has produced is not only large but very complex. We hope instead to give you a flavour of some key ideas for understanding social representations theory.

For Moscovici (1976; 1985) social representations are collective, shared knowledge that people use to understand their social world. These ideas about the social world are worked up in the social, cultural context in which they are located. As Moscovici (1981) puts it:

> By social representations, we mean a set of concepts, statements and explanations originating in daily life in the course of inter-individual communications. They are equivalent, in our society, of the myths and belief systems in traditional societies; they might even be said to be the contemporary version of common sense.

(Moscovici, 1981, p181)

In other words, social representations come about, take shape and circulate in and through our interactions and communications with others. Whether it is talking about current issues with lecturers, watching political debates on the news, reading the latest version of a magazine or gossiping with friends, what we are doing is engaging in some sort of communication activity. It is through this communicative process that we build a picture of particular issues and of our social world. As mentioned earlier, these representations are shared among groups of people so they allow a common basis for us to understand each other and thus provide a degree of cohesiveness that bonds particular social groups together.

We have alluded to the idea that social representations are images or pictures. A social representation is composed of both concrete images but also abstract ideas that are structured around what could be thought of as a core *complex of images* – what Moscovici (1984) called the *figurative nucleus* (p38). As an example, let's take a social representation of intimate partners or couples. Abstract ideas might include romance, commitment and togetherness, and concrete images might be of handholding, running though cornfields together and close physical embraces. This is not to say that the images and ideas that make up social representations are necessarily consistent. Moscovici (1988) suggested that a social representation might well contain paradoxical, divergent ideas.

At this point we can ask: how do social representations relate to attitudes? In social representations theory, our attitudes are based upon and shaped by these shared social knowledges. It is not the object of the attitude – the thing our attitude is about – that shapes our attitude but rather the *social representation* of it. If our attitudes and what we know about an object is built up in and through our social representations of it, then how can we ever know what the object is really like? How can we obtain objective, neutral knowledge of it? The short answer is we can't. The social world as we know it is ultimately built up and constructed in and through our collective social/cultural representations of it. For this reason, social representations theory can be seen as using a constructionist framework that questions the degree to which we can ever know the world objectively.

To illustrate the importance of social representations in orienting us to our social world, we will briefly describe one topical study by Correia and Broderick (2009). This study looked at social representations of making accessible medically assisted reproductive treatment (MART), such as IVF and donor insemination, to single and lesbian women with fertility problems in Australia. Correia and Broderick analysed 180 letters written by the public to editors of newspapers that had reported on this issue. Representations around what could be termed the 'natural' family and family 'love' were identified. The first representation focused on the heterosexual family unit comprising mother, father and children. This family unit was linked to ideas of positive morality, 'goodness' and family ideals. Single and lesbian women were not seen as 'fitting' this representation of the family because they could not provide a father. In addition, lesbian women were variously represented with images of 'man-hating' and of immorality. Correira and Broderick argue that this representation was challenged by the representation of the importance of being a loving parent – the gender or number of parents was seen as unimportant to this representation. Correira and Broderick suggest that the 'loving parent' representation might be key to challenging negative responses to single women and lesbian parents.

While social representation theory locates attitudes firmly back in the social by moving away from the individualising tendencies of mainstream work, it is not without problems. Potter and Wetherell (1987) identified key problems around three issues.

1. The relationship between social groups and representations – social representation theory suggests that groups cohere around shared social representations. Studies then need to identify a group and study their representations. This is the point at which things start to get complicated. This idea suggests that representations mark off the boundaries of who is in the group. It also suggests that we need to identify what the representations are through the members of the group. How can we identify who is in the group if we do not yet know what the representations are? Potter and Wetherell point out that *there is a vicious circle of identifying representations through groups and assuming groups define representations* (p143).

2. Consensus or shared social representations – social representation theory suggests that a group shares social representations. This would seem to make sense, as we tend to develop relationships with people who have similar understandings to us. However, we do also group with people who perhaps do not share all our understandings on all issues, and who perhaps operate with differing social representations to us. Potter and Wetherell argue that in some social representation studies there is a tendency to emphasise consensus and downplay diversity in group representations. In other words, researchers tended to homogenise participant responses. This is a problem as it runs the risk of missing the complexity of the social phenomena being studied.

3. Linguistic or cognitive representations – social representations are located in this theory as mental entities or *cognitive units* (Potter and Wetherell, 1987, p145). Studies in this area identify social representations through, for example, interviewing people, giving them questionnaires, analysing the letters they write, and so on. So what researchers are collecting as data is

language or, more appropriately, discourse. Traditionally, language or discourse has been seen as a passive medium through which we can communicate our internal states. If this were the case there would be no problem – an interview, answers on a questionnaire or a written letter would be a neutral record of the mental entity we are exploring – social representation. But what if language or discourse is not simply a vehicle to our internal world? This has been explored in research that theorises and studies everyday discourse, which we will look at next.

Discourse and discursive action

Like social representations theory, discursive approaches can be located in social constructionist theory. This is because when people talk about an object, event or social phenomenon they are not merely describing it, rather they are constructing a version of it. The version that becomes constructed depends on the function or purpose of the account that has been put together. To make this clear, think about different versions that you have come across of the celebrity Britney Spears – she has been constructed as, for example, one of the most successful artists of our era, as mentally unstable, as a victim of greedy agents, as a bad mother, as a survivor of challenging circumstances – none of these versions gets us any closer to what Britney Spears is objectively like! When studied in context, they do tell us something about the purpose of constructing Britney in these ways, which, in turn, might well tell us something interesting and important about the construction of celebrity. This kind of argument would suggest that language or discourse is doing something more than just describing or reflecting an objective reality. This is the starting point of Potter and Wetherell's seminal book – *Discourse and Social Psychology: Beyond Attitudes and Behaviour* (1987).

Potter and Wetherell make the case that language or discourse is not just a means to express what is going on inside us. Instead, they argue that the use of discourse is a social practice in and of itself. What they mean by this is that people perform social actions in discourse. For example, we can attribute blame, make ourselves seem more or less accountable for a deed done, accuse, justify our actions and so on. Language is not just a representation: it is (also) an action. Key to this perspective is the idea that we talk purposefully (that talk has a function) and what we say varies according to the purpose of the talk and/or what we are trying to achieve. Important to note is that when we say speakers talk purposefully this does not necessarily mean that speakers always talk with specific intentions. It may well be the case that a particular construction of an issue or topic emerges as the speaker makes sense of a topic or issue, or that a particular social activity, such as justifying actions, occurs without deliberation or intent. Variation according to the function of talk can also make talk inconsistent, fragmented and contradictory. In short, talk is extremely messy!

The messiness of talk is not something that is apparent in mainstream psychology. Attitude scales do not allow for messiness to emerge because people are forced to 'tidy' up their responses by answering using predetermined options (for example, agree, neutral, disagree). Potter and

Wetherell demonstrate this with an example from interviews conducted with participants from New Zealand on the topic of Polynesian immigrants.

1. *Respondent: I'm not anti them at all you know* (p46).

2. *Respondent: I'm not anti them at all you know, I, if they're willing to get on and be like us: but if they're just going to come here, just to be able to use our social welfares and stuff like that, then, why don't they stay home?* (p47).

If we look at the first response, it would not be unreasonable to read the respondent's answer as a 'pro' position on the issue of Polynesian immigrants. As Potter and Wetherell argue: *following standard attitude theory . . . this speaker . . . might endorse the sympathetic end of the scale* (p47). However, if we look at the second response, which includes some context around the speaker's answer, we can see that the respondent's answer is much more complex and does not easily fall into a 'pro' position. If we move beyond traditional attitude conceptualisations to look at the discursive actions being performed here, we can start to unpack this complexity. As Potter and Wetherell argue, in the second response the phrase *I'm not anti them* works as a disclaimer, which is a verbal device that functions to disclaim or ward off potential accusations of being racist. The respondent repeatedly uses the word *just* in the second account (for example, *just* going to come here, *just* to be able to use our social welfares) – this repetition creates the impression that the sole purpose of immigration is to make use of social security. This functions to make the Polynesian Immigrants appear selfish and burdensome. As Potter and Wetherell suggest, this representation positions immigrants as:

> *much more blameworthy than, say, coming to provide essential labour but being laid off due to economic recession. By representing it in this extreme way the criticisms [of immigrants] are made to appear much more justifiable* (p48).

The complexity of talk is further highlighted by the issue of variability. Potter and Wetherell illustrate this with two excerpts taken from the same interview with the same person.

3. *Respondent: What I would li . . . rather, see is that, sure, bring them [Polynesian immigrants] into New Zealand, right and try and train them into a skill, and encourage them to go back again* (p49).

4. *Respondent: I think that if we encouraged more Polynesians and Maoris to be skilled people they would want to stay here, they're not um as uh nomadic as New Zealanders are (Interviewer. Haha) so I think that would be better* (p49).

The positions the respondent takes up in the two extracts are variable and contradictory – extract 3 states they should be trained up and then encouraged to 'go home' but extract 4 states they should be trained but encouraged to stay. Traditional attitude research would have difficulty making sense of this inconsistency because there is an assumption that attitudes are more or less fixed and constant. From a discursive perspective, to explore such variability one needs to look at the context. In extract 3, the speaker is making a broader point about the danger of Polynesian immigrants becoming dependent on New Zealand income to support their families 'back home'. Encouraging immigrants to 'go back' is about the need for them to contribute to *their own nation* (p51). Extract 4 is making a somewhat different point – the respondent is discussing the fact that Polynesian immigrants are doing jobs that are disliked by New Zealanders. The implication is that if immigrants stopped doing those jobs and went 'back home', then this could lead to economic problems. The contradictory positions that the speaker takes up now make much more sense. As Potter and Wetherell point out:

> It is, of course, only sensible to adjust one's own response to a topic according to the context. However, this kind of adjustment tends to be overlooked by the attitude researcher who would expect the speaker to be able to articulate on a decontextualised scale a static constant attitude regardless whether Polynesians should stay or return. If it is not static and constant then much of the point of this kind of measurement technology [e.g. attitude scales/questionnaires] disappears.
>
> (Potter and Wetherell, 1987, p51)

A discursive approach then shifts the focus of research from some underlying mental entity (for example, an attitude) to the organisation, function and variability of discourse. From this perspective, the researcher is not trying to access indirectly an internal state or mental process. Instead, they are looking at the social function of interaction – what is the speaker doing? What are they trying to achieve?

Critical thinking activity

Attitudes in context

Critical thinking focus: creative and critical thinking

Key question: *How are attitudes represented in people's talk?*

Select a piece of text in which a person is describing their attitudes or opinions (examples you might want to consider are online blogs, newspaper/magazine articles or a piece of fiction in which the character is describing their attitudes). Attempt to apply the theories and ideas from this chapter to this real-world example. Do the theories/ideas about attitudes we have looked at help to explain features of the text you have chosen?

Use the following prompts to help you identify links between theoretical ideas and the piece of text you have chosen.

– Summarise the piece of text you have chosen by writing down key points about attitudes and behaviour conveyed in your chosen text.

How is the attitude described? Does there appear to be an affective or cognitive or behavioural component, for example?

Does there appear to be a link between the attitude and behaviour described in your text? What are the similarities and differences to this description and the TRA/TPB?

Apply ideas from the discursive approach we have looked at to your piece of text. Identify points of variability in the text by looking for points that seem to contradict each other. For each contradictory idea, ask yourself: What is the point the speaker is trying to make? Does the purpose of the point explain contradiction in their talk?

Critical thinking review

This activity helps develop your skills of creative and critical thinking, and application of theory in relation to a range of theories covered in this chapter. To do this, you were encouraged to apply these theoretical ideas to a piece of text that described a person's attitude. This enabled you to think about the usefulness of these concepts in practice, and also to think critically about alternative understandings of common-sense ideas.

Applying theoretical knowledge in this way, and thinking critically about this knowledge, are important skills that will enable you to evaluate and make critical judgements about psychology research and its application to the real world.

Other skills you may have used in this activity: reflection, recall of key principles and ideas, communication (literacy) skills if you write up the activity, independent learning.

Skill builder activity

Communicating your ideas to an audience

Transferable skill focus: understanding and analysing data

Key question: *Design an attitude questionnaire on the topic of violence in the media.*

In groups, come up with ten questions that could be used in a questionnaire assessing attitudes towards violence in the media. Alongside the questions you devise, you will also need to decide on a response format (for example, yes/no; five-point Likert scale

– strongly agree, agree, unsure, etc.). Based on your questionnaire, we would like you to consider some of the limitations of attitude scales in general.

Use the following prompts to help you prepare your questionnaire.

Identify key areas related to the general topic area of violence in the media. This will help you hone your questions.

Can your questions be answered sensibly with the response format you've chosen?

Have you piloted your questions? A pilot study is a good opportunity to identify any problems with your questions so it would be well worth asking two or three volunteers to try your questionnaire. Ask your volunteers: are there any important issues that have not been included in the questionnaire? Are your questions clearly worded? Are your questions easily understandable?

Use the following prompts to help you prepare class feedback.

To help you identify the limitations of attitude questionnaires, try answering your own questions. Are you able to fully convey what you think about violence in the media? Does the response format allow you to fully express your attitude? If not, why not?

Do the questions cover all aspects of the topic that are important to you and your attitude on the issue? Write down any issues that are missing.

Skill builder review

This activity helps develop your ability to understand and analyse material and data. It has also helped your communication skills, focusing particularly on oral communication. These are important academic and life skills.

Other skills you may have used in this activity: critical thinking, comparison, independent learning, reflection, recall of key principles and ideas, information technology (if you chose to use computer-based presentation materials).

Assignments

1. 'Attitudes predict behaviour.' Critically discuss this statement with reference to relevant psychological theory and research.

2. Compare and contrast two theories of attitudes.

Summary: what you have learned

In this chapter, we have outlined mainstream social psychological theories of attitudes. We have explored mainstream efforts to define attitudes and considered problems associated with pinpointing the boundaries of attitudes. We have considered classic psychological theories such as the theory of reasoned action and theory of planned behaviour. We've highlighted how such theories tend to individualise the concept of attitudes and remove explanations from the social context in which they emerge. We have considered Moscovici's notion of social representations as a more social alternative to the individualist focus of much social psychological research on attitudes. To illustrate the importance of the social context, we looked at alternative concep-tualisations of 'attitude' research, including discursive approaches that highlight the importance of contextualising people's accounts when trying to make sense of them.

To complete your critical thinking and skill builder activities, you have developed and used your skills in creative and critical thinking, communication of ideas, comparison, independent learning, reflection, recall of key principles and ideas, and information technology.

Further reading

Potter, J and Wetherell, M (1987) *Discourse and Social Psychology: Beyond Attitudes and Behaviour*. London: Sage.

This classic textbook provides an excellent review of core issues within traditional attitude research that remains relevant today. It provides the building blocks for the radical shift from attitude research to discursive approaches.

Chapter 2

Attributions

Learning outcomes

By the end of this chapter you should:

- *have an understanding of classic theories of attribution and attributional processes, which seek to understand how we explain and make sense of our everyday lives;*

- *be able to apply the concept of attribution theory to real-life examples;*

- *understand some of the limitations of attribution theory, particularly in relation to its mechanistic and individualist terms of reference;*

- *be able to demonstrate an understanding of how we form our everyday explanations of our social world within a complex social context, and understand that such attributions are not just cognitive phenomena in the way that many mainstream social psychological accounts suggest but that they are also socially constituted phenomena;*

- *be aware of concerns about applying abstract theory to important real-life issues (such as criminality);*

- *have had an opportunity to develop your oral communication skills by delivering a presentation, and have developed your critical thinking skills.*

Introduction

Much of our everyday life is devoted to figuring out why things happen in our social world. Human beings are motivated by a desire to understand, and our understandings of our social experiences are often framed in terms of *why* questions: Why did that happen? Why did you do that? Why now? Why me? In other words, people can be understood as continually looking for, proposing and explaining the *causes* of behaviour (their own as well as others'), experiences and phenomena in general. The everyday causal explanations we give to events and actions in our world are described in social psychological theory as attributions. **Attribution theory** is generally concerned with explaining and exploring the processes we use to attribute different kinds of causes to particular behaviours and events. In this chapter, we will explore attribution theorists' attempts to explain *why* it is that people in general need to know *why*. We will ask questions such as: how do we go about looking at the causes of social phenomena? When are we likely to make mistakes about causes? Why do we make these mistakes? A word of warning – early or classic research in attribution does tend to use a large number of technical terms, but we will bring these to life by applying them to real-life contexts, specifically the areas of criminality and violence.

Social cognition and the development of attribution theory

The development and popularity of attribution theory is tied up with changing emphases in psychology as a discipline in the late 1950s and 1960s. At around this time, there was a shift away from the predominance of **behaviourism** and **psychodynamic** theories to social cognitive psychology. This approach rejects the idea that people respond passively to their environment (behaviourism) or that they are, to a greater or lesser extent, at the mercy of their emotional responses (psychodynamics); see also Stainton Rogers et al., 1995). Social cognitive approaches blend social psychological and cognitive explanations of the person, framing individuals as active doers and rational thinkers in the social world. The social cognitive understanding of people as active thinkers can be considered as the lynchpin of attribution theory. In this section we will explore this representation of people in attribution theory in a little more depth. We will illustrate the ideas contained within attribution theories using some examples around sexual violence and offending more generally, to demonstrate both the importance of understanding how we explain our social world, and also to challenge some of the ways that attribution theories represent our everyday explanations.

Early attribution theory: the work of Fritz Heider

Early developments in attribution theory have been attributed (pardon the pun!) to the work of Fritz Heider (1958) who first noted the importance of our everyday explanations for social psychological research. He was interested in what he referred to as **common-sense psychology** or **naive psychology**, which is how laypeople – non-scientists or, as he called them 'naive scientists' – develop their own ideas or theories about people and events.

Heider argued that investigating everyday common-sense understandings was of critical importance to psychology's scientific understanding of human relationships. This argument was made in the context of psychology's disdain and mistrust of intuitive understandings of the world. Perhaps rather arrogantly, Heider's psychological and social scientific contemporaries suggested that 'ordinary people' engaged in confused, biased misreadings of the social world – *at best [as] a superficial and chaotic view of things, at worst a distortion of psychological events* (Heider, 1958, p5). Heider argued that understanding how people interpret the behaviour of others, attribute causes and make predictions about what others might do in particular situations is crucial because it:

gives us the principles we use to build up our picture of the social environment and which guides our reactions to it. An explanation [from psychology as a scientific discipline] of this behaviour, therefore, must deal with common-sense psychology regardless of whether its assumptions and principles prove valid under scientific scrutiny. If a person believes that the lines in his palm foretell his future, this belief must be taken into account in explaining certain of his expectations and actions.

(Heider, 1985, p5)

In other words, Heider argues, we need to understand how people explain their world, even if, according to scientists, those explanations are wrong.

We can see how important our common-sense explanations are when we consider the example of moral reasoning around issues such as sexual violence and criminality. Because of the perception that such experiences are out of the ordinary, individuals are particularly strongly driven to make sense of both their own and other people's experiences of these phenomena. For example, consider the recent case of the violent death of Baby P. This child suffered lifelong abuse at the hands of his mother, her partner and the partner's brother, ending in Baby P's death at the age of two. The incident fuelled a commission of inquiry into the actions of social services and other professionals working in child protection, and also provoked considerable public debate about the nature of motherhood, child violence and family life in modern society. Alongside the moral outrage that people expressed about this tragic case, there was also a strongly expressed public need to understand *why* incidents like this take place. In contemporary culture, this kind of public response to tragedy is often framed in terms of the question of who, or what, is to blame for what happened. For example, questions were asked about why a mother might fail to protect her child from harm; why social services failed to act to protect the child; and why and how this could have happened in the 'developed' world. Questions were asked as to whether this kind of incident reflected a social crisis in 'Broken Britain'. These questions signal our powerful need to make sense of our social world, particularly when experiences and events are outside what we would perceive as the norm. However, considering the explanations and attributions people did make in relation to the Baby P case, it is also important to remember that these do not occur in a social vacuum – something mainstream attibution research seems to forget. When considering attribution theories in this chapter, it is important to consider the degree to which our social psychological understandings of everyday explanations fail to take into account the complexity of the social processes involved in our daily theorising of our worlds. We would like you to bear this issue in mind, as we continue to explore Heider's version of the attribution process.

For Heider, the development of people's naive or common-sense ideas/theories of their social world happens in the context of what he called their *subjective environment* or life space. This subjective environment is made up of different ways of characterising people, events and objects. According to Heider, the relations that make up the life space of something as everyday as a trip to the garage might include *spatial relations, as when the person believes that the gas station is on the Northeast corner of Main Street; functional relations, as when the person recognises that a gas station is for servicing cars; and evaluations, as when the person thinks that the attendant is dishonest* (p15).

Alternatively, in the case of people's attributional processing around Baby P, the life space might include spatial relations of, for example, the family home; functional relations of the role of the family in contemporary society and in the protection of children from harm; and evaluations, such as judgements of what constitutes good and bad parenting.

Using the notion of **phenomenal causality**, Heider explores the 'naive'/common-sense causal theories that we use when perceiving and making sense of the nature of other people. Our understandings of other people are mediated by the perceptions we have formed of them, based on behavioural information. From these we infer from this about the other person's personality. We might also use information we may have obtained about them from third parties. Based on this process of observation and information gathering, we begin to form theories and ideas about the person we are perceiving. This process of person perception involves building reasonably stable and invariant concepts of that individual, from the variety of diverse behaviours that people are capable of in ongoing interaction. In other words, we build up our notions that, for example, Bob is a grumpy person, that Hilda is domineering, and that Sarah tends to gloss over her upset and focus on the positive. We then use these notions of inferred, stable character traits to inform our understanding of why people do what they do. So if Bob flies off the handle in a meeting, well, that is just Bob, being Bob – his behaviour is caused by the character trait of 'grumpiness'.

A key component of Heider's theory of attribution involves a distinction between our internal and external attribution processes. In the case of Baby P, internal attribution processes would explain the tragedy as a function of the mother's personality defects. In public discussions of this case, for instance, she was often described as 'evil', inferring stable internal personality traits and character defects that explain her behaviour. Individual behaviour is attributed to internal, stable and personal characteristics. Heider argued that what could be considered stable or invariant is not just the other person's personality traits or attitudes but, more importantly, the motives or intentions of the person. In contrast, the external attribution focuses on features of the environment, factors beyond the individual that might motivate that person's behaviour. In the Baby P case, these explanations might include ideas around poverty, class and social deprivation as a framing context for this tragedy.

The focus on people's motives or intentions is a key aspect of Heider's theory – he is concerned with our attempts to answer the question: why do people do what they do? He argues that we are driven to make sense of what others *intend* and not simply what they *do*. When ordinary people engage in this kind of everyday theorising about other people's behaviour, they may use inferences of **impersonal causality** – the idea that actions might produce unintentional effects. For example, if Ann pushes Sarah because Ann has accidentally tripped up then Ann's action can be seen as unintentional – Ann didn't mean to bump into Sarah. Impersonal causality is used to explain not just human behaviours but also events involving objects in the world. So if Ann gets hit on the head by a falling tree branch, then this can be understood as unintentional and thus an example of impersonal causality. **Personal causality** attributes behaviour to intentional actions, and therefore can only be used to explain human behaviour. So this is about doing something and *meaning* it – for example, if Ann deliberately hit Sarah then this would be an example of personal causality.

Social psychology textbooks often focus on Heider's formulation of internal versus external attributions. However, Heider also argued that impersonal and personal causality does not simply map on to internal and external causes. There are not simply two forms of attribution process – the internal/personal attribution versus the external/situational one (Malle, 2004). By focusing just on external versus internal attribution processes, we risk ignoring the concept of intentionality – and this focus on our understanding of motivation is really what Heider is all about. However, at the same time, our argument, as illustrated by our consideration of the Baby P case, would be that we also need to take seriously the idea that intentions, and our understanding of intentions, are framed by a social and political context that cannot be reduced to mere cognitive perception of causality. This is a theme we will return to later in the chapter (see page 39).

Task

Think about the last time you felt moved to explain a situation in the real world – a time when you were driven to ask the question 'why?'

- In wrestling with real experiences, do you think you behaved like a 'naive scientist'?

- In what ways were you like a scientist in resolving your 'why' question? In what ways were you not?

Inside/outside: correspondent inference

Jones and Davis's (1965) theory of **correspondent inference** developed Heider's early work on internal and external attributions. They argued that we infer attributions for other people's behaviour on the basis of two assumptions:

1. that the individual's behaviour is an expression of an underlying stable and enduring disposition (internal) or;

2. that the behaviour has been produced because of the situation that the person is in (external).

For example, consider how we might make sense of Jackie's experiences of domestic violence. One possible explanation given for women's experiences of domestic violence is that they become involved in, and remain in, violent relationships because of their particular character or personality style. For example, a popular image of domestic violence suggests that women like Jackie like the violence (they are masochistic by nature). This is an example of a dispositional inference. An alternative explanation is that Jackie's experiences are a result of cultures of masculinity and femininity that make her both socially and economically unable to leave the situation of domestic violence. This is an example of a situational or external attribution.

So how do ordinary people make decisions about whether behaviours are internally or externally produced? According to the theory of correspondent inference, we make judgements about whether someone's behaviour is freely chosen. If we conclude that the person chose to do it, then we would infer that the behaviour corresponds, or is indicative of, an underlying disposition. For example, if you drop something and another person stops and picks it up, you might infer that they are by nature a nice and helpful person. If we conclude that someone's behaviour is not freely chosen – that there were external circumstances that produced the behaviour (for example, they were forced to in some way or there was some sort of reward for doing a particular behaviour) we are likely to infer that the behaviour is shaped by external rather than internal influences. In Jackie's case, if we see evidence that social and structural factors (like being financially dependent on her partner, or having poor access to alternative shelter) make her unable to leave the situation of domestic violence, we are less likely to attribute her behaviour to dispositional factors.

External influences that may impact our judgements include social desirability – behaving in ways that are considered socially legitimate because they are in line with dominant social norms or rules about how one should behave in particular situations. When people act in socially desirable ways, this does not necessarily tell us anything about their dispositions, because we would infer that their actions are being mediated by the external influence of societal norms. However, when people behave in ways that are not socially desirable or acceptable, then we are more likely to infer that their behaviour corresponds to an underlying disposition or trait.

Our judgements are also shaped by our assessment of the effects of behaviours. Jones and Davis distinguished between the common and uncommon effects of behaviour. Common effects are those understood as produced by a wide variety of different actions or behaviours, whereas uncommon effects are those that are seen as unique to a particular action or behaviour. This all sounds very complicated but it is much more straightforward than you might think. As an example, imagine that Elizabeth has become involved in an amateur dramatics group. The group does a lot of different plays, all of which will involve things like performing to an audience, wearing costumes, learning lines, using stage equipment, and so on – these things can be understood as common effects; they are shared outcomes or effects that come about when one takes part in different plays. Now suppose that Elizabeth is given a choice between being the star of the show or an extra in the chorus and opts for being the star – this can be understood as an uncommon effect – the choice of being the star will mean that she is the centre of attention and is unique to that role. As you might have guessed, Jones and Davis argued that we use information about uncommon effects to infer whether behaviour corresponds to an underlying disposition. In the case of Elizabeth, we might well infer from her choice to be the star that she is by nature extroverted.

What you may have noticed is that this theory departs from Heider's concerns about how we make sense of other people's intentions when they perform particular actions or behaviours. Correspondent inference theory is primarily concerned with whether we attribute causes to a person's disposition (inside the person) or to external circumstances (outside the person). To make this clear, let's take the example of Elizabeth's choice to be the star of a play. We make a dispositional inference by saying that she chose to be the star because she is extroverted. But what is her intention? Why did she do it? Did she want to steal the limelight from her friend Bob? Did she believe that the lead role would further her future acting career? Did she feel compelled to make that choice because she thought that none of her friends were keen to do it? This theory does not explain how we explain the actions of others or infer other people's beliefs or intentions. It only explains how we infer dispositions (see also Hamilton, 1998). Furthermore, while the theory incorporates notions of social norms and attempts to make sense of the way that attribution processes might be shaped by our understanding of what is typical, nonetheless the approach does not take into account the complex ways in which such norms are built in the first place. Neither does it consider how we form judgements of what is typical and atypical for particular people at particular moments in time. Such limitations led to a decline in the popularity of correspondent inference theory.

Kelley's covariation model

Drawing on Heider's notion of people as naive scientists, Kelley (1967) developed the **covariation model** to explain our everyday attempts at attributing causes to people's actions. In Kelley's view, we attribute causes to actions by cognitively running a procedure that is similar to a complex statistical procedure called analysis of variance (or ANOVA). This lay version of doing an analysis of variance involves identifying factors that appear to be associated or correlated with a particular behaviour. Based on the outcome of our analysis, we attribute cause to a factor that appears to be the most likely impetus for the behaviour we have observed. So, for example, Kay notices that her boss André frequently calls her 'pet' and 'love'. Recently, she has also noticed that he tends to touch her a great deal when explaining her work projects to her, stroking her arm, and occasionally patting her on her bottom. Kelley's model would predict that to explain her boss's behaviour, Kay would engage in a complex analysis of possible causes before arriving at a conclusion about the most likely and plausible factor driving his inappropriate behaviour. According to Kelley, we run this analysis to decide whether behaviour is caused by factors internal to the person or by external, situational factors. So in André's case, is his behaviour a result of a lecherous character? Is it a feature of the environment in which Kay works (a culture of being friendly and informal in the workplace)? Importantly, this analysis involves making assessments about three kinds of information, which include:

1. consistency – does the person behave in the same way in the same situation across time?;

2. distinctiveness – is the person's behaviour unique to this situation or do they often behave in this way?;

3. consensus – do other people behave in the same way in a particular situation?

We use this information in our analysis of cause by making judgements about the extent to which a person's behaviour is consistent, distinctive and similar to other people's behaviour (consensus) to work out whether the behaviour is internally or externally caused. The formula that we use looks like this:

Internal attributions = high consistency + low distinctiveness + low consensus

External attributions = high consistency + high distinctiveness + high consensus

How do we use these equations in practice? In the case of Kay trying to explain her boss's behaviour and understand whether his behaviour is inappropriate, she might ask herself about consistency – does André always try to touch her when they speak? If he does, then consistency is high. You will notice that in both equations consistency information needs to be high for any potential cause of behaviour to be considered. According to Kelley, attribution processes are only triggered when a pattern of behaviour is detected. In addition to considering consistency of behaviour, we might also ask about distinctiveness – is the workplace generally very touchy-feely (low distinctiveness), or is this behaviour specific to André (high distinctiveness)? Lastly, we consider consensus information – does everyone see André's behaviour as inappropriate (high consensus), or is his behaviour generally accepted (low consensus)?

Important to note is that Kelley's model is somewhat different from both Heider's and Jones and Davis's theories in the description of how we use the mass of information available to us to make causal attributions. For both Heider, and Jones and Davis, it is assumed that we make causal inferences based on an action made by one person in a given instance. In practice, however, we make attributions based on the wealth of information available to us, which includes comparisons with how other people behave, and how the person we are making attributions about has behaved or might behave across time and in other situations (see also Augoustinos and Walker, 1995). It can be argued that the covariation model takes into account at least some of the complexity of how we make causal attributions in everyday life because it highlights ways in which we use information that we have gleaned across different times, situations and about other people to make attributions.

While there has been a body of experimental research that lends support to Kelley's model causal inferences (for example, McArthur, 1972), it is not without problems. For example, Ahn et al. (1995) suggest that most studies focus on how information is used to attribute cause. However, they point out that this approach ignores the possibility that just because people are able to use certain kinds of information does not mean they necessarily do so when making attributions in everyday life. Ahn et al. ran a series of experiments asking people to articulate what information they would want when making judgements about the causes of particular events. The results from these studies suggest that when making attributions people wanted to know more about aspects of the event and how particular factors might have caused an effect (which they refer to as mechanism information) rather than information about covariation between particular factors and effects they might have. For example, in a car accident, they might prioritise information such as 'was John drunk?' (mechanism information) over less salient information such as 'has John had other accidents?' (covariation information) when attributing causality. Individuals draw on mechanism information to find out further 'facts' about the event, then use this information to test hypotheses that they have developed to account for the cause of an event. While Ahn et al. point out that this does not entirely discount Kelley's covariation model, it can be argued that it does point to ways in which the process of doing covariation analysis in everyday life might lack **mundane realism** (see Hesketh, 1984). In other words, Kelley's model has experimental **validity** and some explanatory power, but arguably lacks real-world application.

Task ── Imagine that you do rather better on your next social psychology assignment than you had predicted.

── Think about the attribution processes you would go through to explain this.

── Reflecting on these attributions, do you think that your processing resembles the mathematical model that Kelley describes?

Making mistakes: attributional errors and bias

Early accounts of attribution are based on the assumption that people are rational information processers: much like a computer, people run analyses to identify the causes of events in their everyday lives. However, cognitive psychological research has often highlighted that, unlike computers, our capacity for processing information is limited (Harrington and Sawyer, 1992; Marois and Ivanoff, 2005; Baddeley, 2007). Since we are limited information processors, it has been argued that we use cognitive shortcuts (known as heuristics) to make sense of the social world. Attributional processes are often characterised by the use of such heuristics. While shortcuts help us process the vast amount of information with which we are continually bombarded, they can also create problems by increasing the possibility that we will make errors or use biased thinking. In the following sections, the main kinds of attributional errors and sources of bias are outlined.

Fundamental attribution error or correspondence bias

Originally referred to as the **fundamental attribution error** (Ross, 1977), this error/bias is concerned with our tendency to attribute the causes of behaviour to internal dispositions, such as personality traits, rather than to external or situational influences. This source of bias is also sometimes described as **over attribution** (Jones, 1979), or more commonly **correspondence bias** (Gilbert and Jones, 1986). One of the most widely cited studies demonstrating this error or bias asked American participants to consider a speech written about political figure Fidel Castro who was hugely unpopular in the USA at that time (Jones and Harris, 1967). Participants were given speeches that were pro-Castro, anti-Castro or equivocal. Jones and Harris also manipulated what the participants were told about the writer of the speech: participants were told either that the writer had freely chosen to take a pro, anti or equivocal position or that the writer had been instructed to take a particular position by the debating adviser. Participants were then asked to decipher what the writer's 'true attitude' was towards Castro. The results suggested that the speech was seen as reflective of the writer's true attitude when the writer was free to choose the position they could take (a dispositional attribution). Somewhat counterintuitively, the results also indicated that participants inferred some correspondence between the position taken in the essay and the writer's 'true attitude', even when they were told that the writer had little choice about the content of the speech. In other words, participants still made a dispositional attribution even when there were clear situational constraints on the writer. Correspondence bias – the tendency to attribute dispositionally rather than situationally – is seen as a key source of attributional error.

Returning to examples of criminality, internal dispositions are often used to explain why perpetrators did the things that they did. As an example, let us consider the Soham murders – an infamous UK case of child abduction and murder – where Ian Huntley was convicted of the murder of two young girls (Jessica Chapman and Holly Wells). Huntley's girlfriend Maxine Carr was charged with providing him with a false alibi. What was particularly interesting is that Maxine Carr was a key figure of discussion in public debates about the murders and was often described as inherently evil (internal disposition) even though there was no evidence of her direct involvement in the murder, or evidence that she knew anything about it until she was asked by Huntley to provide him with an alibi. External attributions could have been made about Carr's behaviour (for example, that she was following social norms about trusting your partner in romantic relationships; she was pressured into providing an alibi; she herself was a victim of Huntley's manipulation and brutality), but what newspaper and media accounts predominantly opted for were internal dispositional attributions.

A body of work has suggested that we make this particular mistake because of our (over)reliance on heuristics or cognitive shortcuts. The correspondence bias suggests that we tend to make dispositional attributions over external ones because the individual and their behaviour is what appear to be prominent in most events or situations. We come to favour dispositional explanations because they are immediately available to us and usually offer plausible explanations of events. Consequently, we tend not to focus on less obvious situational influences (for example, Nisbett and Ross, 1980; see also Gilbert 1998).

Tetlock (1985) argued that such explanations of attributional errors paint a rather unflattering picture of humans, positioning us as 'cognitive misers' *whose preference for simple, easy to execute heuristics (the principle of least effort) renders them vulnerable to inferential bias such as the overattribution effect* (p228). In short, such explanations portray us as fundamentally lazy (Taylor, 1981). In contrast, Tetlock explored the possibility that people were *cognitive motivators* rather than misers – that is, people move beyond the use of simple heuristics when making attributions when they have an incentive to do so. To test this idea, Tetlock devised an experiment similar to Jones and Harris's study mentioned above. He asked participants to read an essay about minority quota systems (**affirmative action**) in university admissions. The essay took an either pro or anti stance. Participants were informed that the writer had either freely chosen the pro or anti stance or that they were instructed to take a particular position. However, Tetlock also built an incentive for attribution into his experiment. He told participants that they would either have to justify their judgement to a member of the research team, or that their responses would be kept completely anonymous and confidential. The presence or justification was included as a cognitive motivator because it was predicted that participants would be more motivated to carefully consider the attribution they made because they would be accountable for it – they would have to justify themselves to another person. Like Jones and Harris's findings, participants in this study tended to make dispositional attributions when they were told that the writer had freely chosen to take a particular pro or anti position in the essay. However, they were more likely to make an external attribution when:

- they were told that that writer had little choice in what they wrote, and

- participants knew that they would be held accountable for their decision because they would be expected to justify it.

Arguably, while Tetlock challenges the underlying assumption that humans are fundamentally lazy, he may well have introduced a new assumption – that we only consider the shortcomings of our understandings of the world when there is a chance we might look bad in front of others!

The actor-observer effect

While the fundamental attribution error explains that people tend to overuse internal attributions to make sense of the behaviour of others, it does not explain why it is that people tend to overuse external attributions when accounting for their own behaviour. For example, if Gertrude shouts at Sally for no apparent reason, the fundamental attribution error predicts that Sally will see that as a reflection of Gertrude's aggressive character. In contrast, the actor-observer effect suggests that Gertrude's attribution would be that she was having a bad day, and that her outburst was not a reflection of her personality. When someone is the actor (the person doing the actions or behaviour under consideration), they tend to attribute their own behaviour to external or situational causes. However, when they are the observer of another person's behaviour, they tend to make internal attributions about the causes of behaviour. This distinction in the kinds of attributions we make depending on whether we are the actor or observer is known as the **actor-observer effect** (Jones and Nisbett, 1972).

This distinction can have powerful real-world implications. For example, the actor-observer distinction has been used to make sense of jurors' responses to cases of domestic violence where the person on trial has killed their abusive partner. The act of killing in this instance could be attributed to external factors (for example, the defendant felt that their life was in imminent danger and so acted in self-defence). However, Plumm and Terrance (2009) suggest that the actor-observer effect means that jurors involved in such cases become positioned as observers, and are thus more likely to attribute the defendant's actions to internal causes such as deficiencies in personality or errors of judgement rather than to the complex and difficult situation that the defendant has been in. This effect may intersect with an existing social tendency to blame victims of domestic violence for their experiences of being abused, and can be seen to have serious implications in terms of how such defendants are treated by the legal system.

The point should be made, however, that the very definition of error or bias means that attributional mistakes are the exception rather than the rule. Some psychologists have argued that the impact of the actor-observer effect in people's sense-making has been, on occasion, overstated (Quattrone, 1985). The business of attributing causes to both our own and others' behaviour is complex. The distinction made between being an actor and observer, as well as the difference between internal and external attributions, is far from clear-cut in everyday practice.

False consensus effect

Some psychologists have argued that when people make attributions they do so because they believe their judgement is reasonable and typical of what other people would do when forming explanations of similar events (for example, Marks and Miller, 1987). If a person thinks that other people would have reasonably made the same attribution as they have, then that person can also assume that their attributions are sensible and realistic. The problem is that sometimes people overestimate the degree to which other people would act in the same way as them. This overestimation is known as the **false consensus effect**.

In their classic study, Ross et al. (1977) asked university students if they would be prepared to advertise an eatery wearing a large sandwich board displaying the slogan, 'Eat at Joe's'. Those who agreed to wear the board reported that they thought that a large percentage of other students would do the same. Similarly, students who refused to take part reported that they thought that the majority of other students would also opt out of participating in this form of advertisement. This experiment shows that we tend to assume that our view of the world is a shared one, and that our social perceptions are the same as everyone else's.

Attribution errors rooted in a perception of false consensus have been considered by some psychologists as evidence of the limits of laypeople's explanations – they point to illogical thinking and irrational judgements (for example, Nisbett, 1981). This argument positions psychologists as superior rational thinkers, wielding a logic that eludes laypeople's 'naive science'. As we saw earlier, Heider's representation of ordinary theorists of everyday life implicitly contains an assumption that the everyday theories are lacking in scientific robustness. Implicitly, this kind of representation of scientific versus lay knowledge suggests that psychological thinking is somehow less prone to error than lay explanations are. The question that should be asked, however, is whether psychologists ever make attributional errors and mistakes. Psychologists are, after all, people as well. Do the rigours of scientific experimentation really protect them from the everyday errors of processing that they observe in their participants? We will look at this issue in the following section.

Just an excuse? Making sense of offenders' attributions

As we have seen so far, attribution theory suggests that people tend to attribute their own behaviour to situational or external causes. These attributional processes come into stronger focus when people have done something wrong. Under these circumstances, people often reason that their bad behaviour is the result of situational factors – the dog ate my homework; I was grumpy because I was having a bad day; I'm late because my car broke down. This sort of attribution can be thought of as excuse-making, which involves acknowledging wrongdoing (for example, I can't hand in my homework; I was grumpy; I'm late) but denies responsibility for it (for example, it's the dog's fault; my bad day made me do it; the car broke on its own accord). In other words, excuses allow people to say: 'I did wrong, but it wasn't my fault!' Weiner et al. (1987) argue that excuses involve different dimensions of attribution. These include:

- appeal to external/situational causes (aliens made me do it);

- uncontrollability – that the person could not stop or control the thing that caused their behaviour or event (the spaceship landed in my back garden – it was out of my control and there was nothing I could do);

- unintentionality – the person did not mean to do it (I didn't mean to flatten the neighbour's shed while fleeing the scary aliens).

It is perhaps unsurprising that psychological studies have often reported that excuse-making is a common social practice that people do in everyday life (for example, Weiner et al., 1987; Schlenker et al., 2001).

What is perhaps a little more surprising is that psychology has treated offenders' excuse-making for their crimes as fundamentally different from everyday behaviour. This is well illustrated in Maruna and Mann's (2006) consideration of how psychology has conceptualised offenders' causal attributions for their behaviour. They point out that, like people in general, offenders often use excuses for their behaviour through appeals to situational causes that are represented as beyond their control. However, the majority of psychological work on offenders sees offenders' excuse-making as evidence of their deficient internal cognitive processes. This cognitive deficiency is seen as producing erroneous thinking and distortions in perceptions of reality. Many psychological studies have understood excuse-making and justifications (a person accepts responsibility but denies that the behaviour is actually wrong or bad) as an expression of this erroneous thinking. By arguing that excuse-making is a result of internal cognitive deficits, psychologists are attributing a dispositional/internal cause to explain this behaviour. This is quite different from their theorising about 'ordinary' people's attributional processes, which position people as 'normally biased'. Criminals are, in this kind of thinking, represented as a different class of person in social cognitive terms.

Maruna and Mann point out that psychologists represent everyday excuse-making as a common social practice. They suggest that, just like 'ordinary people', offenders' excuse-making can be represented as an expression of the fundamental attribution error. To support their argument, they review literature on excuse-making that has highlighted the functions of disclaiming individual responsibility to a greater or lesser extent in everyday social practice. Consider the possible implications for the wrongdoer and for the rehabilitation process if they do not make an excuse. The process of taking full responsibility for bad behaviour has implications for self-identity – their sense of who they are (for example, I am by nature a bad person). This might limit the extent to which they believe they are capable of change (for example, I am always going to be a bad person because I am by nature bad), which might then mean that they do not try to change (for example, there is no point in trying to be good because I am ultimately going to fail). Thus, making excuses might have an important role to play in allowing people to see the possibilities for personal change and behavioural change, which can be considered particularly important for offenders, especially in relation to recidivism. Maruna and Mann also argue that research has shown that many people who have been wronged in some way prefer to hear excuses (I didn't mean to do it) rather than forms of internal attribution (I did it because I felt like it) as it is generally preferable to hear that someone didn't mean to upset or harm you! This has important implications for the notion of **community reparation** and **restorative justice** prevalent in, for example, the contemporary British judicial system.

At the beginning of this chapter, we argued that it was possible that psychologists (and other scientists) might themselves engage in attributional errors. This argument challenges the representation of psychologists as an intellectual elite, whose methodologies are so objective as to render a mistake unlikely. Our consideration of offenders' excuse-making highlights the ways in which the academic study of cause and effect cannot be divorced from the social context in which theories and research emerge. The idea that offenders are inherently different from the majority of people has been a common representation in both academic and popular discussions of offending. In books and movies we see the image of the incorrigible and unrepentant prisoner, constantly excusing his criminal behaviour and asserting his innocence. We would argue that this image remains popular because it allows people in everyday life to distance themselves from bad behaviour (for example, I am not like offenders and I can't be like them because they are just plain bad, there is something inherently wrong with them). In the research examples cited above, it is clear that psychologists are themselves not exempt from being influenced by these kinds of social representations of criminality. The individualising arguments which say that offenders' excuse-making is a result of cognitive distortion make it very easy to forget the broader social, cultural and structural issues that might give rise to offending behaviour, such as poverty, deprivation and social practices that render some problematic behaviour as normal. These issues will be explored in greater depth in Chapter 7 in our exploration of aggression and masculinities. A key point in this textbook is that psychologists are not isolated from dominant social ideas and practices; like everyone else, they are immersed in their social context, and this context is reflected and reproduced in psychological theories and ideas.

Who's to blame? Attribution, responsibility and morality

Attributions and excuse-making often become salient when something goes wrong. We often see this in the media frenzy that emerges around crises and tragedies. Our newspapers are littered with questions such as 'Who is responsible? Who is to blame?' In everyday life, people tend to make attributions, excuses and justifications when something happens that is a little strange, out of the ordinary and/or when an individual's actions fall outside social norms for acceptable behaviour. As Semin and Manstead (1983) argue, in everyday life people do not usually question events or behaviour that are considered routine. When people make excuses, it is usually because they have been asked to provide an account of their behaviour. The question 'Why did you do that?' often carries with it an implicit accusation of wrongdoing, which, in turn, might lead to being positioned as responsible and to blame for a particular incident or event.

Notions of responsibility and blame highlight a key point about everyday causal explanations: people's accounts of causes, responsibility and blame can be considered to be a social activity (for example, Edwards, 2006). In attributional processes, assigning or avoiding blame is complicated by what people are trying to achieve in a given social context (see, for example, Billig, 1987; Antaki, 1994). This functional and contextually oriented aspect of causal explanation tends to be missing from traditional attribution theories. Mainstream theories are based on a view of the individual as a detached information processor who passively makes calculations on (some) of the information available to them to determine cause-and-effect relationships. This conceptualisation of the individual removes them from the social context in which their causal accounts are made. If we represent individuals as information-processing machines with faulty circuits, it is easy to miss the ways in which people's causal accounts are actively performing particular social functions in specific situations. (Computers do not have agency – their processing simply happens. They lack the intentionality to orient their processing to a particular desired social effect.) This point can be seen in the example provided earlier of the Soham murder case. We argued that the dominant portrayal of Maxine Carr as evil might be interpreted by traditional attribution theorists as a fundamental attribution error – that is, many laypeople who made this claim had erroneously attributed Maxine Carr's action of giving a false alibi to an internal cause (she's evil) rather than considering possible situational causes. However, a different explanation can be advanced for this attribution when causal explanations are seen as a social activity. For example, the blame attributed to Maxine Carr can be seen to reflect and reinforce moral outrage that was bound up with broader societal concerns about all individuals' responsibility to protect children from danger. It also plays into dominant representations of 'good' versus 'bad' women. Good women look after children. Bad women place them in harm's way. Attribution theory focuses on the individual processing of information, but fails to locate everyday accounts of cause and effect within a social context. As a consequence, these theories fail to address questions such as 'Why do we make the attributions that we do?' and 'What social function do these attributions serve?' This is perhaps why attribution theory tends to remain a very descriptive account of human sense-making and everyday explanations.

As psychologists, it is important to critically consider the impact of applying assumptions made in attribution theories (like the use of the computer metaphor) to the study of important social issues. This is demonstrated in Anderson and Doherty's (2008) review of the implications of attribution research on the issue of sexual violence. Attribution work on sexual violence has been largely concerned with identifying factors that lead people to assign cause, responsibility and blame in sexual violence scenarios. One central issue that has been investigated is myths about sexual violence that are sometimes used in everyday explanations to assign blame to the victim. In explaining this, some attribution research uses **vignette**-based experiments to understand how judgements about cause and effect are made in the sexual violence context (for example, Calhoun et al., 1976). In these experiments, information about the hypothetical victim is manipulated so that the victim might be seen as more to blame (for example, the victim's personality traits are linked to their experience of sexual violence) or less to blame (for example, it was simply bad luck that the victim was in the wrong place at the wrong time). Participants are asked to make judgements about whether the victim or the perpetrator is to blame. Anderson and Doherty point out that such research sets up the victim and the perpetrator as having an equal chance of being selected as the cause of sexual violence. Thus, in such research, the question of who is to blame is positioned as a matter of debate – the idea that victims might somehow be responsible for their own victimisation is implicit in the structure of the experiment. This assumption can be considered highly problematic because it reinforces myths about sexual violence (for example, that the victim asked for it or deserved it), reflecting the problematic social activity of victim-blaming rather than challenging sexual violence. We see again here how social psychologists are themselves influenced by their social context. Researchers draw on dominant social ideas about victims, reproducing problematic notions of victim-blaming within their experiments. This highlights the reality that research does not take place in a social vacuum, and draws attention to the importance of being **reflexive** about our own assumptions when we engage in research.

Critical thinking activity

Attribution processes in the media

Critical thinking focus: critical and creative thinking

Key question: *How do the media use attributional processes in crime reporting?*

Choose two recent newspaper articles that report on a criminal act. Choose one 'red top' newspaper article (for example, from *The Sun*, *Daily Star*, *Daily Mirror*) and one 'broadsheet' newspaper (for example, *The Guardian*, *The Times*, *The Daily Telegraph*, *The Independent*). Compare the attributional processes in the article, and use attribution theory to build your own account of how attribution works in real-life contexts.

Use the following prompts to help you develop your comparison.

- Read the articles carefully, and list the attributional processes that are engaged in the two reports.

- What are the similarities and differences in the explanations offered by the journalists in the two accounts?

- Look for evidence of internal and external attributions, for elements of Kelley's model, and for error processes in the journalists' thinking.

- Can you see evidence of the influence of factors beyond individual cognitive processes in the explanatory frameworks the journalists use? Is an attribution-theory-based explanation enough? What would you want to add to an attributional model to make sense of the explanatory processes evident in the newspaper accounts you have read?

Critical thinking review

This activity helps develop your critical and creative thinking skills. While it is very important as a student to learn to synthesise the ideas of others, and to make claims that are rooted in evidence, it is also important not to stifle your own creative and critical thinking. When we critique theory, it is important to ask ourselves, 'What has this theory missed?'

Other skills you may have used in this activity: critical thinking, comparison, analysis of textual data.

Skill builder activity

Make a poster

Transferable skill focus: communication (visual) and IT skills

Key task: *Prepare a poster, using appropriate software (for example, PowerPoint, Open Office) to present your findings.*

Drawing on the analysis of newspaper articles you completed for your Critical thinking activity (above), prepare a poster in which you present how attribution theory might help you to analyse the way that newspaper accounts offer explanations of criminal activity.

Your poster should:

show the key explanatory themes you have identified in the newspaper articles you have explored;

show how you have applied attribution theory to make sense of the explanatory processes in evidence in the articles.

To prepare a good poster presentation, remember to:

keep it clear – text explanations should be succinct, readable and clear;

be selective – you can't include everything in a poster, so make sure you select the key information to present;

keep it visually interesting – use pictures, graphic representations etc. to make your poster visually pleasing;

don't clutter – while you want to have a visually interesting poster, you don't want to overwhelm your audience with a poster that is too busy, or too crammed with information.

Skill builder review

To complete your poster, you have developed your IT and visual communication skills. Making research posters is an important academic skill, used at conferences, workshops and in other contexts in which you need to present your findings to your audience in an immediate, accessible and digestible way.

Assignments

1. Critically discuss the importance of understanding sources of attribution error in everyday life.

2. Explore the role of attributions in everyday understandings of criminal behaviour, and consider critically the value of traditional attribution theory in the context.

Summary: what you have learned

In this chapter, we have outlined mainstream social psychological theories of attribution – the causal explanations we build to make sense of our everyday lives. We have used 'real-life' examples (for example, looking at the attribution of blame in criminal activity) to explore the value of these kinds of attribution theories in the 'real world'. Beginning with Heider's account of human beings as 'naive scientists' motivated to explain the social world within which they are located, we considered how distinctions between internal and external attributions might be useful, looking at how factors like perceptions of free choice, social desirability and common/uncommon effects influence the explanations we give to everyday events. We have explored Kelley's suggestion that when making causal explanations about observed behaviour human beings consider three factors: how consistent that behaviour is; how distinct that behaviour is; and whether most people would behave that way. Based on these three considerations, we decide whether a behaviour is caused by internal or external factors. In this sense, Kelley suggests that our social cognitive processes function like a maths problem – a presumption that has been criticised for its lack of mundane realism. We have considered common social psychological accounts of social cognitive sources of error in attribution, like the fundamental attribution error, the actor-observer effect and the idea of false consensus. We have highlighted the way that these kinds of accounts of attribution processes position human beings a little bit like faulty computers, not quite making accurate sense of the world within which we live. In this sense, we have also highlighted a key criticism of attribution theory. In making sense of our social worlds, in providing causal explanations of our environment, we are not simply quirky, slightly faulty machines, processing information from our social worlds and producing individual explanations of behaviours. Attributional processes are not (just) individual, they take place within a social context. So, for example, when explaining criminal behaviour, we do not just look at the behaviour itself, we consider that behaviour in relation to social representations of criminality, masculinity, femininity, dominant ideas about sanity and insanity, about justice and fairness. In this sense, attributions are not just cognitive phenomena in the way that much of these mainstream social psychological accounts suggest; they are also socially constituted phenomena.

To complete your critical thinking and skill builder activities, you have developed and used your skills in creative and critical thinking, communication of ideas, comparison, independent learning, reflection, recall of key principles and ideas, and information technology.

Further reading

Hewstone, M (ed) (1983) *Attribution Theory: Social and Functional Extensions*. Oxford: Basil Blackwell.

Hewstone is the recognised British authority on attribution theory, and this book is regarded as one of the classic texts.

Hewstone, M and Jaspars, JMF (2010) Intergroup relations and attribution processes, in Tajfel, H (ed) *Social Identity and Intergroup Relations*. Cambridge: Cambridge University Press.

An up-to-date account of attribution theory, exploring its intersections with approaches like social identity theory.

Chapter 3
Stereotypes, prejudice and racism

Learning outcomes

By the end of this chapter you should:

- *have an understanding of the constructs of 'race', 'ethnicity', 'prejudice' and 'racism';*

- *have an overview of key theory and research in the area of race and racism;*

- *have a critical understanding of the framing of race, racism and prejudice as an aspect of 'intergroup relations';*

- *understand the social cognitive approach to the understanding of race and racism;*

- *be able to contrast this social cognitive approach with more materialist understandings of race and racism (for example, realistic conflict theory);*

- *understand the core limitations of mainstream social psychological research on race and racism;*

- *consider the value of discursive accounts of race and racism;*

- *have developed your skills of textual data analysis, and visual communication, by analysing a piece of text and building a collage.*

Race and ethnicity

Race is often understood in lay terms to be a biological inheritance – the possession of certain chromosomally determined physical features that produce variations in skin tone, hair colour, etc. However, it is often pointed out that, at a genetic level, there is far more within group variation among members of a racial group than there is between group variation – that at a biological level, racial categorisation is not really something that can be sustained. In social psychological terms, race is better defined as a socio-politically constructed category, composed of people who share biologically transmitted traits that members of a particular society view as important. To understand race in Britain, for example, it is probably more fruitful to look at the way that ideas about race were produced in times of empire and colonisation, how it was produced and reproduced within the ideology of the Commonwealth, and how it continues to be deployed within 'multicultural' Britain today in our talk about disadvantage, immigration, etc.

Another important construct in talk around race and identity is the idea of 'ethnicity': an ethnic group is one that has a shared cultural heritage (for example, religion, language, ancestry) and an assumed common and distinct social identity. The term 'ethnicity' is often used in a manner that suggests that ethnicity is a property of 'ethnic minorities'. However, it is important to remember that this is a misuse of the concept. For example, it is perfectly reasonable to talk about white British ethnicity (or ethnicities).

Understanding prejudice and racism

Prejudice is understood within most social psychological work as an attitude, with three components – emotional, cognitive and behavioural. Prejudice is a general term for any negative attitude towards a social group. Thus we can have racial prejudice, gendered prejudice, anti-gay prejudice, etc. The first component – the affective or emotional aspect of prejudice – involves a negative emotional feeling towards groups – so, for example, a pervasive aversion to black people based on their simply being black. It also includes a negative stereotype (a cognitive schema) – the second component – based on the idea that all members of the group share particular (usually negative) traits. For example, a common racist stereotype associates black people with violence. The third aspect of prejudice is the behavioural component, the act of discrimination. Discrimination involves behaving in a way that is negative or harmful to people, based on their group membership. For example, the tendency for police stop-and-search tactics to be disproportionately directed towards young Asian and black men has been seen as a form of discrimination, a behaviour that disproportionately targets and disadvantages individuals based on their perceived ethnic group membership.

Human history is blighted by problems of race, racism and/or **ethnocentrism**. Racism takes many forms, from the extreme racial hatred exemplified by neo-Nazi political groups, or genocidal violence, to the more subtle institutional racism and covert racism more typical of modern British life. Racism is an ideology of superiority, an ideology that functions to justify the political dominance of one racial group over another, and to ratify avoidance of or discrimination against other racial groups. It can function at the individual level, as an expression of personal prejudiced attitudes and discriminatory behaviour based on group membership. For example, one individual may express an individual attitude of dislike for members of a particular racial group, and indicate their racially motivated preference not to associate with members of that group. A South African author, Annelie Botes, recently stated publicly that 'I don't like black people', arguing that her fear of violence at the hands of black people justified that view (see *The Guardian*, 29 November 2010). This statement might be read as her personal expression of a racist attitude. However, we would suggest that this kind of statement is not simply an expression of individual processes, but that Botes' expressed racial attitude is one that is constituted within a particular social and political context (post-**apartheid** South Africa) and that analysing her response as purely a personal one is inappropriate. Furthermore, much racism functions at an institutional level. For example, the Stephen Lawrence Inquiry, which explored the police handling of the racially motivated murder of a young black man, revealed the British police force to be **institutionally racist**, suggesting that pervasive practices within the police force as an institution acted in a way that was significantly prejudicial to and discriminatory against black people (Macpherson, 1999). This analysis of institutional racism suggests that racism is not (just) an individual phenomenon, but that it is expressed and constructed within the social arrangements and practices of organisations, institutions and societies. Looking at racism within the British National Health Service, Allan et al. (2004) suggested that *racism and institutional racism are reproduced through personal and interpersonal as well as structured social relationships* (p117). This suggests that in order to understand the operation of racism, we need to explore its expression and construction at the individual, interpersonal and intergroup level.

In this chapter we explore the social psychological study of racism as an individual, interpersonal and intergroup phenomenon. We will review the literature on race and racism, including a consideration of ideas such as stereotyping and intergroup behaviour. We will also give some consideration to the place of race and ethnicity in identity.

The authoritarian personality

Research on authoritarianism emerged from an attempt to understand how seemingly 'ordinary' people would comply with extreme orders, as in the case of Nazi Germany. Researchers were concerned with the question of what makes ordinary, apparently decent human beings do terrible things when instructed to do so. Research on authoritarianism has been used in two contexts in social psychology – as an explanation of how and why people comply, and also as an understanding of how a particular form of racism might have emerged socially. In Chapter 5, we will consider the role of the **authoritarian personality** in conformity and obedience. In this chapter, we focus on the application of this theory to an understanding of racism.

Adorno et al.'s (1950) understanding of authoritarianism suggests that particular personality types are susceptible to fascist ideology, and that this has its roots in a particular family type, characterised by harsh discipline and dogmatic ideas. Authoritarianism is associated with ethnocentrism, which is a belief in the superiority of your own ethnic and cultural group, and an associated aversion to members of other ethnic and cultural groups. High levels of authoritarianism, as measured on the **F scale**, were found to be a significant predictor of prejudiced and racist views. Thus racism, within this theoretical framework, is essentially a personality flaw – a kind of **psychopathology**. Altemeyer's (1981) adaptation of Adorno et al.'s original theory suggests that the right-wing authoritarian personality is associated with high levels of conventionalism (a tendency to conform), authoritarian submission (excessive deferral to authority figures such as parents, government, other leadership figures), and authoritarian aggression (aggression directed to out-group members). Racism is understood as a projective process. In early childhood, children who are raised by authoritarian parents experience harsh, punitive parenting practices, particularly at the hands of authoritarian fathers. This punitive treatment produces an infantile rage, but fear of their fathers' reprisals mean that this rage cannot be expressed directly, and so is projected outwards – on to socially powerless others – for example, on to black people. Measures of right-wing authoritarianism (RWA) do correlate with negative expressed attitudes to other racial groups in a broad range of contexts. For example, Altemeyer (1998) found that high scores on the RWA scale strongly predicted anti-African-American prejudice; Duckitt (1992) found that it correlated with anti-black prejudice among white South Africans; Verkuyten and Hagendoorn (1998) found it was linked to anti-Turkish sentiment in the Netherlands; Heaven and St Quintin (2003) found it predicted racial prejudice in Australia. Further, Duriez and Soenens (2009) found that RWA is one of the mechanisms for transgenerational transmission of racist attitudes – this kind of ideology is literally 'passed on' from parent to child within the home environment.

However, Adorno's representation of racism as a feature of an authoritarian personality type has been criticised by many authors. Tajfel and Fraser (1978) point out that racism is too widespread a phenomenon to be explained as some kind of **deviance** or personality disorder. Also, it has been noted that many forms of racism have no particular association with the kind of upbringing and early history that the authoritarian personality theory would predict (Sidanius et al., 1986). Duckitt (2001) has suggested that the link between authoritarianism and racism relates to perceived membership of social groups, and cannot be explained by personality dynamics. In keeping with the intergroup theories we will discuss later in this chapter, Duckitt suggests that prejudice is mediated by our group membership. If we see another group as a threat to the interests of our own, and we score highly on the RWA scale, then we are very likely to express racist ideology.

Perhaps one of the key difficulties with the idea of the authoritarian personality as an explanation of racism is that it only accounts for one form of racism – that associated with relatively extremist right-wing views. However, racism and prejudice are often far subtler in their expression than this, and the model does not take into account **modern or symbolic racism** (Billig, 1982). Modern or symbolic racism is expressed less directly through institutional processes. It might be expressed in the way we talk, in patterns of inclusion and exclusion. For example, symbolic racism in Britain includes the way that black people from African and Caribbean backgrounds are far less likely to be represented on the boards of major companies, are less likely to receive a higher education, and are more likely to be represented among those 'excluded' from secondary education. These phenomena are hard to explain as expressions of the kind of overt, personal and direct racism that is expressed in the phenomenon of the authoritarian personality, and are far too widespread and too clearly built into social and institutional structures to be explained as a function of an individual's personality disorder.

In contrast to these pathologising, individualising accounts of racist practices and beliefs, more modern social psychology focuses on the social cognitive processes that produce prejudice and racism as a larger social phenomenon.

Stereotypes

A **stereotype** is an over-generalised belief about the characteristics of people, based on their group membership (Allport, 1954). Lippmann (1922) suggested that a stereotype is the image that comes to mind when we think about a particular social group – our idea of the 'typical example' that is then generalised to all members of that social group. Stereotypes are cognitive schemas that contain information about particular social groups, including assumptions about shared characteristics, shared **social roles**, etc. The stereotypes, for example, that 'white men can't jump' or that 'black people have natural rhythm' clearly involve attributing to an entire group a particular set of social characteristics. The stereotype may emerge from a number of possible sources: for example, it may be based on observation of the behaviours and traits of members of the social group and the over-generalising of these observations to all members of the group on the basis of available information or pervasive social attitudes.

The underpinning mechanism of stereotyping is **social categorisation**. This involves categorising people into groups on the basis of the perception of common attributes (Schneider, 2004). Basically, the theory of stereotyping suggests that, in much the same way as we categorise the material world into plants and animals, chairs and tables, so too, we categorise our social world. We are naturally oriented to perceiving our world categorically, and racial stereotyping is understood as an extension of this hardwired cognitive tendency to categorise the physical and social world. This facilitates the formation of heuristics, or common-sense social rules, which we use to simplify and understand our complex social worlds. In the case of, say, 'black people have natural rhythm', we might use this stereotype as a common-sense rule of thumb when making judgements about which young people we might want to include in a community dance project. Social categorisation is understood by most social psychologists who study prejudice to be the process that underlies the formation of **in-groups** and **out-groups** – groups we perceive to be 'like me' or 'not like me'. (We will return to this concept later in the chapter.)

Stereotypes often cluster together, and may be hierarchically organised. For example, we may hold a general stereotype that British Asians are generally quite religious and very family oriented. To this we may add specific exemplars – the Muslim man next door prays twice a day and often has his parents and his wife's parents visiting. The exemplar is seen as 'evidence' of the general rule of thumb we have constructed in association with the category we form. Stereotypes may also be structured and organised hierarchically – from the general category to the more specific. Think, for example, about the way that stereotypes around 'Islamic extremism' function. There is a general category of 'British Asians', to which a broad range of stereotypical characteristics might be attributed (for example, culturally embedded, committed to family life), within which the lower order category of 'British Muslim' is nested. The category 'British Muslim' incorporates the category of British Asian but we might add to it other stereotypical attributions (for example, religiously devout, holds 'traditional' ideas of gender relations). Within this there might be a further category of 'radical Muslim man', with increasingly stereotypical attributes such as 'sexist', 'violent', 'jihadist' etc.

How rigid are stereotypes, and what happens when our stereotype is challenged by new information? For example, an individual, Bob, may hold the Islamophobic view that 'all Muslims are sexist and potential jihadists', but he has a neighbour, Safiya, who he likes very much. Safiya is helpful, supportive and neighbourly, and does not conform to Bob's stereotype of followers of Islam. This presents him with a conundrum – how does he resolve the disparity between his existing stereotype and this additional information? The cognitive processes that underpin stereotyping ensure that, while they are open to some revision, they are also relatively stable. Because we are 'cognitive misers', human beings tend not to shift too far from their established beliefs in processing information – they are motivated to roughly maintain their existing stereo-types (Fiske and Taylor, 1984). Allport (1954) noted that one way in which stereotypes are maintained is by excluding counter-stereotypical individuals to maintain the original stereotype. So in the case of Bob and Safiya, Bob may position this friend as 'the exception that proves the rule', and will look for information that enables him to exclude the neighbour from the general stereotype, leaving the stereotype itself relatively untouched. He may find that his neighbour attended a Western school, is married to a white British man, and so is positioned as 'not typical'. So his stereotype is re-rendered as 'All Muslims are potential jihadists, except for Safiya, who has been exposed to Western values a lot when she was growing up, and therefore isn't like other Muslims'.

If presented with an accumulation of instances of 'exceptions' to the stereotype, it may need to be revised. Safiya introduces Bob to several of her friends, who are all pleasant, friendly and kind, and do not express any of the views that Bob holds in his stereotype, but who, unlike her, went to Muslim faith schools and are married to Muslim men. This may then result in the construction of a 'subtype' of 'good Muslims' versus the general and unchanged existing stereotype. Alternatively, if the disconfirming evidence is not too extreme, and if the disconfirmers are otherwise 'typical' in terms of Bob's stereotype, he may simply revise his stereotype to fit the new evidence. This involves reworking the stereotype to widen the existing category to include the disconfirming examples, and is typically a slow and incremental process. This happens most frequently when disconfirming examples are otherwise representative of their group (Bob can categorise them as 'typical Muslims' in lots of ways, but they don't fit his stereotype of being either sexist or jihadist).

The effect of stereotypes on their targets

We have considered the implications of stereotyping for the formation of racist attitudes and behaviours above. However, stereotypes also have implications for individual members of the stereotyped group too. For example, Steele and Aronson (1995) investigated the effect of the common stereotype that black students underachieved academically. They found that black students performed in a manner similar to their white counterparts on standardised tests of ability, except when their race was emphasised. The stereotype of black students as academically weak seemed to become salient when race was activated in tasks. If race was highlighted, this tended to predict poorer performance for black students. Essentially, this study suggests our academic performance might be negatively affected when we think it will be judged in terms of racial stereotypes. Steele and Aronson term this phenomenon 'stereotype threat', and suggest that it is a consequence of the perception that we are somehow at risk of confirming a negative stereotype as a personal characteristic. It has been suggested that stereotype threat can explain phenomena such as reduced practice time for a task (Stone, 2002) – rather than 'fail' and confirm the racial stereotype, individuals do not try as hard, offering an alternative possible explanation for their failure (it is about lack of practice, not lack of ability). Stereotype threat will be stronger in conditions that highlight the stereotype, and where the individual is strongly associated with the stereotyped social category (Marx and Stapel, 2006). So, for example, if you see yourself as a black boy, and a prevalent stereotype is that young black boys perform poorly in literacy tasks, then when presented with a literacy task your category membership as a black boy becomes salient. This results in a (not always conscious) self-talk along the lines of 'I am a black boy, black boys aren't good at literacy. This is a tricky literacy test'. This kind of perception of the self in terms of category membership, and in terms of association with the negative stereotype, can disrupt performance because of anxiety about reproducing and confirming negative group stereotypes. Schmader and Johns (2003) suggest that the stereotype threat might have a negative impact on working memory, which, in turn, will have an effect on performance. Stereotype threat is often offered as an explanation for the phenomenon of underachievement by black boys and young black men in education.

Task — Read through the extract below from an article in *The Observer*.

Do you think that the idea of stereotype threat is a sufficient explanation for the phenomenon?

Can you think of social or political issues that might be neglected in the social psychological suggestion that these differences are a result of young black men's own *perceptions* of racial stereotypes?

Is this really a purely cognitive phenomenon in the way social psychologists suggest?

Take exclusions, for example. Pupils from non-white British backgrounds were as likely in 2008–09 to be permanently excluded as pupils overall. But a more detailed analysis shows large differences between groups.

The lowest permanent exclusion rates were among the Asian community, with five out of every 10,000 pupils being excluded, followed by children with one white and one Asian parent.

Those closer to the average of 10 permanent exclusions per 10,000 were white British, black African, Irish and mixed white/black African children. Yet children with one white and one black Caribbean parent were 2.5 times more likely to be excluded than average, with a rate of 25 per 10,000 pupils. The highest rates of exclusions were found among Gypsy/Roma children, who were more than three times more likely to be excluded, followed by black Caribbean pupils.

. . .

Rob Berkeley, director of the Runnymede Trust, a leading race equality think-tank, said . . . "tomorrow's report makes clear that ethnicity still matters" – even if you control the factor of class, he added. So it is a little early to declare "mission accomplished".

He said the issue of race inequality had become complex and it was urgent to highlight what parts of disadvantage were about racial discrimination and what were about something else.

(Astana, A (2010) Britain's Divided Schools, *The Observer,* 10 October 2010)

(Reproduced from *The Observer* newspaper with the permission of the Guardian Media Group plc (copyright Guardian Media Group plc))

Using an understanding of stereotypes to reduce racism, prejudice and discrimination: the contact hypothesis

Allport (1954) suggested that a key aspect in understanding racism and intolerance was the lack of contact between racial groups. He suggested that both formal and informal practices of **segregation** meant that members of varying social groups did not have the opportunity to get to know one another, and that lack of knowledge increased the likelihood that individuals who were members of these groups would develop negative stereotypes about the other group. The impetus behind the contact hypothesis as an approach to understanding racism is a plea for political tolerance (Shamir and Sagiv-Schifter, 2006). This understanding of racism works with the assumption that prejudiced attitudes and behaviour emerge as a result of a poor understanding of the culture and practices of particular groups: we are racist primarily because we are ignorant of others' social values. It is suggested that to challenge the rigidity, over-generalisation and inaccuracy of racial stereotypes requires the development of a more detailed and accurate understanding of the racial groups on which they are based. In other words, reason, education and information will reduce racism.

Recent work investigating the contact hypothesis has been quite mixed – sometimes contact appears to be very effective in reducing racial prejudice, but in other contexts it has no effect, or may even increase it. For example, Vezzali et al. (2010) explored Allport's hypothesis in the Italian context, using a questionnaire to study the attitudes of Italian (majority) and immigrant (minority) secondary school students. They found that, consistent with Allport's hypothesis, as contact increased longitudinally, young people held fewer negative stereotypes about members of the other group, and positive attitudes increased. However, Smith et al. (2006) investigated the common-sense understanding that is embodied in the contact hypothesis (that familiarity and understanding will reduce the formation of stereotypical attitudes) and found that often the opposite is true – familiarity can function to actually increase stereotyping.

What factors might predict whether contact is effective as a means of reducing intergroup conflict and challenging racial stereotypes? Rothbart and John (1985) extended Allport's basic concept, suggesting that contact works as part of *the general cognitive process by which attributes of category members modify category attributes* (p82). So essentially, Rothbart and John suggest that our contact with individuals who challenge the general categories we have formed will act to modify the stereotypical category. They suggest that contact will reduce prejudice and racial stereotyping if three criteria are met.

1. *Contact is with members of the group who behave in a way that is inconsistent with the stereotype.* In the context of apartheid South Africa, Duckitt (1992) pointed out that many white South Africans continued to hold racist stereotypes about black people despite daily contact with them in their places of work and in their homes where black women often served as domestic workers. He suggested that mere contact is not sufficient to reduce prejudice. In this context, contact with poor, black working-class people, performing menial tasks such as factory work and domestic labour, did not function to disrupt racist views, but rather could function to reinforce stereotypes that suggested that black people were a 'labouring class'.

2. *Contact occurs in a range of different contexts and is fairly frequent.* To reduce prejudice, the contact experience needs to be generalisable. Having contact with people from other racial groups as part of, say, a church group, would do little to reduce prejudice if that were the only context in which contact took place. Knowledge gained from contact limited to just one setting is easily dismissed as somehow extraordinary, and therefore the stereotype is not challenged. Brown and Hewstone (2005) suggest that for contact to be successful it needs to take place in a context where group membership is significant as this encourages generalisation to other members of the contact group.

3. *Contact is with members of the social group who are seen as typical.* If the contact is with someone who you can see as 'just a regular member' of the social group, it will be much more effective. The contact experience cannot be dismissed as atypical and the members are not seen as 'exceptions that prove the rule'.

In addition to these criteria, subsequent research has suggested that other features of the contact situation have a significant impact on the value of the contact experience for reducing prejudice.

For example, Hamberger and Hewstone (1997) highlight the importance of the context, noting that contact at work often does not function to reduce prejudice, and in some cases can actually function to intensify prejudice. They suggest that this is because workplace relationships are often not seen as being substantial or intimate, and that the workplace itself can be a competitive environment in which ethnic minority colleagues may be viewed as rivals. Similarly, research suggests that superficial but regular contact can function to intensify intergroup hostility, rather than reduce it, as familiarity without interaction makes it more likely that we will rely on stereotypes rather than real knowledge and understanding to evaluate our peers (Smith et al., 2006). Smith et al. suggest that this is a feature of the laziness that characterises human cognitive processing. Because we are familiar with a person or situation, we are likely to use heuristics (common-sense rules of thumb) more rather than less, because we process familiar material more shallowly.

Evaluating stereotypes

When considering research that is based on the notion of stereotypes, it is important to remember that the link between attitude and behaviour is always imperfect – holding a stereotyped attitude about, say, British Asian people does not necessarily directly produce racist behaviour. Indeed, a key problem in research around stereotyping is the question of what mediates this behavioural response. A further problem in work on stereotypes is a methodological one. Fiske et al. (2010) point out that while discrimination involves an overt behavioural act that can be perceived by other people, stereotyping is primarily an intrapsychic process and is not necessarily easily observed by the outside world. This means that we have to operationalise stereotyping in some way in order to observe and measure it.

Stereotypes are understood within social psychology as cognitive phenomena. The social significance of stereotyping is that it does not simply function at the level of thought, but that it has emotional and behavioural outcomes. Stereotypes are not just cognitive phenomena, but also include an emotional component. Fiske and Taylor (1991) suggest that stereotypes activate *a range of preferences, evaluations, moods and emotions* (p410). Associated with the stereotype are emotional reactions such as like or dislike, evaluations such as good or bad, and preferences such as 'I will socialise with them' or 'I will not socialise with them'. Stereotypes therefore do not just predict what we think about members of other social groups, but also how we feel and act towards out-group members. When considering this affective component, it is important to remember that stereotypes do not always function in a way that is straightforwardly negative. Fiske et al. (2002) explored stereotypes by placing attitudes on scales of warmth and competence, and found that stereotyping was often an ambivalent process. For example, stereotypes of older people tended to blend high warmth (positive feelings) and low competence, while stereotypes of rich people tended to blend high competence and low warmth (negative feelings).

Finally, as with all social cognitive research, it is important to consider the degree to which stereotyping offers a sufficiently social explanation of racism, ethnocentrism and prejudice. If we understand racism as a feature of human cognition, as an aspect of 'natural' cognitive processes, are we not running the risk of ignoring important social, economic and material processes that underpin racism in the modern world?

Realistic conflict theory

There has been much concern in Europe in the past few years about the rise of the extreme right, and particularly the rise of neo-Nazi and fascist organisations whose politics hinge largely on assumptions of white superiority and concerns about immigration into the EU. In Austria in 2008, 30 per cent of the general election vote went to ultra-right parties. Similarly, the ultra right gained 15 per cent in popularity in Austria, Slovakia, Holland and Denmark in the 2009 EU election. The discourses of the extreme right often draw on notions of competition and encroachment to justify the more racist aspects of their ideology. Comments about 'Britain being full', or it being a 'small island' that would sink under the weight of immigration exemplify this kind of position. In this way, these ultra-right parties produce anxiety around competition for territory and other material resources as a means of galvanising anti-immigrant sentiment.

The **realistic conflict theory** was developed by Muzafer Sherif, Carolyn Sherif and their colleagues (Sherif and Sherif, 1953; Sherif et al., 1955, 1961) to explore the possibility that intergroup phenomena such as racial conflict might be linked to conflict over limited material resources. Essentially, if we perceive that we are in competition with members of other social groups for resources, and if those resources are not plentiful, then we are more likely to develop negative attitudes and behaviours towards that group. Therefore, Sherif and his colleagues propose that hostile **intergroup behaviour** is produced by intergroup competition.

To investigate the relationship between competition, conflict and the development of prejudice and discrimination, the Sherifs attempted to set up a series of naturalistic experiments at a Boy Scout camp in the Robbers Cave National Park (Sherif and Sherif, 1953; Sherif, et al., 1955, 1961). The research set out to consider the hypothesis that, when individuals come together to interact in a group they will construct a group structure with its own hierarchies and roles, and that if two such groups come into contact and are positioned to compete with each other, particularly under difficult circumstances, that hostile intergroup behaviour will emerge. This piece of research is referred to as the Robbers Cave Experiment. Posing as the camp janitor, Muzafer Sherif observed the boys who attended the camp, paying particular attention to the formation of intergroup behaviour. A group of 22 middle-class boys from intact families and similar backgrounds, all apparently emotionally and physically healthy, were taken to the Robbers Cave campsite.

This first phase of the experiment (Sherif and Sherif, 1953) involved the formation of in-groups. The boys were divided into two groups of 11, with any pre-existing friendships being split up across the two groups. The boys arrived at the camp on separate buses, neither aware of the existence of the other group. For several days, the boys lived at the camp in their two separate groups, enabling natural intergroup social ties to be established. They named themselves 'The Eagles' and 'The Rattlers'. Each group developed its own social hierarchy, with the emergence of clear leadership figures.

After a few days, the boys became aware of the presence of the other group. The boys' sense of their own group membership seemed to be quite strong, and they expressed concerns and became defensive about the other group's use of camp facilities. Both groups also requested that the camp staff set up competitions between the two groups. In-group activities were performed more enthusiastically as the whiff of possible competition was in the air. The presence of an out-group seemed to make the boys want to do better within their groups at swimming, baseball and tent pitching, all of which seemed to become ways of competing at a distance with the other group of boys.

In the next phase of the research, the 'friction phase', researchers brought the two groups together in direct competition with each other. They arranged a series of competitive activities, with a trophy to be awarded at the end of the competition to the group with the highest score, and with pocket knives to be given out to individuals from the winning team. The announcement of the intergroup tournament brought out strong intergroup behaviour. 'The Rattlers' claimed the ball field as their own practice site, putting up a 'Keep Off' sign to ward off their competitors. They spent a lot of time discussing tactics and making disparaging remarks about the chances of their competitors. They put up their own flag, and even made threatening comments about what would happen to The Eagles if anyone disturbed the flag. When the two groups were formally brought together in the dining room, a great deal of intergroup behaviour was observed – including name-calling, jeering and singing rude songs about each other. Members of The Eagles refused to eat with The Rattlers. The intergroup behaviour intensified, and included a flag-burning incident and the raiding of each others' cabins. The Eagles won the competition – this produced a string of hostile incidents and name-calling became commonplace. The boys would hold their noses as they passed out-group members. Both groups refused to share meals.

The final stage of the research involved the researchers de-escalating the hostility that the friction phase had produced. In the first instance, they tried simple contact-based activities such as getting together for fireworks or to watch a film. This produced no real reduction in intergroup hostilities (one attempt at reconciliation ended with a food fight . . .). Once simple contact had failed, the research team introduced co-operative activities focused on a unifying superordinate goal. For example, boys were told that vandals had damaged the water system that supplied the camp with water from the local reservoir. The boys went out to try to resolve this problem and found a full tank of water with a tap that had been blocked with a sack. If the boys wanted to drink or use the toilets, they would have to fix the problem. Faced with a problem that threatened both groups of boys, they began to work co-operatively to solve the problem, suggesting and trying out solutions together. When the water came through, the boys celebrated together and were gracious in the distribution of water. Several co-operative tasks of this sort were introduced as part of camp life, and functioned to reduce intergroup hostility. Sherif and his colleagues suggested that the reduction of hostility was a result of joint activity in pursuit of superordinate goals as well as the joint celebration of achievement. On the final day, most of the boys agreed that they would prefer to share the bus home, and boys did not sit in their in-groups on the bus on the way home.

So what does the Robbers Cave Experiment tell us about intergroup prejudice and racism? Dixon and Durrheim (2003) suggest that conflict and threat often precede racial intolerance. When groups are perceived as having different goals, or goals that clash with each other, and are competing for resources such as housing, jobs etc., intergroup conflict is often an outcome. While this kind of threat perception can produce conflict between groups without interference in the modern world, we often see this manipulated by interest groups. For example, the British National Party campaigned on the slogan 'British Jobs for British Workers' for several years, suggesting essentially that British livelihoods were threatened by immigration, and that the scarce resource of available jobs should be reserved for (white) British people. It might be argued that by galvanising anxiety about scarce resources (jobs and housing), the party was able to drum up anti-immigrant sentiment, effectively producing racist sentiment in areas where they were most successful.

In modern accounts of the realistic conflict theory, authors are at pains to point out that the competition is not just about material resources, but also about symbolic resources in which our sense of group identity is often rooted. Again, considering the example of the British National Party, much is often made of the notion of 'Britishness' in the discourses of the BNP. Consider, for example, their use of Winston Churchill and other symbols of the Second World War in their campaign materials for the 2010 election. This was a clear attempt to galvanise a sense of British identity through the use of national symbols of pride. Referring to real-world conflicts such as the prolonged conflict between Palestine and Israel, Shamir and Sagiv-Schifter (2006) suggest that the conflict between these warring sides centres on land and boundaries as well as statehood and national identity. They suggest that the question of material resources (land, access to cities, national boundaries) is intermingled with the notion of the right to exist as a people, as nation states, for both parties to the conflict. Disputes over Jerusalem, or of Palestinians' right of return to Israel, are not simply about the places, but about the sense of identity bound up in those spaces. Further, Shamir and Sagiv-Schifter suggest that while conflict elicits threat, *it also enhances people's identification with the collective: their attachment to their ingroup becomes more salient, more functional, stronger; "ingroup love" as well as "outgroup hate" increase* (p371).

They are arguing that when trying to understand intergroup conflict, it is important that it is not simply about hostility to the out-group, but that the experience of intergroup conflict also often brings with it a strengthening of in-group bonds. In the next section, we will consider one attempt to understand how this in-group identification is built up in the first place.

Task —— Think about your experience of school. Think particularly of things like sports days, being put into groups to compete for academic prizes, being in a 'house' at school, etc.

— Do you think these experiences have anything in common with the Robbers Cave experiments?

— Did they produce intergroup conflict?

Social identity theory

How is our sense of identification with a particular group built up? How do we come to identify ourselves as raced, as classed, as gendered? How do we arrive at a place where we see ourselves as members of a team, as part of a community? How is that sense of belonging constructed? Tajfel and Turner (1986) suggest that our group membership is a source of pride and self-esteem, and that how we feel about the groups we belong to has significant implications for how we feel about ourselves. Their **social identity theory** offers an important theoretical account for an understanding of this sense of belonging to a group, and this theoretical tradition offers important insights into our understanding of race and racism.

Social identity theory is concerned with the formation of in-groups and out-groups – groups we feel we belong to, and groups we perceive to be different from us – and the implications of these groups for our identities. As we noted earlier in the chapter, the key mechanism for the formation of in-groups and out-groups is social categorisation. Social identity theory suggests that because we base such a large part of our self-esteem on our group membership, we are strongly motivated to feel positive about groups we belong to. This can result in us overstating the positive aspects of the groups we belong to, and being overly negative about the groups we do not belong to.

Minimal groups

How are in-groups and out-groups formed? In 1968, distressed by the violence and racism she observed in the storm around the American civil rights movement, Jane Elliott, a school teacher from Iowa, conducted an informal experiment with the children in her class to help them to understand racism and its impact. The exercise she developed involved identifying the children in her class with blue and brown eyes, and then suggesting that the group with blue eyes was superior, would have privileges and would succeed in life, while the other group, with brown eyes, was inferior, unpleasant, associated with negative social characteristics, would take second place in class to the blue-eyed children, and were unlikely to succeed in life. Imitating the racist and eugenicist language of American racism in the 1950s and 1960s, she taught these children 'facts' about the inferiority of brown-eyed children. After a relatively short period of time, the blue-eyed children started to take on superior and arrogant attitudes, while the brown-eyed children began to accept their positioning as 'inferior', exhibiting some characteristics of internalised oppression and learned helplessness. She then reversed the situation, with brown-eyed children in the superior position and blue-eyed children in the inferior class, and found similar results (though the brown-eyed children were more sensitive to the experiences of the blue-eyed children in the reverse condition, having had such a recent experience of discrimination themselves). Her basic premise was that racial prejudice was based on relatively trivial physical distinctions between people – that race lacks any ontological reality. By recreating what are essentially racialised dynamics based on the perception of group difference rooted in very trivial distinctions, Elliott was able to support this idea with the evidence produced in her classroom.

The minimal group experiments are an attempt to systematically study the way that in-groups and out-groups are formed as a function of perception of difference. Rabbie and Horwitz (1969) conducted the first formal 'minimal group' experiment to explore the processes of social categorisation that underpin the formation of in-groups and out-groups. Essentially, minimal groups research is interested in establishing the minimal conditions necessary for these group categorisation processes to be triggered – the conditions under which in-groups and out-groups will be formed. Rabbie and Horwitz suggested that simply perceiving interdependence is sufficient to provoke group feelings, and intergroup behaviour – group feelings emerge if we feel we and other group members have a 'common fate'. In their study, schoolchildren were randomly divided into two groups of four, members of each group were given either blue or green name badges and were seated together, unable to see the other group. In the control group, this was all that occurred. In the experimental group, group members were either given or deprived of a radio, based on their group membership. Once group members had been told this, the screen separating the two groups was removed, and individual members were asked to read out some information about themselves, while the members of the two groups rated their contributions. In the experimental condition, Rabbie and Horwitz noted that ratings were affected by group membership (ratings for in-group members were higher than for out-group members), but no such effect was noted in the control group. They concluded that group membership itself was not enough for intergroup behaviour to emerge, and that there needed to be an added dimension of reward or loss for group perceptions to develop.

Tajfel et al. (1971) revisited this idea of minimal groups in a piece of research that suggested that Rabbie and Horwitz might have underestimated the impact of 'mere perception' of group membership. Initially interested by the Sherif's Robbers Cave Experiment, Tajfel had queried whether the element of actual competition was a necessary component for the production of intergroup behaviour, or whether mere perception of group membership was sufficient for the production of in-group favouritism and out-group discrimination. In the Tajfel et al. experiment, schoolboys were shown images of abstract art, which they rated. They were then told that they were part of a group that exhibited a preference for either Kandinsky or Klee. (In fact, the assignment to groups was random.) They only knew their own group membership – they had not been told who else was in the group with them. They were then told they were taking part in a study about decision making, and were asked to use specially designed booklets to allocate money to other participants in the experiment. When allocating money to each group member, they knew what group they were in (Klee or Kandinsky), but they did not know who that individual actually was. Tajfel et al. found that boys in this experiment consistently allocated money in a way that maximised the difference in the money allocated to group members, and that this was done along in-group lines. In other words, despite not even knowing who the individuals in their group were, participants consistently favoured in-group members over out-group members. The tendency to allocate money to maximise difference between the in-group and the out-group was so strong that it even functioned in conditions where allocating money to maximise difference actually meant that the final amount of money allocated to the in-group was less overall. This tendency to favour in-groups at the expense of out-groups is called the in-group–out-group bias. Based on these results, the authors developed their minimal group paradigm, which suggests that the mere perception of group membership is enough for the beginnings of group identity to emerge. The study has been replicated extensively, using various conditions to form the minimal conditions for group membership and a range of tasks to enable participants to reward or discriminate against in-group and out-group members (for example, Tajfel, 1982; Wilder, 1990; Hartstone and Augoustinos, 1995; Ben-Ner et al., 2009).

The formation of in-groups and out-groups has consequences for the way that both groups are perceived. In addition to research around in-group favouritism, studies have also identified an out-group homogeneity bias – a tendency to see all members of the out-group as sharing similar characteristics and traits. While in-group members are often seen as more heterogeneous (for example, Linville et al., 1996), views of out-group members are far less differentiated (Judd et al., 1991).

Social identity theory suggests that the process of categorising people into in-groups (people like me) and out-groups (people not like me) is a natural and universal one. The theory suggests that these social categories may hinge on trivial differences, but nonetheless will have consequences for how we relate to other people, who we favour and who we don't. This is the case even if the groups have no significant basis, and even if the in-groups and out-groups we perceive lack any substantial social anchor (Tajfel, 1981; Tajfel et al., 1971). It is important to note that this body of research involves experimental conditions that remove both conflict of interest between the groups and self-interest (you cannot allocate rewards to yourself in these experiments), and the formation of the groups is nominal (they are anonymous, and based on very trivial distinctions) (Kinder and Kam, 2009).

Minimal groups and social identity

How then, according to social identity theory, do these minimal groups impact on our **social identity**? Social identity is defined as *that part of an individual's self-concept that derives from his knowledge of his membership of a social group . . . together with the value and emotional significance attached to that membership* (Tajfel, 1981, p225).

It is the aspect of individual self-concept that emerges from our perception of social group membership (Hogg and Vaughan, 2002). Social identity theory is essentially about the social and cognitive processes that underlie the way that 'I' becomes 'we'. The theory suggests that we do not have one personal self, but multiple selves, corresponding to our various group memberships. So, for example, I am a woman, a white person, a mother, a lecturer, a choir member, a cellist, a geek . . . All of these examples are clearly part of my personal identity, my sense of I, but are derived from my membership of various social groups, my sense of we. Varying social contexts make particular identities more salient at particular times. Turner et al. (1987) suggest that we have varying levels of self (personal, family, or national), which are linked to different kinds of social identity.

As we have seen in the previous section, human beings engage quite quickly in processes of self/other categorisation, a process that forms in-groups and out-groups, and that leads us to favour in-groups and discriminate against out-groups. How does an understanding of social identity help us to understand why the mere formation of these groups seems to be sufficient for the beginnings of intergroup behaviour to stir? Tajfel and Turner (1986) suggested that we are motivated to feel positively about ourselves and that a positive social identity is a key component of a positive identity. Once in-group/out-group classification has taken place, the particular group membership becomes incorporated into our sense of identity, and we begin to look for ways of building positive self-esteem through a process of **social comparison** (Tajfel and Turner, 1979). They suggest that the process of group formation involves three processes. First, we engage in social categorisation, the process whereby groups are formed (perceiving groups or categories of person). The second stage involves social identification. We identify ourselves as members of a particular group, and probably begin to behave in a way that fits our perception of how members of that group behave. As the definition of social identity above suggests, this is not merely a cognitive process as there is a strong affective component. Our group membership has an emotional significance to us – we care about the groups we belong to. Belonging itself has a certain emotional valence to it. Think about the things that you care about, the things that you are passionate about (sport, parenting, reading, being a student, being a member of a particular ethnic or religious group): most of the time, these are linked in some way to our social identities – our sense of where we belong, and with whom. The third stage of the process is social comparison. Having categorised ourselves as a member of a particular group, and having identified with it, our desire for positive self-esteem means that we start to compare our group with others. Think, for example, of the rivalry that builds up between supporters of various football teams. Arsenal supporters make scathing comments about Spurs or Chelsea, and the hostility between Manchester City and Manchester United supporters has been known to provoke riots! Because our group identity is an aspect of our personal identity, we are motivated to maintain a positive image of the groups we identify with, and this is done through the process of comparing in-groups and out-groups. Groups distinguish themselves from, and discriminate against others, in order to maintain positive self-esteem through a positive social evaluation (Jenkins, 2009). The important mechanism here is distinctiveness – in order to enable positive comparisons to be made, we need to demonstrate how our social groups are distinct. In the minimal groups context, where the distinction between groups is so arbitrary and trivial, research participants maintain this positive distinction by the only means available to them – the allocation of positive rewards to in-group members at the expense of out-group members (Brown, 1996). This process of social comparison is crucial to the understanding of prejudice and racism that social identity theory offers. The world is organised in various social categories, and racial and ethnic groups are a major form of social categorisation. Consequently, social comparison based on ethnic and racial lines is, according to social identity theory, an inevitable social cognitive process.

What do we do if our social comparison process leaves us with a negative evaluation of our group? Social identity theory predicts that this depends on the intersection of three variables: stability (our perception of how easily social categories can be changed); legitimacy (whether the status structure of social categories is seen as fair and just); and permeability (how easily group members are able to move from one social category to another). If social categories are seen as permeable, an obvious option would be to simply leave the group (**social mobility**). Where this is more difficult to achieve, and particularly if the stability of the social system is perceived to be high (and thus social change is unlikely), individuals might disidentify with the group. Tajfel and Turner (1979) term this strategy **individual mobility**, suggesting that we tend to distance ourselves psychologically from low-status social groups with which we might be identified.

Ikegami (2010) looked at how a belief in 'elite academic institutions' impacts on individuals in moderate-status universities. He found that participants who had a high belief in the elite status of particular kinds of universities (such as Oxbridge, Harvard etc.) tended to disidentify with their own moderate-status universities and disparage lower-status universities. This kind of research supports the view that if we perceive our in-group to be low status, we are likely to attempt to leave the group, either physically or symbolically through disidentification. Early social psychological research yielded many examples of this kind of strategy. For example, in the Clark and Clark (1947) study of black American children, they found that many black children did not identify strongly with being black, appeared to have negative evaluations of being African-American, and identified more strongly with the dominant white social group. Social identity theory would suggest that this is a result of negative social comparison. As Tajfel and Turner (1986) point out, this strategy is an individual one that does nothing to change the low status of our social group.

A more group-based strategy to deal with the problem of a negative social comparison is the possibility of **social creativity**. This typically happens when the group status hierarchy is seen as unjust, when permeability is limited, but when we think that **social change** is possible. This strategy involves redefining the characteristics of the derogated social group as positive. The black consciousness movement, with its slogans like 'black is beautiful', is a clear example of this kind of social creative process.

This strategy can produce the conditions under which a third strategy – social change – becomes possible. If the status quo is viewed as illegitimate and if the possibility for changing the categorisation hierarchy is possible, then social change is entertained as a possible solution to the problem of negative social comparison. Social change involves changing the definitions of in-groups and out-groups, and engaging in processes of recategorisation. This kind of thinking also underpins the late twentieth-century celebratory discourses of multiculturalism, which suggest that we should redefine the idea of status hierarchies themselves. So, for example, in the UK ethnic distinctions were seen as being swept away by the logic of a culturally diverse Britain. In the UK context, the definition of Britishness, for example, has been significantly widened socially to include British Asian and black British identities, representing a clear shift from the narrower reading of Britishness as simply referring to white British people.

However, it is important to remember that social change can occur quite superficially, and may not always have lasting and permanent effects. Across the UK and Europe, the twenty-first century has seen a shift in the valuing of the ideology of multiculturalism, which is increasingly seen as outmoded (Verkuyten, 2008; Scroggins, 2005; Entzinger, 2003). Public discourses in particular focus heavily on the ideal of cultural assimilation (the view that ethnic minority members should simply fit in with dominant cultural norms), making the creative strategy of celebratory multi-culturalism difficult to maintain (Fredrickson, 1999). Most political parties in the last general election in the UK had a policy on 'curbing immigration', and the idea of Britain (and other European countries) as being 'threatened' by immigration is now a powerful and widely accepted public discourse (Capdevila and Callaghan, 2008).

What about the 'social' in social identity theory?

In the experimental context, the removal of real-world drivers of prejudice, such as conflict of interest, competition over real material conditions and self-interest is both the strength and the weakness of this body of research. There is a question as to whether an abstract set of experimental conditions, deliberately stripped down to the barest possible social cognitive processes, really has much to contribute to the complexity and messiness of real-world racism, ethnocentrism and prejudice. Tajfel (1982) was quite diffident about the use of the minimal groups paradigm in an explanation of real-world conflicts (noting that this focus on perceptual processes underpinning group formation cannot take the place of social and economic analysis). Nonetheless, the tradition of social identity theory has often been guilty of neglecting social context, and focusing overly on perceptual processes, often in laboratory settings explicitly designed to strip the social context away. Indeed, recent research has attempted to further individualise social identity theory, suggesting that in-group favouritism includes a stronger individual component than Tajfel and Turner's original work had predicted, emerging, for example, as a function of the link between evaluation of in-group status and of positive self-image (Clement and Krueger, 2002; Gramzow et al., 2001). Some researchers suggest that our self-description is a core aspect of personal identity, and that we tend to project that self-image as an aspect of the in-group. Most people evaluate themselves positively, and it is suggested that this generalising of personal self-esteem to the group as a whole is a sufficient explanation for in-group favouritism – it is an extension of personal regard (Koole et al., 2001). Effectively, this research flips round the assumptions of social identity theory – that group identity becomes an important component of personal identity – suggesting instead that how we feel about, say, our racial group, is a reflection of how we feel about ourselves. This process of projecting how we feel about ourselves on to our in-group is referred to as social projection (Clement and Kruger, 2002) or in-group self-anchoring (Cadinu and Rothbart, 1996). While this line of research might illustrate that the popular social identity theory is not the only possible explanation of the connection between personal and social identity, we would argue that it is a politically very problematic account of in-group and out-group processes. While the argument is perhaps unproblematic when explaining positive social identity, we would suggest that it becomes rather more oppressive when accounting for negative social identity. Say, for example, a young black woman is a victim of racist abuse, and feels negatively about herself and her racial group as a consequence of this experience. The social projection argument heavily individualises this process, suggesting that the negative identity is a consequence of the group member's poor self-esteem. Essentially, she is positioned as feeling bad about being black because she has personal self-esteem issues. This feeds into potentially racist discursive constructions, which suggest, for example, that ethnic minority members have 'chips' on their shoulders, and can function to further oppress minority groups.

In contrast, many researchers seek to extend social identity theory by attempting to explore more fully how the perceptual processes of categorisation involved in the establishment of minimal groups intersect with social and economic processes. Context has a clear impact on the importance of social categorisation, shaping the way that in-group/out-group classifications might result in positive or negative social comparisons, and consequent negative intergroup behaviour (prejudice, racism, etc.). As Brewer (2001) suggests, it is our social context – our norms, ideologies, cultural values and social practices – that determines *when ingroup love becomes outgroup hate* (p17). While positive in-group identification may have a strong influence on the development of prejudice towards out-group members, it is not the only factor that predicts this (Brewer, 2001; Duckitt, 2003). Social processes, and in particular social conflict, have a potent influence on whether social categorisation predicts hostility in real-world conflict situations (Duckitt and Mphuthing, 1998).

Shamir and Sagiv-Shifter (2006) suggest that the insights of realistic group conflict theory might help us to extend the application of social identity theory. They note that perception of threat increases intolerance under conditions of real-life conflict, and that the intensity of our in-group identification also mediates the relationship between real-world conflict and political intolerance. Looking at hostility and political intolerance in the Palestine–Israeli conflict around the time of the Al Aqsa intifada, they suggest that conflict increases threat perception, but that it also strengthens in-group identity, and that both these factors act to increase political intolerance. They suggest that the effect of both in-group identity and threat perception on political intolerance is activated by conflict. For example, during times of significant conflict and perceived threat of violence *salience and attachment to Jewish collective identity* increased (p587) and tolerance levels declined – in other words, social processes intensified the in-group favouritism aspect of social identity and bolstered out-group hostility. In-group–out-group distinctions increased through the intifada, hinging on the Jewish-Arab distinction. Attitudes shifted from more pluralist to focused intolerance throughout the conflict. Shamir and Sagiv-Shifter concluded that, in relation to real-world conflict, intergroup processes are strongly influenced by perceptions of threat and hostility, and cannot be simply understood as a function of social-perceptual processes.

Critical thinking activity

We're not racists, but . . .

Critical thinking focus: creative and critical thinking

Key question: *How do these theories of intergroup processes help us to understand textual accounts of race and racism?*

Read the following extract from interviews with two prominent representatives of the British National Party.

Example 1: Nick Griffin on BBC *Question Time*, 22 October 2009.

I say that Churchill would belong in the British National Party because no other party would have him [for what] he said in the early days on mass immigration into this country, or the fact that 'they're only coming for our benefit system', and for the fact that in his younger days he was extremely critical of the dangers of fundamentalist

Islam in a way which would now be described as Islamophobic. I believe that the whole of the effort of the Second World War, and the First, was designed to protect British sovereignty, British freedom, which Jack Straw's government are now giving away lock, stock and barrel to the EU, and to prevent this country being invaded by foreigners. Finally, my father was in the RAF during the Second World War while Mr Straw's father was in prison for refusing to fight Adolf Hitler.

The indigenous British . . . skin colour is irrelevant . . . Jack Straw wouldn't dare go to New Zealand and say to a Maori, what do you mean indigenous? He wouldn't go to North America and say to an American Red Indian what do you mean indigenous, we're all the same. The indigenous people of this island are the English, the Scots the Irish and the Welsh . . . colour is irrelevant, it's the people who have been here overwhelmingly for the last 17,000 years. We are the aborigines here. I'm sorry if you laugh.

Example 2: Andrew Norfolk, BNP advances on Middle England to exploit 'fear' of Polish migrants, *The Times*, 23 April 2007. (Available at www.timesonline.co.uk/tol/news/politics/article1690422.ece)

Since 2004, however, North Yorkshire has become home to thousands of migrant workers from eastern Europe, the majority of them young Poles who have found jobs in employment sectors ranging from farms and factories to hotels, restaurants and care homes. Tom Linden, the BNP organiser for North Yorkshire, says their willingness to accept relatively low rates of pay is driving down wages, undercutting British workers and leading to reduced investment in training.

"Why would an employer put British teenagers through apprenticeships when he can advertise for some workers in Poland and get them the next day?" The BNP, he said, saw "a massive untapped potential in North Yorkshire. Local people are suffering every day, not just because the country is being taken over by non-native British people, but because of things like crime and antisocial behaviour."

Use the following prompts to guide you through an analysis of these extracts.

– Summarise the key points made by the two interviewees. What do they say about Britishness; immigration; race; indigenousness; nativeness or non-nativeness? What traits are associated with British people, and with immigrants?

– Do you see evidence of race and racial talk in the extracts? How are these references to race made, and what strategies do the speakers use to hide their racialised references?

How do you think the theoretical models we have considered so far would make sense of these extracts? Is there material here that could be explained by: authoritarian personality theory?; an approach focused on stereotyping?; realistic conflict theory?; social identity theory?

What does your analysis of these extracts tell you about the usefulness of each of these theories in the analysis of contemporary racist talk?

Critical thinking review

This activity helps develop your skills of creative and critical thinking, and application of theory, in relation to two extracts from interviews with prominent members of the British National Party. To do this, you have broken the extracts down into their component parts, analysing the textual material for evidence of talk about race and national identity. You have applied your theoretical social psychological knowledge to help you to extend this textual analysis. This enabled you to think about the usefulness of these concepts in practice.

Applying theoretical knowledge in this way, and thinking critically about these knowledges, are important skills that will enable you to evaluate and make critical judgements about psychology research and its application to the real world.

Other skills you may have used in this activity: reflection, recall of key principles and ideas, independent learning.

Discourse, postcolonial theory and intersectionality

The idea of race and racism that is advanced by much modern social psychology is overly simplistic, rooted in understandings of race and race politics that emerged between the 1950s and 1970s, and emerging primarily as an expression of the concerns of the American civil rights movement. Social identity theory emerged in Europe in the 1980s as a corrective to the over-focus on simple notions of stereotypes but, as we have seen, to a degree this approach falls into the same trap of oversimplifying social processes and editing them out of laboratory-based experiments. While many of its proponents suggest that we need to consider the complexity of the social world within which categorisation takes place, this approach has nonetheless been criticised for its failure to do so, and for its consequent naturalisation of racism as an inevitable feature of hardwired human cognitive processes.

A discursive account of race and racism suggests that race itself is a social construct – that it is not a pre-given biological phenomenon – but is formed in social practices, social institutions and, primarily, in discourse. Hall (1996) suggests that discourses of race refer to a particular way of *representing 'the West', 'the Rest' and the relations between them* (p56). Discourses are symbolic practices through which we produce social meanings. Race itself is produced in the language we use to describe it. There is nothing inherently or necessarily white or black about the racial designations 'white' or 'black', but when we carve up the world according to these categories we are essentially producing them as a social reality. These categories bear with them a long social history – of colonisation, slavery, modern social practices of exploitation, religious ideas about purity (associated with the colour white) and wickedness (associated with darkness, black-ness) etc. – that is invoked when we use the terms 'black' and 'white'. These terms are therefore 'productive' (they produce a set of social distinctions and social relationships when we use them) and 'reproductive' (our social relations are formed by the history of the use of this kind of language).

In contrast to the social cognitive approach we have reviewed in this chapter, discursive accounts of race and racism emerged as an attempt to engage with the social context within which notions of race themselves are produced. In their classic text *Mapping the Language of Racism,* Wetherell and Potter (1992) argued that to combat racism we need to understand it in its everyday expressions, not just in the extreme actions of bigots and racists. They suggest that the everyday expression of racism is often to be traced in subtle rhetorical and discursive forms rather than in overt acts of aggression and violence. As van Dijk (2000) suggests:

> many forms of the new racism are discursive: they are expressed, enacted and confirmed by text and talk, such as everyday conversations, board meetings, job interviews, policies, laws, parliamentary debates, political propaganda, textbooks, scholarly articles, movies, TV programmes and news reports in the press, among hundreds of other genres. They appear mere talk, and far removed from the open violence and forceful segregation of the old racism.

> (van Dijk, 2000, p34)

This approach suggests that the perniciousness of contemporary racism is in its subtlety of expression, and in its cultural pervasiveness (Billig, 1995; Hook, 2001; van Dijk, 2000; Dixon and Durrheim, 2005).

Discursive psychology has drawn attention to the multiple ways in which racism is constituted and defended within everyday speech. For example, the common rhetorical device of 'I'm not a racist but . . . ' functions to enable individuals to make racist statements while simultaneously dis-avowing a racist identity. Billig (1988) suggests that this is an outcome of a *norm against prejudice* (p95). In twenty-first century society, overt expression of racist views is generally not regarded as acceptable. However, this does not mean that racism has somehow disappeared. Rather, racism has gone 'underground' and its expressions are more subtle and hidden. As Goodman (2010) notes, racism is produced in a manner that enables speakers to avoid racist talk. By using phrases such as 'I'm not being bigoted but . . . ', these kinds of rhetorical moves construct race and racism as relatively unspeakable – something delicate and faintly socially embarrassing, which has to be approached with kid gloves (van Dijk, 2000; Capdevila and Callaghan, 2008).

A lot of the talk around race in contemporary Western culture centres on debates around immigration and asylum. Consider the following extract from Goodman's (2010) article about discourses of race and immigration.

> *The trouble with this country is that we are not allowed to tell the truth about certain things – such as immigration, asylum, multiculturalism and race – without being pilloried. But straight talk is needed.*

(Robert Kilroy-Silk, Sunday Express, 23 January 2005)

In this extract we see the 'problems' of race and immigration constructed as a 'truth' – the idea that seeing immigration as a racial problem is not really racism but simply *straight talk*. Kilroy-Silk can be seen seizing a kind of 'reverse racism' victim position, locating himself and those who wish to 'talk straight' as being stifled by liberal discourses that position anti-immigration arguments as racist. Goodman suggests that his potentially racist remarks are *therefore presented as designed to preserve the value of free speech (or 'straight talk')*.

Discursive approaches enable us to consider the more subtle and complex forms of prejudice expressed in what Billig has termed *modern racism*. However, discursive approaches are not without their problems. As Burman (2003) has noted, an ethnographically rooted linguistic analysis enables a detailed consideration of everyday and political discourses of racism, but it is still possible for these accounts to lose their contextual and political focus. Furthermore, Hook (2001) and Dixon and Durrheim (2005) have pointed to the failure of much discursive analysis to engage sufficiently with the material realm. Racism is not just practised in linguistic interaction, but remains embedded in institutional practices and material conditions, which continue to position some categories of people in more privileged ways than others. So, for example, it remains the case in the UK today that you are still more likely to be subject to police stop-and-search practices if you are a black or young Asian man; you are more likely to be sectioned under the Mental Health Act and diagnosed as schizophrenic if you are black; you are more likely to be excluded from school if you are a black male youth. These kinds of social practices are not explicitly challenged by discursive analysis of racial talk. The implications of these practices for people's real lives are not adequately addressed by an engagement with discourse. While discursive practice is an important way of deconstructing modern racism, it cannot be our only tool in the development of a progressive social psychology able to engage with and deconstruct racist institutions and discriminatory practices in contemporary Western society.

Skill builder activity

Visual presentations

Transferable skill focus: visual communication and visual analysis

Key question: What does it mean to be British?

Over a period of a week, document the images you see of Britishness. Bring these to class with you, and in groups, build a collage to represent British identities. (If you are not working with a class group, you can build this collage on your own, but may want to ask friends and family to help you by adding their found images of Britishness.)

Use the following prompts to help you build your collage.

- Write your thoughts on what you think Britishness is.

- Through the course of the week, be aware of visual images around you that either support or challenge your notion of Britishness. Look for magazine articles, buildings, groups and activities you see when you're out and about, adverts and political events.

- After a week of observation, bring your images together with the other images in the group.

- Discuss in what sense the images might be seen to represent Britishness.

- Agree a strategy for arranging the images for maximum visual and analytic impact. Think about grouping images together on the basis of similarities and differences. What patterns and tensions do you see in the visual data?

- Discuss how you identify or disidentify with the images represented. What does this tell you about the construction of ethnic identity and ethnic difference?

- What theoretical material from the chapter helps you to reflect on the experience of identifying or disidentifying with the images of Britishness?

- Look back at your original definition of Britishness. Has it changed or is it still the same? How do you make sense of this?

Skill builder review

This activity helps develop your visual communication skills, and your capacity for visual analysis and visual communication. These are important academic and life skills.

Other skills you may have used in this activity: critical thinking, comparison, independent learning, reflection.

Assignments

1. Consider critically the strengths and weaknesses of a social cognitive explanation of race and racism.

2. What are some of the key differences between social identity theory and a discursive explanation of racism?

Summary: what you have learned

In this chapter you have developed your understanding of race and ethnicity, prejudice, racism and ethnocentrism. You have further developed your understanding of the authoritarian personality, with a particular focus on how it helps us to understand racism. We have considered stereotypes as an explanation of racism and prejudice through the processes of social categorisation and the development of schemata. We have explored the contact hypothesis, which suggests that contact between in-group and out-group members can, under specific conditions, undermine stereotypical thinking and reduce intergroup prejudice. We have considered the insights offered by the realistic conflict theory, which explains how intergroup behaviour might be explained in terms of competition for scarce resources between in-groups and out-groups. In contrast, social identity theory suggests that competition is not necessary to explain intergroup behaviour, and that mere perception of group membership is sufficient for in-group favouritism and out-group hostility to develop. The limitations of social cognitive models of prejudice, racism and discrimination were considered, and a discursive framing of racism considered.

Further reading

Hogg, MA (2006) Social Identity Theory, in Burke, PJ (ed) (2006) *Contemporary Social Psychological Theory*. Palo Alto: Stanford University Press.

This chapter provides a detailed and up-to-date account of social identity theory, and includes a consideration of its theoretical and practical limitations.

Wetherell, M and Potter, J (1992) *Mapping the Language of Racism*. Hemel Hempstead: Harvester Wheatsheaf.

This is a classic discursive text on the social construction and reproduction of race and racism.

Chapter 4

Social influence: persuasion

Learning outcomes

By the end of this chapter you should:

- *have an overview of key research in the area of social influence and persuasive communication;*

- *understand the theoretical construct of persuasion;*

- *understand mainstream models of persuasive communication (the Yale model, the elaborated likelihood model and cognitive dissonance theory);*

- *understand the core limitations of mainstream research on social influence;*

- *understand the importance of social context and emotionality in persuasive communication;*

- *have developed your skills of analysing, evaluating and reflecting by applying theoretical models of persuasion to an advertisement and a political speech.*

Introduction

Human beings are social beings. We live our lives and form our identities, views on the world and behaviour in interaction with others. Social psychologists have long been interested in how individuals influence one another – how people are persuaded to act in ways that they might otherwise not have, what makes us obey others, and what makes us conform in social situations. **Social influence** is the process whereby one person or group of people affects the thoughts, attitudes, feelings or behaviours of another person or group of people. We have learned in Chapter 1 that the link between attitudes and behaviour is often quite tenuous, and that we do not always act in ways that are in keeping with our professed beliefs and value systems. To a degree, this disparity might be best understood as a feature of social influence. In this chapter, we consider the social phenomenon of persuasiveness as an instance of social influence, exploring social cognitive theories of persuasive communication, and the notion of cognitive dissonance. We explore the limitations of these models, questioning the degree to which they can really be understood as social psychological theories. We conclude the chapter with a consideration of discursive approaches to persuasion, exploring whether these take better account of the social aspects of influence in persuasive communications.

Persuasion

One of the main sources of social influence in everyday life is **persuasion**. By appealing to the emotions and/or reasoning of the person for whom it is designed, persuasion involves the direct and deliberate attempt to influence someone's attitudes, feelings and behaviour via persuasive communication (Miller and Boster, 1988). The most obvious forms of persuasive communication are advertising, political campaigning and lobbying, and propaganda.

Using an internet search engine (Google Images is useful for this), search for a few political posters from the 2010 UK election campaign. A good example would be, for instance, the Conservative party poster, including the famously airbrushed image of David Cameron, the then leader of the Conservative Party, looking straight at camera, an earnest expression on his face. Alongside his picture is the slogan, *We can't go on like this. I'll cut the deficit, not the NHS* (see, for example, http://tinyurl.com/yf9uhe4). Looking at these posters, think through what elements the advertiser used to make this particular poster persuasive.

The most important aspect of a persuasive communication is likely to be seen as the message itself. In this poster, David Cameron is seen trying to persuade the electorate to vote Conservative. The message itself is fairly straightforward: 'Vote Conservative, because we will both cut the budgetary deficit, and protect the National Health Service'. In everyday life, we are bombarded with such persuasive communications – buy this, vote for that, watch this programme, listen to this music, agree with this, support that. We evaluate these communications by considering the logical validity of the argument, and if the argument is sufficiently coherent, then, in theory at least, we might be swayed into changing our attitudes and then changing our behaviour. Thus the message-based approach to persuasive communication would suggest that our attitudes and behaviour will shift if the argument presented is sufficiently compelling, and that we engage in a careful cognitive process to weigh up the strengths and weaknesses of the arguments we hear.

While this is clearly an important part of persuasive communication, it is also obvious that the most rational and logical arguments do not always win hearts and minds. Clearly, pure logical reasoning is not enough to change most people's views and behaviours. Furthermore, we do not always engage in a careful evaluation of the arguments we hear – sometimes we do not have enough information to be able to do so, and sometimes we do not have the motivation.

The Yale model

In contrast to this message-based model, the **Yale model of persuasive communication** suggests that persuasive communication is made up of three components: characteristics of the source or sender; characteristics of the message itself; and characteristics of the audience/receiver/ decoder (Hovland et al., 1953). The combination of these variables determines how effective the communication is, i.e. how persuasive a message is depends largely on who says what to whom (and with what intent).

So, in the case of the Conservative Party poster, the extent of our attitude change will depend on:

- who the speaker is (Do we see Cameron as attractive, intelligent, and competent? Do we see the Conservative Party as trustworthy?);

- how compelling the argument is (What kind of message is it? Does it appeal to fear – the dread of what will happen if we do go on like this? Is the message rational – is it logical to assume that the Conservative Party will cut spending without placing public services like the NHS at risk?);

- how we see ourselves as the person to whom the message is directed (Are we the 'we' to whom the poster is addressed – can we see ourselves as one of the people who 'can't go on like this'? Do we, for example, see ourselves as traditional Labour supporters, swing voters, Conservatives? Do we see ourselves as people likely to benefit from the changes he proposes?).

The Yale model predicts that the interaction of these variables will predict the degree to which we are persuaded by the piece of political propaganda.

While this model may seem intuitively correct, in application it produces increasingly confusing and contradictory results. For example, sometimes an attractive source increased the likelihood of persuasion, but sometimes it reduced persuasiveness – perhaps because people paid less attention to the message, being distracted by the source's attractiveness; perhaps because they didn't identify with the very attractive source (Eagly and Chaiken, 1993).

The elaboration likelihood model (ELM)

The **elaboration likelihood model** (Petty and Cacioppo, 1986) extends the Yale model, retaining Hovland's focus on cognitive factors, but focusing more on what motivates us to pay sufficient attention to the persuasive communication to even be open to social influence. The elaboration likelihood model uses Hovland's variables (source, message and receiver) and adds to them a focus on emotional and contextual factors, and heuristics (see Chapter 2). What this model strives to understand is how the same communication might produce different outcomes, and how the same variables within the source, message or audience might have differing effects. It focuses not just on the arguments of the persuader, but also on the arguments of the persuaded – their counterarguments (points of dispute with the persuasive message) and their consonant arguments (points of agreement).

The ELM suggests that how we understand and are influenced by a persuasive communication depends on how motivated we are to engage with it, and how well we are able to understand it. This approach suggests that there are two ways in which persuasion can occur: a central and a peripheral route.

The central route

The central route to persuasion involves a very full and detailed argument, and encourages the audience to engage in a full and detailed consideration of the message (Stephenson et al., 2001). Using this central route to persuasion presumes an audience that is concerned about the issues, and sufficiently attentive to evaluate the argument carefully and arrive at a reasoned position on the issues at hand. We have to be really interested in and concerned about an issue to be influenced via the central route.

The problem with the central route to persuasion is that to be swayed by a detailed argument requires a highly motivated audience. Think about election campaigns: generally, the detailed political speeches are reserved for party conferences or for quite select audiences. What most of the communication parties do with the electorate is in the form of short, attention-grabbing bits of information. The reality is that, even in something as important as who we vote for, we are often not swayed by the complex and detailed arguments, simply because to engage with that level of argument requires more energy and investment than most people are prepared to devote (Howitt et al., 1989). As an audience, we often want our messages delivered in sound bites, not in complex, hard-to-digest chunks.

The advantage of the central route to persuasion is that because the audience spends so much time considering and digesting the message, the attitude change it engenders is characterised by greater commitment – it is more enduring and resistant to further change (Scott, 1966). However, very few people have the staying power to engage with lengthy and detailed communication and debate.

Task — Refer again to your election poster (http://tinyurl.com/yf9uhe4).

Does the poster attempt to use the central route to persuasion?

Does it present a detailed and complex argument about party policy to sway voters? Why do you think it does not do this?

The peripheral route

In contrast to the central route, the peripheral route to persuasion has low receiver involvement, low receiver motivation and weaker, less elaborated messages. This persuasive approach does not involve a conscious, cognitive processing of the message. Rather, it succeeds as a result of persuasive powers that are extraneous to the message itself. Celebrity endorsements and catchy slogans are both ways of persuading the audience, without taxing them too much to think about the message itself. This kind of persuasive communication might also involve associating the message with something the audience has perhaps already thought about.

In the poster we have been considering, the message itself is minimally elaborated. What other appeals does the poster use to persuade the audience through peripheral means? Think about how it appeals to the audience in less direct ways. How does it represent the source? Think about the implicit messages it contains about the previous government, about the Conservative Party, about David Cameron, and about the target audience it presumes.

Source variables

According to the ELM, each variable within the model can have different persuasive effects, depending on the receiver's motivation to analyse the information presented (Petty and Wegener, 1998). In addition, source variables such as expertise (Hovland and Weiss, 1951) have been found to be highly influential. This influence is mediated by personal relevance – information that matters less to us is more likely to be persuasive if presented by an expert (Petty et al., 1981). Sources who were seen as trustworthy and authentic (Eagly et al., 1978) or as credible (Petty and Wegener, 1998) were also seen as more variable. An attractive source can be persuasive in certain circumstances (Chaiken, 1979), perhaps because people draw on an 'attractiveness = likeability' heuristic when considering persuasive messages from an attractive source. However, the significance of the attractiveness variable depends in part on the importance of the message to the receiver: where the message was seen as something that really mattered to the receiver, the attractiveness of the source can have no influence on the persuasiveness of the message, or might even reduce its impact – perhaps because it is seen as being trivialised by a 'pretty face' (Chaiken, 1986).

As we have noted, the ELM suggests that the receiver of persuasive communication is often persuaded not by the message itself, but by peripheral cues that function less consciously to shape attitudes and produce attitude change. For example, Samman et al. (2009) studied individual attitudes to charitable giving. They found that celebrity endorsements had a strong influence on attitudes to charities and intention to donate. Looking at the example of poverty reduction through international aid schemes, the researchers found that the causes themselves were less powerfully persuasive than the perceived characters of the celebrities who endorsed them. This was judged by perceptions of how committed the celebrity was to the cause, demonstrated by longstanding commitment and by being seen as maintaining a relatively low profile in relation to the cause (being visible, but not being seen as too pushy or self-promoting). This demonstrates that the persuasiveness of the argument itself might be less significant than peripheral factors.

Message variables

In terms of message variables, the issue of the relevance or importance of the message itself is highly significant, and a clever persuader will try to raise the personal relevance of the message (Boninger et al., 1995). However, people are also not easily persuaded by a too obviously targeted message – the message needs to have personal relevance, without appearing to be too deliberate an attempt to persuade, in other words, the personal relevance is often more persuasive when it is implicit rather than explicit (Walster and Festinger, 1962; Stayman and Kardes, 1992). Fear arousal is a powerful tool of persuasion. Messages that suggest strong negative consequences if you do not adopt the attitude and behaviour they promote can be very persuasive (Petty and Wegener, 1998), but only if the person targeted by the message has a sense of **self-efficacy** in responding to the message – that is, if they feel they can actually do something about the message they receive (Mulilis and Lippa, 1990). However, Thompson et al. (2009), looking at campaigns designed to persuade smokers to give up, warn that fear-based messages can have contrary effects for those who do not have high self-efficacy, by reinforcing their self-identity as 'hardcore smokers'. Guilt arousal is a strategy commonly used in campaigns around, for instance, charitable giving, but these strategies only work when they contain the implicit message that participants will feel better about themselves if they comply with the message (Hibbert et al., 2007). In contrast, feelgood messages can be a powerful way of increasing the persuasive impact of messages through positive associations (Hogg and Vaughan, 1998). For example, looking at the impact of road safety messages, Lewis et al. (2008) found that negative messages produce greater immediate persuasive impact, but that if you want to change attitudes and behaviour over time, positive appeals that make people feel better about themselves have a greater long-term impact.

Audience variables

The persuasiveness of the communication can also be shaped by the way in which it appeals to the target audience. So, for example, in terms of receiver variables, perceived similarity between source and receiver is an important feature of persuasion (Petty and Cacioppo, 1981). It was also found that young people might be more susceptible to persuasion (Ceci and Bruck, 1993; Messerschmidt, 1933). Van 't Riet et al. (2008) found that health promotion campaigns about smoking cessation were more persuasive for those individuals who felt that they could successfully quit – those who had a sense of self-efficacy. Three persuasive messages were shown to research participants – one that emphasised the negative aspects of continuing to smoke (a loss-framed message), one that emphasised the health gains involved in giving up (a gain-framed message) and a control condition. Participants with high self-efficacy were more strongly motivated to quit by the loss-framed message, but for those with low self-efficacy, motivation to stop smoking was unaffected by any of the messages. This suggests that the persuasive effect of communication is moderated by traits that are internal to the audience and shape the impact of the persuasive argument itself.

Similarly, Sher and Lee (2009) found that participants' reactions to online reviews of consumer goods were mediated by the personal trait of scepticism. Highly sceptical individuals tended to base their reaction to a consumer review drawing on their intrinsic beliefs, not situational factors. The sceptic tended to be biased against the idea of the consumer review itself (perhaps thinking that most people who write consumer reviews have some kind of vested interest in selling the product). This meant that they tended to exhibit a particular, negative reaction to the review, regardless of the quality of the message itself. This study emphasises the importance of considering the traits of the audience in building a persuasive communication.

A further role for the receiver in this communication is the importance of the way that the target audience processes the information that they receive – a process that may be open to cognitive distortion. A pervasive moral panic in our society relates to the role of the media in shaping and influencing attitudes and behaviour. But how significant is the impact of the media on us? Are we mere passive recipients of persuasive media messages? In estimating the persuasive power of the media, social psychologists have noted the influence of the third person effect (Davison, 1983). This refers to a tendency to assume that others are more likely to be influenced by the media than we are ourselves. Think, for example, about people's reactions to the size zero debate, and the ongoing discussion of the role of the media in influencing people's perceptions of the ideal woman. Do you feel women's perceptions of beauty are likely to be shaped by media representations of ultra thin models? Do you feel *you* are likely to be influenced by such representations? Generally, people will answer 'yes' to the first question and 'no' to the second question – this is the operation of the third-person effect. Douglas and Sutton (2004) found that this was not because people overestimated the extent of attitude change in others, but rather that they underestimated media influence on their own attitudes.

In addition to the direct cognitive processes that individuals engage in when exposed to persuasive communication, Petty and Briñol (2008) suggest that we are also influenced by metacognitive processes – these involve our reflections on our own thought processes, the way we think about our thinking. Petty and Briñol suggest that, in addition to our perceptions of the various source, message and audience characteristics, the persuasive impact of a particular communication is mediated by our own confidence in our thoughts about the issue. If we tend to doubt our own judgements, we will read a persuasive communication differently from if we tend to have great confidence in our own discernment. Petty and Briñol argue that, when we are responding to a persuasive communication, we are not simply influenced by our judgements, but the judgements we make about the communication are strongly influenced by our confidence in our own judgements.

Task   ⌐   Look again at the poster we have been considering.

        ├─ How does it use the variables of source, message and receiver to craft a more persuasive message? For example, how is perceived similarity constructed in the communication?

        ├─ How is the source represented as more credible and trustworthy? To what extent is fear arousal used? What about self-efficacy?

Criticisms of the Yale model and the ELM

One of the difficulties with these kinds of models of persuasion is that they remain essentially cognitive models. Persuasion is seen as a feature of perceptual processes – how we see the source, how we read and process the message, how we understand ourselves. However, as Howitt et al. (1989) point out, it is often the case that we simply do not think about things this carefully – by and large, we do not carefully weigh up arguments that are presented to us. Further, it might be argued that, as social psychological theories go, these kinds of ways of thinking about persuasion and social influence are very asocial. They do not take adequate account of the role of the 'social' in social influence.

Burgoon (1995) suggested that the Yale model and the ELM rely on an individualised model of persuasion that does not make adequate sense of the interactions between source and target that produce persuasive processes. In contrast, researchers like Hsiung and Bagozzi (2003) point out that most social influence and persuasion are exerted in the interpersonal domain. Looking at social influence in the family, they found that persuasion and social influence are shaped by our **interdependence**. They explored the interaction patterns associated with social influence, looking at the degree to which they were independent or **co-constructed**. Most social psychological work on persuasion would suggest that it is largely determined by cognitive processing done by the individual (i.e. how the individual understood the message, how they saw themselves, how they saw the source of the message). However, looking at how family members influence each other in the process of making a decision over which car to buy, Hsiung and Bagozzi found that the process of persuasion is dynamic (i.e. it changes considerably over time) and reciprocal. So, for example, at various points in the decision-making process, parents within a family function as a dyad (for example, when agreeing on a price range for purchasing a vehicle), or might be influenced differently by their children (when weighing up how a more expensive car might impact family life, or when thinking about the colour of the vehicle). Ultimately, what emerges, though, is a sense of variable social influence, producing an outcome that is a reflection of interdependent processes of influence and persuasion. What is clear from this example is that persuasion is not something that a source does to a target, but rather that it is an active and dynamic process that is negotiated through complex interactions.

Stewart-Knox et al. (2005) suggest that when looking at young people's decisions to take up smoking, young people are rarely influenced by direct persuasion. Using a longitudinal, qualitative interview approach, the researchers found that smoking uptake is largely influenced by the young person's attempts to conform to their peer group's perceived normative behaviour. Thus, their decisions around smoking depend on how they see themselves (identity) and what group they feel they belong to (self-categorisation). Direct persuasion was rarer and less influential than this kind of conformity pressure. The ELM has been generally criticised for underestimating the importance of social factors such as interdependence and conformity pressure in persuasiveness.

Cognitive dissonance

A key difficulty identified with the Yale model and ELM is that they presume an interested and motivated audience. However, generally, individuals are not sufficiently motivated to attend to the messages offered in persuasive communication to actually be persuaded by them. The theory of **cognitive dissonance** addresses this theoretical gap, offering an explanation of how persuasion works by playing with the sense of discomfort produced when we realise that we are contradicting ourselves! This discomfort motivates us potentially to be persuaded.

Cognitive dissonance theory is essentially an equilibrium or balance theory. As human beings, we are motivated to feel that our attitudes and behaviours are in harmony. When we experience psychological inconsistency, or a contradiction between two views we hold, or between our views and our behaviour, this produces discomfort that requires some kind of resolution. Consider the following example.

- I like to smoke.

- I want to live a long and healthy life.

- I understand that smoking causes lung and heart disease and shortens lifespan.

These contradictory values and behaviours construct a sense of cognitive dissonance, which we need to resolve in one way or another. For some people, the only resolution, ultimately, is to stop smoking. For others, they will engage in all kinds of justifications to deal with the dissonance. For example, most committed smokers will trot out anecdotes about their Great Uncle Billy, who smoked 50 a day from the age of 10 and drank like a fish, but lived to be 164, or their cousin Jane who was a healthy-living teetotaller who never smoked a day in her life, but inexplicably dropped dead at the age of 22. These kinds of anecdotes serve as a defence against the psychological discomfort produced when our value systems and behaviour are in disharmony.

Festinger and Carlsmith (1959) set up an experiment to explore how people deal with the experience of cognitive dissonance. Using an induced-compliance paradigm, they set up a task where research participants were paid to turn pegs a quarter turn in a peg board, over and over again, or similar tasks that were extremely dull and uninteresting. Participants were then asked to talk to another potential subject about the task in order to persuade them to participate in the research task (this second participant was, in fact, a confederate of the research team, and not really a potential subject at all). Participants fell into two conditions – those who were paid $20 (a large amount of money in 1959) and those who were paid $1 to talk to the other participant about joining the research. Once they had spoken to the confederate, participants were then asked themselves to rate the tasks. Participants in the $1 condition routinely rated the tasks as more enjoyable than those in the $20 condition.

Festinger and Carlsmith suggest that this is evidence of the operation of cognitive dissonance, and illustrates its implication for persuasion and attitude change. All participants held conflicting views: *I told another potential participant the task was interesting* and *I was bored by the task*. However, those in the $20 condition had a reasonable justification for telling the lie – they were well paid for it. Those in the $1 condition lacked that justification, and to deal with the discomfort created by the dissonance, they adjusted their attitude to reconcile the conflicting cognitions. They persuaded *themselves* the task was more interesting than it was.

Steele et al. (1988) asked participants to answer an essay about tuition fees. They were assigned either a pro- or anti-tuition fees position. Their attitudes were measured before and after the essay-writing task. The researchers found that for those whose essay was counter-attitudinal, their attitudes were likely to change over time to be more in line with the argument of their essay. This suggests that their compliance to the essay-writing task had implications for attitude change.

Aronson and Carlsmith (1963) explored cognitive dissonance and self-justification in children, using a 'forbidden toy' experiment. Children were left in a room with a range of toys, and told not to play with one, highly desirable toy. Half the children were told that they would receive a severe punishment if they played with the toy, the other half of the children were told there would be a mild punishment. None of the children actually played with the forbidden toy. Later, children were told they could play with all the toys in the room, but while the children in the high punishment condition did play with the toy when permitted, the children in the mild punishment condition did not. The researchers concluded that this was further evidence of the operation of cognitive dissonance and its persuasive power. They suggest that the children in the low threat condition had greater dissonance, because the punishment itself was not sufficient to justify compliance with the instructions of the researchers. Consequently, they persuaded themselves that the toy itself was not that desirable, and that they didn't really want to play with it. Essentially, the children in the low threat condition did not really have the level of justification for not playing with the toy originally. This aspect of cognitive dissonance is sometimes termed the insufficient deterrent paradigm.

Using a free choice paradigm to produce cognitive dissonance, Brehm (1956) asked female students to rate household appliances. They were then allowed to choose one of two appliances on the list to take home as a gift. When asked to rate the appliances again, participants increased the rating of their chosen appliance, and decreased the rating of the one they had rejected. Their attitudes to the appliances shifted to fit with the choices they had made.

Aronson and Mills (1959) found similar self-justificatory attitude shifts in an experiment designed to induce an effort-justification paradigm. They had participants go through an initiation ritual in order to become a member of a club. Some had to go through a lot of effort and embarrassment in order to become a member, while others went through a much less intense initiation. Once they had gone through the initiation, they found that, in fact, the group they had joined was rather dull, but those in the high-effort initiation condition had a more positive evaluation of the group than the others.

Festinger and subsequent theorists of cognitive dissonance suggest that dissonance occurs under several conditions. These are when we:

- have incongruent thoughts or beliefs;

- freely behave in a way that is inconsistent with our attitudes;

- commit ourselves to an activity or course of action or put a lot of effort into something that doesn't turn out as we had expected;

- make a decision that excludes more desirable outcomes for us;

- cannot find evidence to support an existing attitude, or to justify a behaviour.

While some people cope very well with cognitive dissonance, for many, feeling this sense of disparity between what we had hoped and what occurs, between what we think and what we do, or between competing but cherished value systems, is resolved by attitude change. With a focus on the way that dissonance produces attitude change, cognitive dissonance theory suggests there are three main ways in which we reduce dissonance between attitudes, or between attitudes and behaviour. First, we might avoid people and situations that might directly challenge our views, with the prediction that selective exposure itself prevents dissonance. If we stick with people 'like us', read newspapers and television articles that keep us comfortable and don't challenge us too much, then we will not be affected by dissonance. Second, dissonance often occurs after a decision has been made, and creates a need to feel reassured about our decisions. For example, let's say we buy a shiny new smartphone, and then experience 'buyers' remorse', worrying that perhaps our new phone wasn't the best choice in terms of battery life or signal power; we seek out reassurance that we have made the right decision.

Dissonance is raised by three conditions.

1. How important the issue is (Is the phone an important work tool? Do we use it extensively?).

2. How long it took to make the decision (Did we weigh up all the options and dither about accessories?).

3. How hard it is to change the decision once it has been made (Are we stuck with a 24-month contract, or can we send the phone back and exchange it?).

The combination of factors in these three conditions can make the individual really question the choice they have made. Having made a difficult choice, the person is highly motivated to seek support, reassurance and even justification for their decision.

Finally, the level of incentive to make a particular decision or engage in a particular action plays a role in the level of cognitive dissonance experienced, and in predicting whether this dissonance will produce attitude change. Here, research findings are counterintuitive. Historically, it has been suggested that people need large incentives to produce attitude change. We need to know that there's 'something in it for us' before we're prepared to give up cherished values. However, what cognitive dissonance theory teaches us is quite the opposite. Large incentives can justify our decisions without us needing to change our underlying attitudes. It is small incentives that are more likely to produce attitudinal change, by forcing us not to rely on extrinsic motivators to justify our decisions, actions and beliefs.

While other social cognitive theories of persuasion fail to fully account for persuasive communication simply because people in the real world are often not that motivated to engage in substantial thought about the issues at hand, cognitive dissonance theory shows a route through which people become very motivated to deal with their attitudes and their behaviours. The persuasive effects of cognitive dissonance are, however, limited to very specific conditions – routes for self-justification and rationalisation need to be cut off in order for attitudinal change to be the most desirable resolution to the disharmony.

Applying cognitive dissonance theory

Cognitive dissonance theory has been applied in a range of contexts, from health promotion campaigns, therapeutic interventions and motivational interviewing through to advertising strategies, political campaigns and anti-bullying campaigns.

Mullainathan and Washington (2009) explored patterns of cognitive dissonance and voters' attitudes to politicians. They questioned whether people were more likely to hold favourable attitudes to candidates they voted for, and in line with the prediction of cognitive dissonance theory, they found that support was likely to be stronger and more stable under conditions where an individual's specific vote might be seen as more salient. For example, they found that favourable opinion was likely to be more stable in support for senators elected during low turnout non-presidential campaign years than for high turnout presidential campaign years. Furthermore, those who were eligible to vote tend to show more polarised views on presidential candidates than those ineligible to vote. This has clear implications for political campaigning and advertising that is geared towards swaying voter opinion and voting intention.

In the health sphere, for example, Rodriguez et al. (2008) explored the use of a dissonance-based eating disorder intervention to prevent the development of eating disorders. In this study researchers highlighted the contradictions in participants' desire to be healthy, and their desire to be ultra-thin. By intervening in attitudes around thin ideal internalisation and body dissatisfaction by intensifying dissonant attitudes around health, appearance and ultra-thinness, the study found that the intervention was effective in reducing eating disordered behaviours in several different ethnic groups. This approach brings two value systems (for example, health and thinness) into direct conflict, by highlighting that fitness and extreme thinness are antithetical. This kind of inconsistency motivates people to consider their value system closely and can stimulate attitude change. Miller (1983), applying cognitive dissonance theory in motivational interviewing, found similarly that increasing cognitive dissonance by highlighting the contradictions between problem behaviours in heavy drinkers and the client's awareness of the negative impact of the negative behaviour, they enhanced attitude change and increased motivation to change drinking behaviour.

A significant problem for theorists attempting to understand the links between attitudes and health behaviours has been that mere knowledge of what is healthy, and what we need to do to produce optimal health, is often not sufficient to bring about behaviour change. This is nowhere more stark than in the example of health professionals who understand better than most people the health risks associated with, say, smoking, unsafe sex, unhealthy eating or lack of exercise, but who themselves do not 'practise what they preach'. For example, Clark et al. (2004) explored undergraduate nursing students' understanding of smoking and its impact on health and their attitudes to smoking behaviour. They found that a sizeable proportion of their sample of 365 student nurses were still smoking, and that most of the smokers had begun to smoke in high school. They had extensive knowledge of the health implications of smoking, but this knowledge had not filtered through to them changing their smoking behaviour. Furthermore, the research team noted that, while non-smoking nursing students had positive attitudes to smoking cessation campaigns and initiatives designed to protect non-smokers' rights, participants who still smoked tended to be more negative about the potential effectiveness of these kinds of interventions. It is clear here that smokers, confronted by the dissonance between their own smoking behaviour and their knowledge of the health implications of that behaviour, sought to reduce that dissonance by engaging in justificatory attitudinal practices around public health initiatives oriented towards smoking cessation.

Problems with cognitive dissonance theory

Cognitive dissonance has proved a popular and enduring theoretical contribution to the social cognitive understanding of persuasion and attitude change. However, critics have suggested that it may offer an unnecessarily complex explanation of the cognitive processes it describes, and that more parsimonious explanations are available. For example, Rosenberg (1965) suggested that rather than changing attitudes in line with the predictions of dissonance theory, participants might be concerned that their honesty or integrity was being tested by the early experimental situations, changing their expressed attitudes deliberately and consciously to create an impression of consistency and personal integrity. Subsequent research has adjusted design to take these concerns into account, and continues to produce outcomes that are in line with dissonance theory (for example, Aronson, 1969).

Tedeschi et al. (1971) suggest that participants are engaged in impression management rather than dealing with the impact of dissonance. They argue that, in our society, we tend to be rewarded for consistent behaviour and punished for inconsistent behaviour, such that we are socialised to appear consistent in behaviour and attitudes. Essentially, they suggest we are trained to manage the impressions we give others of ourselves, to ensure an appearance of consistency. Inconsistent and hypocritical behaviour is heavily socially sanctioned. Think, for example, of the 'bigotgate' incident in the run-up to the 2010 election. The criticism levelled at Gordon Brown was not so much that he had suggested a member of the electorate was bigoted, but that being nice to the voter's face and critical of her in private was evidence of inconsistency and hypocrisy. Tedeschi et al. argue that the traditional cognitive dissonance experiments produce situations in which people try to rationalise or justify inconsistency to 'important others' (such as high-status experimenters), to avoid social sanction. This approach is different from cognitive dissonance in that it does not argue that we have an inner need for consistency, but rather that we have learnt to manage impressions others have of us by producing the appearance of consistency. In this sense, the theory offers a behaviourist critique of the social cognitive framework of the theory, querying whether we need to posit a notion of inner needs to explain behaviour and expressed attitudes.

The question of impression management certainly appears as an important issue to consider when thinking about cognitive dissonance, though it may not be a sufficient explanation in and of itself. It seems likely that the processes that underpin the apparent attitude change produced by dissonance are more complex than being simply designed to convince the experimenter.

A further criticism of dissonance theory is that the conditions that have to be met to produce dissonance are actually quite difficult to achieve in real-world settings. To provoke situations in which behaviour and attitudes, or two held attitudes, are inconsistent can be tricky. To establish situations where minimal rewards are present, or where individuals expend considerable effort in undesirable situations, is complicated and often very artificial (or in the case of Zimbardo et al.'s (1965) grasshopper-eating experiment, perhaps a teensy bit unethical!) This can limit the real-world applicability of the theory. While it is easy to think about situations where existing inconsistencies might be exploited, it is rather harder to plan, for example, advertising campaigns or political messages that combine all the elements that predict real attitudinal change as an outcome of cognitive dissonance.

Task — Consider the following vignette.

Ned is a third-year student with a large student grant. He worries a lot about student debt, particularly because he comes from a family with limited financial means. He voted in his first election a year ago. In the election, one party explicitly stated in its manifesto that it would scrap university fees if it came to power. Ned became very enthused about this, and actively campaigned for this party, and voted for them in the national election. The party has now indicated that it intends to raise student fees.

What does the theory of cognitive dissonance predict that Ned will do? What factors do you think this theory might leave out in explaining Ned's situation?

Critical thinking activity

Persuasive communication

Critical thinking focus: analysing, evaluating, reflecting

Key question: What makes adverts persuasive?

Reread the sections above on persuasive communication.

Select three adverts – one from the press, one from TV and one from other media (YouTube/internet/radio).

Analyse the adverts' structure and content for 'persuasiveness'. Use theories of persuasive communication to make sense of why the adverts have, or lack, persuasive power.

Use the following prompts to guide your analysis of the adverts and to form links between the theoretical material reviewed and the adverts you have chosen.

- Summarise the key verbal messages, visual images and other elements of the adverts that are intended to persuade the viewer/reader/listener to change their attitudes or behaviours, or to buy a particular product.

- Look at the elements of source, audience and message. How are these elements used in a persuasive manner?

Are the adverts attempting a direct or peripheral route to persuasion?

Can you see any evidence of attempts to exploit or intensify cognitive dissonance in the adverts? (In the Conservative Party poster we have been looking at, for example, the appeal 'We can't go on like this' explicitly plays with a range of dissonances. For example, there is an implicit appeal to the warring views that 'we want to be happy' and 'if we continue as a nation as we are, disaster will strike'. Can you see evidence of similar intensification of dissonant views?)

What do you think is left out in the social cognitive analysis in which you have engaged? Are there elements of the Conservative Party poster that are persuasive but are not accounted for by the theoretical models we have considered?

Critical thinking review

This activity helps develop your skills of analysis, evaluation and reflection by applying theoretical material from the chapter to adverts. By applying the three theoretical models to the adverts you have chosen, you were able to analyse textual and visual images, and evaluate critically the robustness of the theoretical models under consideration. You were also encouraged to think critically about social issues that might be left out of a more cognitively focused social psychological model.

Applying theoretical knowledge in this way, and thinking critically about these knowledges, are important skills that will enable you to evaluate and make critical judgements about psychology research and its application to the real world.

Other skills you may have used in this activity: recall of key principles and ideas, communication (literacy) skills if you write up the activity, independent learning.

But where is the 'social' in social cognitive research?

Perhaps a more general issue with social cognitive research on social influence and persuasion is the degree to which it prioritises cognitive processes over both emotional and social ones. Does social influence in general, and persuasion in particular, happen as a consequence of cognitive processes – things that occur in the heads of the individuals who are influenced? Can these complex interactions really be understood with reference to the cognitive processing of messages, perceptions of self and of source and inner needs for consistency, without paying careful attention to the social context within which such cognitive processing and inner needs are constructed? For example, the impression management critique of dissonance theory suggests that we are conditioned socially to manage our behaviour to create an impression of consistency. However, what it does not do is understand what it is about late industrial Western culture that values consistency so highly, that pressures us to smooth over the contradictions inherent in social life, and present ourselves as seamless, unitary individual subjects. What is it about our society that leads us to be so critical of someone who is nice to a voter's face, but goes back to his car and calls her a bigot?

An alternative to understanding social influence and persuasion might be to see persuasive communications and rhetoric as produced within broader networks of social representations, appealing not just to an individual's thoughts, but to their sense of who they are. In other words, persuasion is to do with more than just what we think and how we process information, and more to do with our social and cultural location, our history, and the social symbol system within which the persuasive communication is located. We illustrate this with one example of a discursive account of political rhetoric and persuasive communication.

Loseke (2009) argues that a key criterion for persuasive communication is emotionality – precisely that which is left out in traditional social cognitive theories. She explores the question of how speeches and other persuasive communications might appeal to the emotions of diverse audiences, suggesting that this is achieved through the use of 'emotion codes', which are commonly agreed on ideas about what emotions are appropriate in particular contexts and times. Analysing one of President Bush's speeches about the 'Story of September 11', Loseke argues that these 'emotion codes' are constructed using particular rhetorical strategies and appeal to broader social constructs such as 'heroes', 'villains', 'victims' and being a 'good American'. In some senses, these ideas reproduce the traditional pantomime context, in which we all know when to boo and hiss, when to cheer, and when to yell 'He's BEHIND you!' The use of emotion codes appeals to audiences to feel particular ways.

For example, Loseke considers the way in which Bush invokes the image of 'victim' in his speeches as a justification for war, exploring how the emotional appeal to common ideas about victims as good people who suffer functions as a persuasive rhetorical device. She argues that the symbolic code of 'victim' contains within it a socially agreed expectation that the victim suffers harm. This is emphasised by Bush's use of terms like *airplanes flying into buildings, fires burning, huge structures collapsing*, referring to *deadly attacks* and *unimaginable horror*. He goes on to locate the victims as ordinary, good American people, with phrases like *thousands of lives suddenly ended*, and *children whose worlds have been shattered*. Bush suggests that *all* Americans are de facto victims, suggesting *[g]reat harm has been done to us. We have suffered great loss*. In this way, Bush constitutes America itself as a victim of this attack, and invites the listening audience to identify itself with this victim position. He suggests the attacks are a *wound to our country*.

It is clear in this analysis that what is persuasive about this speech is not simply to do with source and audience variables, or cognitive dissonance. The appeal here is not to individual cognitive processes. Rather, Bush is appealing to commonly agreed views of good and evil, of victim and aggressor, and is also making an identity appeal to notions of 'Americanness'.

In her analysis, Loseke does two key jobs. She recentres the importance of emotionality in persuasive communication, highlighting the degree to which thought and emotion intersect, and arguing that cognitive processes cannot be understood as separate from emotional life. She also highlights the importance of emotionality as something that is not constituted individually, but rather which functions in a social and cultural sphere. In this way, she positions persuasive communication as something that is socially constituted, not individually or merely inter-personally located as social cognitive theories of persuasion would predict.

Skill builder activity

Political speeches

Transferable skill focus: analysis of data

Key question: *What strategies do politicians use in political speeches to persuade their audiences?*

Use the following prompts to help you prepare a presentation.

- Read Capdevila, R and Callaghan, JEM (2008) It's not racist, it's common sense: A discursive analysis of political discourse around asylum and immigration in the UK. *Journal of Community and Applied Social Psychology*, 18: 1–16.

- Visit the website of a political party and select a speech for analysis. Here are some suggested sites you might use (there are many others).

  www.conservatives.com/News/Speeches.aspx

  www2.labour.org.uk/gordon-brown-speech-conference

  http://bnptv.org.uk/

  www.carolinelucasmep.org.uk/speeches/

- Summarise the key message of the speech. What is it that the speaker is trying to persuade us of?

- Think about the elements of the speech that are persuasive. Look at the source, target and message variables.

- Think about appeals to emotion in the speech. Can you see where there might be pauses for the audience to applaud? Where the speaker might anticipate an emotional reaction? What emotional reaction is the speaker hoping for and how does he or she aim to produce it?

How might these emotional appeals be persuasive?

What social representations are drawn on to build the persuasive power of the speech? Who is represented as good or bad? What images are used to build that impression?

How is the audience invited to identify with the speaker, and with their aims? (For example, in the article you have read analysing the Michael Howard speech on immigration, the construct of 'decent Britons' and 'good immigrants' were used to draw in the identification of the target audience.) Who is included, and who is excluded? How does this function to persuade the audience of the politician's position?

Write a 500-word report on the speech, discussing how well it works as a piece of persuasive communication.

Skill builder review

This activity helps develop your written communication skills, as well as analysis of textual data. These are important academic and life skills. The activity also encourages you to reflect critically on the more social aspects of persuasive communication.

Other skills you may have used in this activity: critical thinking, independent learning, reflection, recall of key principles and ideas, information technology (to search for the speech).

Assignments

1. 'To understand persuasive communication, we need simply to look at the power of the message.' Critically evaluate this claim, with reference to two theories of persuasion.

2. 'A full understanding of how people are persuaded in the real world must include a consideration of the social context.' Draw on discursive accounts of persuasion to consider the importance of the social in understanding social influence.

Summary: what you have learned

In this chapter, we have outlined mainstream social psychological theories of persuasion. We have explored three mainstream social cognitive models of persuasion: the Yale model, the elaborated likelihood model and cognitive dissonance theory. We've highlighted how these approaches focus on cognitive, and to a lesser degree interpersonal, factors, and neglect the social context and the emotional side of persuasion. To illustrate this point, we explored a discursive account of a political speech, focusing on both emotionality and social context.

To complete your critical thinking and skill builder activities, you have developed and used your skills in evaluation and analysis, communication of ideas, creative and critical thinking, independent learning, reflection, recall of key principles and ideas, and information technology.

Further reading

Capdevila, R and Callaghan, JEM (2008) It's not racist, it's common sense: A discursive analysis of political discourse around asylum and immigration in the UK. *Journal of Community and Applied Social Psychology*, 18: 1–16.

Every, D and Augustinos, M (2008) Taking advantage or fleeing persecution?: Opposing accounts of asylum seeking. *Journal of Sociolinguistics*, 12(5): 648–667.

These articles explore attempts by politicians, legal advocates and laypeople to provide persuasive accounts of the role of immigration and asylum in contemporary Western society. They use a discursive frame of reference to explore how arguments are constructed socially and linguistically.

Petty, RE, Briñol, P and Priester, JR (2009) Mass media attitude change: Implications of the Elaborated Likelihood Model of Persuasion, in Bryant, J and Oliver, MB (2009) *Media Effects: Advances in Theory and Research*. New York: Routledge.

This interesting chapter considers the history of persuasion in the media, and outlines the strengths and weaknesses of ELM in understanding media campaigns.

Chapter 5

Social influence: conformity, compliance and group processes

Learning outcomes

By the end of this chapter you should:

- *have an understanding of the concepts of conformity and compliance;*

- *have a critical understanding of the operation of social influence in small groups and large groups;*

- *be able to explore critically the way that social psychological research tends to portray social influence as a negative phenomenon;*

- *demonstrate a critical understanding of the processes of minority influence;*

- *be able to explain the way that crowds might shape behaviour, and how crowd behaviour in turn is constituted within a complex social context;*

- *be able to apply theoretical material to an understanding of soldiers' behaviour 'under orders', considering the role of agency in our understanding of social influence, and have built your oral communication skills and ability to build reasoned arguments through a debate on the question of crowd behaviour.*

Introduction

One of the most frequently expressed anxieties that parents have about their children is to do with 'peer pressure' and 'bad company'. Peer pressure is blamed for every teenage ill from smoking through underage sex to membership of occult groups. This anxiety seems to reflect concerns that, despite individual thoughts, feelings and values, other people still have the power to influence us. As we noted in Chapter 4, social influence refers to the way that the thoughts, feelings and behaviours of one person (or a group of people) are influenced by the real, imagined or implied presence of other people. Three forms of social influence should be distinguished.

1. **Compliance** involves changing your behaviour on the instruction or under the influence of another. It also involves a response to a direct instruction from another person. Compliance

differs from persuasion in the sense that compliance targets behaviour change (regardless of shift in attitude), while persuasion is intended to change people's attitudes.

2. **Obedience** involves compliance with the instructions of an authority figure.

3. **Conformity** involves changing your attitudes or opinions as a result of social pressure. This can include conformity to the behaviour or a group, conformity in large groups (**crowd behaviour**, or what is sometimes termed 'mob psychology') and conformity to social norms.

Think about the way you dress, the way you style your hair, the kind of shoes you wear. How much of this is really individual choice, and to what degree is it influenced by issues such as fitting in, following a style or trend etc.? Even the least fashion-conscious person in the world will often still dress with a sense of what might be appropriate (or if they wish to shock, inappropriate) to the context they are in. We often dress to blend in, or to stand out, but either way there is an element of social influence in our choices. Conformity is often represented as a negative thing – as in the case of 'peer pressure'. However, is fitting in always a bad thing? To what degree is a level of conformity necessary for social life?

In this chapter, we will consider various social-psychological perspectives on social influence at the individual and at the group level. We will be asking questions such as: what makes us comply with the wishes of others? Why might we obey the instructions of an authority figure? How and why do people conform? How do groups influence our behaviour? What about resistance to conformity pressures?

Compliance and obedience

Compliance involves acceding to the request of another person. The request might be explicit ('Go to the office and fetch my case') or implicit (as in the case of some of the less direct forms of social influence considered in Chapter 4), but the hallmark of compliance, rather than conformity, is that the individual being influenced is aware that someone is trying to influence them.

Robert Cialdini (2001a, 2001b), summarising the findings of social psychological work on compliance, suggests that several principles determine whether we are likely to comply with the requests of others. We are more likely to accede to a request if it is delivered by someone we like, or if there is a reciprocity to the relationship (if there is a level of 'give and take' attached to the request). We are more likely to agree to something if it is consistent with our expressed values and beliefs, or if acceding to the request makes us feel like a more worthy social being (for example, a request to give to charity). Expert advice tends to produce compliance more often than lay views.

But how do we explain people who obey instructions that do not fit with their past views or actions, that are not given by someone likeable and where there is no clear advantage to the person who complies? How, for example, do we explain why perfectly reasonable men and women in Rwanda obeyed the instructions of those who ordered them to slaughter their neighbours during the Rwandan genocide? How do we understand the ordinary German soldier who complied with instructions to perform horrific acts of violence against individuals and groups during the Holocaust?

Adorno et al. (1950) questioned whether some people had a personality that was more vulnerable to compliance with figures of authority. As we saw in Chapter 3 they argued that social attitudes (like racism) were an *expression of deep-lying trends in personality structure* (p1). Following Freud, Adorno et al. suggested that personality is dependent on early childhood experiences, particularly experiences of parenting, and that social attitudes are an expression of repression. The authoritarian personality theory suggests that parents who were harsh and punitive in their parenting practices produced in their children an excessive compliance to authority figures (Heaven, 2001). Conformity and prejudice are understood as an expression of unconscious hostility to these overly punitive, rigid and demanding parents. The fear and compliance that children feel in relation to their authoritarian parents is projected on to other authority figures. The hostility they feel to their parents as a consequence of the parents' disciplinary behaviour cannot be directly expressed to the parents (or to other authority figures) because of a deep-seated anxiety about reprisals. Instead, this hostility is projected on to derogated out-groups – people who are perceived as safe targets for authoritarian aggression. Adorno et al. suggest that the authoritarian personality explains the tendency both to conform and comply, and the tendency to racism, which is displayed by right-wing authoritarians. Adler (1917) suggested that authoritarian personalities are characterised by a *will to power* over others – a driving need to assert your authority over others to protect against, and compensate for, an overwhelming sense of inferiority, inadequacy and insignificance. This, he suggests, is also a consequence of authoritarian parenting practice, which makes children feel small, undervalued and worthless.

Adorno et al. suggested that the authoritarian personality was characterised by nine personality traits. These are:

1. conventionalism – a concern with being normal, and a distaste for individuals who are non-conformist;

2. authoritarian submission – excessive deference to authority figures;

3. authoritarian aggression – hostility to derogated out-groups;

4. anti-intraception – resistance to change, and a strong desire to maintain the status quo;

5. superstition and stereotypy – a belief in powers beyond our control that shape our lives and behaviours, like luck, destiny, fate, extreme religiousness, and a tendency to develop ritualised and rigid behaviours as a way of dealing with this belief system;

6. an excessive concern with power and toughness – a tendency to be very concerned about physical and symbolic power and strength;

7. destructiveness and cynicism – generalised hostility, vilification of human beings, a worldview that sees people as basically bad;

8. projectivity – a tendency to project inner conflicts outwards, and consequently to see the world as a bad place;

9. concerns about sexuality – being concerned about others' sexual 'goings-on', being sexually repressed or highly controlled in relation to sex and sexuality.

Developing Adorno et al.'s ideas, Altemeyer (1981) reduced the number of traits associated with authoritarianism. He suggested that the right-wing authoritarian (RAW) personality was characterised by three traits: authoritarian submission, authoritarian aggression and conventionalism. It is easy to see how this kind of personality structure might be more susceptible to compliance to instructions from an authority figure, or to tend to a particular kind of conformity of behaviour.

However, both Adorno et al.'s and Altemeyer's work has been heavily criticised for methodological and theoretical reasons. First, it has been pointed out that Adorno's scale will also easily pick up individuals who are not particularly authoritarian, but who are highly acquiescent or submissive. Acquiescing to authority is not, in itself, evidence of authoritarianism. A significant methodological criticism was that Adorno's original work was largely carried out with a group of white Americans, who were identified by the researchers as being likely to be authoritarian. We could therefore reasonably ask both how generalisable these findings are, and also the degree to which Adorno et al. simply went out and found what they set out to find. These methodological problems were addressed by Altemeyer. Perhaps more significant is the question of whether the theory is really able to explain the phenomenon it set out to consider. Think about conditions like those found during the Second World War. Can we really understand the widespread compliance with the Nazi regime as being an expression of a particular personality type?

Like Adorno et al., Milgram (1974) set out to answer questions about compliance in his now infamous studies of compliance. He was interested in understanding obedience to authority – whether people are willing to obey requests or commands given by authority figures – but unlike Adorno et al., he did not attempt to locate these behaviours within the personality of the individuals who complied. In trying to understand the violence perpetrated in the Holocaust during the Second World War, Milgram questioned whether people who complied with commands to commit atrocities did so from a sense of shared moral conviction, or whether they saw themselves as simply following orders. He set a series of experiments between 1960 and 1963 to investigate this. These experiments took various forms, but in his most famous piece of research, participants were invited to take part in a study on the effect of punishment on learning. They were told by an experimenter that they should 'teach' another participant, the learner, a series of words, and that whenever the learner got the answer wrong, they would administer a shock, increasing the voltage of the shock with each wrong answer. Before the procedure began, participants saw the learner in another room, strapped into a chair with electrodes being placed on them. They communicated via microphone, so although they could not see the learner, they were able to hear them and to hear the effect of the shock on them. In reality, the 'learner' was not a learner at all, but was a confederate of the researchers. The shocks ranged from low voltage to 450 volts, but the learner's protests about the shock treatment stopped when they reached 300 volts.

Four 'prods' were used to secure the compliance of the participants. If a participant expressed reluctance, or hesitated in administering the shock, they were told the following.

Prod 1: *Please continue, or, Please go on.*

Prod 2: *The experiment requires that you continue.*

Prod 3: *It is absolutely essential that you continue.*

Prod 4: *You have no other choice, you must go on.*
(Milgram, 1974, p21)

The real aim of the research was not to explore the impact of punishment on learning, and no actual harm was done to the learner in this situation. Rather the experiment was designed to explore whether people would obey a figure of authority (an experimenter in a white coat), even if the effects of their action appeared to them to be harmful. Milgram (1974) reported obedience rates of between 50 and 65 per cent – that is, between 50 and 65 per cent were prepared to issue the maximum shock, even after the learner had fallen silent. Milgram felt that this was evidence of a fairly general human tendency to obey authority figures.

The key characteristics of the Milgram experiment for social psychologists are that obedience was secured in a stressful situation in which high-pace commands were issued, gradually escalating over time. Participants were 'acclimatised' to the idea of shocking someone, by the initial mildness of the shocks, which intensified over time. This creates a subtle pressure to conform – a sort of 'you've gone this far, why stop now?' situation. The visible authority said that they would take responsibility if harm was done. Several conditions made compliance more likely. Participants were less likely to administer the shock if they were in physical contact with the learner. In one condition, they were required to place the learner's hand on the lever that administered the shock, and in this case, obedience dropped to 30 per cent. Participants were more likely to conform if the 'authority figure' (the apparent experimenter) was in the room – their proximity seemed to matter, too. The study was replicated, with greater attention to ethics, by Burger (2009), who also reported high rates of obedience. He introduced the element of a 'defiant confederate' – someone who resisted the programme and challenged the moral authority of the experiment – but even in this condition, compliance rates were high.

Milgram suggested that, in the conditions reconstructed by the experiments he conducted, participants lost their sense of an *agentic state*. He suggests that, when an authority figure is present, participants lose their ability to see themselves as individuals with autonomous control over their own actions. He notes that:

the essence of obedience consists in the fact that a person comes to view himself as the instrument for carrying out another person's wishes, and he therefore no longer sees himself as responsible for his actions. Once this critical shift of viewpoint has occurred in the person, all of the essential features of obedience follow.

(Milgram, 1974, pxii)

The person is seen here as deindividualised, as having subordinated their will to the authority figure. Milgram sees this as a clear explanation of people's compliance to authority figures in doing deeds that they might otherwise not perform, as evidence of the *capacity of man to abandon his humanity . . . as he merges his unique personality into larger institutional structures* (Milgram, 1974, p188).

Milgram's theorisation is a little thin here – it is a plausible explanation that fits the findings, but is not well supported by evidence from the experiments themselves (Blass, 2004). Indeed, some critics, like De Vos (2009), suggest that Milgram's experimental situation actually functions to psychologise the question of obedience. Instead of seeing compliance as a social phenomenon, De Vos argues that the entire structure of the experiments Milgram conducted individualises the scenario. For example, after the experiment, De Vos notes, Milgram made interventions such as the following.

Milgram: I'd like to ask you a few questions if I may – How do you feel?

Pozi: I feel alright, but I don't like what happened to that fellow in there, he's been hollering. We had to keep giving him shocks, I don't like that one bit. I mean, he wanted to get out, and he just kept going, keep throwing 450 Volts, I don't like that, he won't even look at that gentlemen.

Milgram: But who was actually pushing the switch?

In his focus on the question of 'how does the participant feel?' and in emphasising individual responsibility through the question 'who was actually pushing the button?', Milgram is clearly shifting the analysis on to the person who engaged in the experiment. In asking how they felt, Milgram is, to a large degree, neglecting the social context within which compliance is secured.

Nissani (1990) suggests that Milgram's findings might be an expression of a cognitive limitation – a difficulty in understanding that an apparently good person expressing good intentions (in this case, wanting to understand more fully how people learn) might nonetheless be doing bad things. In a series of articles, Nissani and colleagues suggest that the ability to understand this requires the understanding that individuals need to engage in a cognitive shift, which might ultimately be difficult for them to make. To test this, participants were taught a complex but false formula to calculate the volume of a sphere. They were then given real spheres and asked to calculate their volume. The formula they had been taught significantly overestimated the size of the sphere. They were asked to use the formula to determine volume, and were also asked to use a more traditional method of filling the sphere with water, and then measuring the volume of the water. While their sensory observations clearly demonstrated that their formula-based calculations of volume were wrong, participants routinely abandoned the sensory evidence in favour of the formula, which they had been given by an authority figure – a maths expert who knew how to calculate volume. Nissani (1989) found that participants did not reject the false formula, and that most continued to use it in later tasks, despite the disconfirming sensory evidence. Nissani's findings suggest a level of *conceptual conservatism* – people will cling to established beliefs, even in the face of disconfirming evidence, particularly if the beliefs were established through interaction with someone who might be regarded as an authority or an expert. In one of the studies, one of the participants, a scientist, explaining his failure to reject the flawed formula noted: *It is difficult to imagine that one could be deliberately deceived in an exercise like this* (Nissani and Hoefler-Nissani, 1992, p105).

Nissani's work has a clear advantage over Milgram's in that the experimental set-up here is more ideologically neutral. The findings from these studies also have clear applicability in real-life. Miller (2009) notes the importance, for example, of understanding an individual's willingness to obey orders, and to inflict pain on others, in relation to issues of torture. Think, for example, of the US's use of waterboarding on political prisoners. What makes a reasonable, presumably well-meaning individual representative of the state inflict such terror on another individual? In the case of waterboarding, this might at least partly be because an American panel of experts insist that this is not 'torture-torture'. Russell (2009) suggests that under circumstances such as these, participants are in a *state of autonomous denial* (p132), knowing that they are ultimately morally accountable, but seeing circumstances in the situation that enable them to evade feeling or being seen as personally responsible, without having to confront the experimenter directly.

But were participants really as compliant as Milgram's formal report of this research suggests? There have been some questions about the authenticity of the experimental situation. For example, when teaching this study to a first-year group, one of our colleagues was impressed that a first-year student, watching the video of the experiment, noticed that the 'learner' was heard to be banging on the walls when asking to be let out – but he was supposed to be bound to his chair. Is it possible that participants in this research did not entirely buy the researchers' experimental ruse? Critics point out that there are many features of the experimental set-up that might clue participants into a reality that all is not quite what it seems (see Orne and Holland, 1968; Brannigan, 2004). The participants draw lots with the 'fake' participants to determine who will be 'teacher' and who will be 'learner' (the drawing is rigged to ensure that participants become teachers and confederates become learners). Logically, there is no reason why experimenters could not have played the role of teachers themselves in the pseudo-experiment: this might well have induced participants to look for other possible motives for their participation in the research.

In his fascinating reanalysis of Milgram's original audio tapes, Gibson (2011) notes that participants were far more resistant to, and challenging of, authority than Milgram's write-up of the experiments might suggest. He draws a distinction between Milgram's reporting of the original transcripts, and his own transcriptions, which are more detailed and follow more closely the protocols of modern qualitative research. For example, in one extract, Milgram reported that a participant asked the experimenter to go and check that the learner in the other room was all right. In the Milgram transcript, the experimenter simply assures them he is OK, and then instructs the participant to continue, which they do. Gibson's transcript, however, looks quite different:

Extract 1b (Participant 0208)

During this time period movement can be heard, and what sounds like a door shutting. From what follows it seems reasonable to presume that E went out of the room, ostensibly to ask L if he wished to continue.

E: He seems willing enough to go on so please continue.

T: Wet, night, grass, duck, cloth.
(Extract from Gibson, 2011)

Gibson argues that it is very clear from his transcript that the participant offers far more resistance to the authority figure than Milgram's report suggests. Milgram's transcript skips over the fact that the experimenter actually left the room – presumably to check on the 'learner' before continuing. Passini and Morselli (2009) make the point that these psychological experiments on obedience and compliance underestimate the significance of resistance, disobedience and non-compliance in human relationships. We will return to this theme later in the chapter. Gibson extends this point, noting that in fact participants often engaged in extensive debate with the experimenters, and that the experimenters were more persuasive, using far more rhetorical strategies than the original Milgram reports indicate.

Social influence and conformity

How does the presence of other people influence our behaviour? Do we act differently when in a group? Is it harder for us to act in a way that flies in the face of what others around us do? These are the kinds of questions that preoccupy social psychologists interested in social influence and conformity.

Social influence and task performance

The effect of other people on individual behaviour has been well established. Some research suggests that the mere presence of others can have a direct impact on, for example, our task performance. Zajonc (1965) noted that for automated or easy tasks, the presence of others improved our performance. So, for example, if we were in a job testing light bulbs, which required us to screw and unscrew light bulbs over and over, our performance at this repetitive task would be enhanced by the presence of other people. This is termed **social facilitation**. But think of the all too familiar experience of trying to read with someone looking over your shoulder. When engaged with more complex and difficult tasks, the presence of others typically diminishes our performance. Zajonc described this as social inhibition. This phenomenon is explained with reference to our state of arousal – Zajonc (1980) suggests that, as a species, we are hardwired for an increase in arousal so that we are in a state of readiness to respond to the actions of others. Cottrell (1972), in contrast, suggests this is a learned rather than an evolutionary response: he suggests that we learn to be apprehensive in the presence of those we feel might evaluate our performance (**evaluation apprehension**). Lots of musicians report this kind of experience: they can play a piece perfectly in their room, by themselves, but the minute they feel there is an audience evaluating them, their performance falls to pieces (Kenny and Osborne, 2006). Robinson-Staveley and Cooper (1990) demonstrated that our expectation plays a key role in mediating the effect of evaluation apprehension on performance. For a computer task where participants had a positive expectation of achievement, the presence of others enhanced performance, but where their expectation was negative, the presence of others reduced overall performance. The effects of the presence of others are mediated by a range of other effects. For example, Ben-Zeev et al. (2006) notice that gender has an impact on children's expectations of maths performance. Social norms and discourses of gender (for example, the 1994 Barbie doll who declared *Math class is tough!* – often misquoted as *Math is hard*) will affect children's expectation of their maths per-formance, which, in turn, will logically impact on evaluation apprehension. While the presence of others in small group interactions plays a role, this is always located within broader social contexts.

The presence of others can have other kinds of effects on task performance. Ringelmann (1913, in Kravitz and Martin, 1986) first noted a phenomenon he termed **social loafing**. He noticed that when men were asked to pull on a rope while in a group, they tended to put in less effort than if they were alone. This observation was further investigated by Latané et al. (1979) who conducted an experiment in which they asked participants to shout loudly, and found that loudness of shouting decreased relative to the size of the group they were in. Latané et al. suggest that individuals reduce their level of effort when their individual contribution to a group effort is not discernible (i.e. their reduced effort is less visible), while Kerr and Bruun (1983) suggested that this effect was more likely if participants felt their effort had little impact on group outcome (this is termed, rather charmingly, in this literature as *free riding*). Kerr (1983) also suggested that individuals will reduce their effort if they perceive that others are not trying hard, to avoid being exploited (what Kerr terms *the sucker effect*). Kerr and Bruun (1983) suggest that these effects are more likely in groups working around disjunctive rather than conjunctive tasks. Disjunctive tasks are ones where group members gather to decide how best to act, or how best to solve a problem.

For example, you are placed in a group together with other students to do a group project, and meet to choose a project focus. Under these circumstances, weaker group members are more likely to show a motivational dip because they do not perceive that it matters how hard they work as their ideas will not be chosen, while stronger members tend to loaf because they see others as relying on them to get things done, and may start to feel exploited. In contrast, in conjunctive groups, where each group member has a contribution to make to the final product, individual motivation and effort is less likely to be affected. So, for example, if each member of your project group is tasked with a different job (one chooses a topic, one chooses a method, etc.), it is more likely that everyone will make a reasonable contribution. More recently, technological advances mean that a great deal of group work is conducted remotely. Alnuaimi et al. (2010) found that even in a virtual environment, similar dynamics are in operation. Group workers are more likely to loaf if teams are large, and if moral responsibility is diffuse (participants do not feel personally responsible). However, perhaps most interesting in the virtual environment, participants are more likely to loaf if they do not perceive their virtual co-workers as 'real' – a feature that is exacerbated by computer-mediated co-operative work. This has clear implications for the idea of virtual offices and workspaces, suggesting a need to make the social contact between co-workers feel more real and substantial in order to avoid social loafing behaviour.

Research on social loafing and related concepts tends to be fairly negative about the effectiveness of working in groups, suggesting that social influence has a negative impact on group efforts. However, there are some studies on social influence and performance that focus on the beneficial effects of group interaction on performance. Köhler (1929) suggested that weaker group members often work harder to avoid being blamed for poor group performance. Stroebe et al. (1992) suggested that there was not much convincing evidence to support the idea of social loafing, and that where individual contributions to group outputs are visible, individuals actually compete and work harder. The models are based on a presumption that individuals are fundamentally selfish, and contribute to groups in a manner that enables them to minimise effort, rather than in an altruistic way. The approach significantly underplays the possibility of effective co-operative and collective action, positioning people's experiences in groups as fundamentally individualistic, selfish and competitive.

Task — Think about a recent experience of group work.

Do you think you put in your best effort? Do you think that others in the group did so, too?

Was your behaviour in the group influenced by the amount of effort you saw others putting in?

Do you think you, or others in the group, engaged in 'social loafing'? Why?

Conformity

Groupthink (Janis, 1972) refers to the condition human beings experience when our need to belong, to feel the same, to think the same as those around us overrides our capacity to think critically or realistically about situations. It refers to conformity in the group context. Asch (1955a) conducted a series of experiments on the nature of conformity, in which he explored the way that individuals 'yield', in their critical judgements and decision-making behaviour, to interpersonal influence. Most of the work inspired by Asch's original experiments has focused on conformity behaviour in small groups. Asch's experiment explored the influence of group behaviour on individual decisions, looking at how group pressure might influence responses on simple tasks. He used an experimental situation in which there was one real participant and seven individuals whom the real participant thought were also experimental subjects, but who were actually confederates of the research team.

The participants and pseudo-participants were asked to identify which line in Set B was the same length as the line in Set A. Participants took turns to answer out loud, and the confederates routinely gave obviously wrong answers. Asch wanted to see whether the real research participants would give the obviously right answer, or would adjust their choices based on what others were answering. He found that participants conformed to the majority answer in 37 per cent of the trials, clearly giving obviously wrong answers when these were the majority answer in the group; 76 per cent of all participants complied at least once. He concluded that individuals conform to group processes as a means of gaining social reward and acceptance.

There are clear flaws with Asch's methodology. It is quite possible that participants guessed the purpose of the study – the answers to the questions posed were so obviously wrong that participants may well have started to query what was really going on in the study. As a measure of how people behave in real-life groups, the study lacks somewhat in naturalism or ecological validity. Nonetheless, the study does suggest that individuals might be subject to normative social influence, and may conform to majority opinion even if it is not in keeping with their personal or private views. Asch suggested that this might be an expression of individuals' need to belong, be accepted and liked.

This study has been replicated in a range of contexts and conditions. Researchers have queried whether Asch's findings can be explained in terms of true attitude change, or mere compliance (i.e. did participants really believe their wrong answer was right, or were they just fitting in with the group?) Deutsch and Gerard (1955) varied the conditions under which individuals made judgements – comparing decision making on simple tasks, like the line judgement task, when in groups and when on their own. They found that participants were more likely to make errors when working in the group conditions where confederates were giving wrong answers than they were when they worked alone. This suggests that behaviour in groups is about mere compliance or public conformity – fitting in with the group – rather than about a real change of belief. It is also clearly not the case that participants are conforming as a result of **informational social influence** (the human tendency to turn to others for information or insights – for example, looking to others to establish how to behave at a club you have never been to before). Rather, their behaviour is consistent with **normative social influence** (changing behaviour in order to fit in, without changing your privately held beliefs).

What factors influence whether and how individuals conform? The size of the majority within the group has an impact. The bigger the number of people holding the majority view, the larger the effect is – up to a point (Asch, 1955b). The effect of the size of the majority on individual conformity tapers off once you reach five or six – perhaps because participants become suspicious of the real aim of the experiment. Participants are more likely to conform in groups if they perceive similarity with other group members, and if the group is cohesive (for example, Hogg, 1992; Nowak et al., 1990). This is borne out in 'real life' by the perhaps obvious research finding that we are more likely to be influenced by friends than by relative strangers (Crandall, 1988).

Kameda et al. (1997) found that members who were seen by others in the group as 'prototypical' would have a greater influence over the group as a whole, regardless of whether their original perspective was a minority or majority position. In other words, the person who seemed most typical, most representative, of the group would hold greater sway. Within groups, individuals whose views were 'cognitively central' and seen as 'prototypical' – as embodying the group consensus – had greater overall influence in subsequent decisions. Kameda suggested that this was because perceived similarity, shared beliefs and shared knowledges, gave people in the group a basis to identify that individual as an expert in some way.

If responses are anonymous, participants are less likely to conform. If no one in the group knows what their answer is, participants' answers appear to be uninfluenced by group processes. This suggests that what we are seeing in the conformity studies is conformity, not attitude change: individuals change their behaviour to be seen to be fitting in, not because their beliefs about the task have changed. If their beliefs had changed, their responses would fit the group regardless of whether they were visibly or anonymously agreeing.

Characteristics of the target individual also play a role in the degree to which they are likely to conform. For example, Moeller and Applezweig (1957) found that individuals were more likely to conform if they had a high need for social approval or popularity, and a low need for self-approval. Crowne and Liverant (1963) found individuals with low expectations of individual success tended to conform more. Low self-esteem and a need for social approval emerge frequently in this literature as a feature of conformity behaviour. For example, Jetten et al. (2006) found individuals were more likely to conform if they felt they had a low social status in a group.

This research on conformity has focused very heavily on factors that increase the likelihood of individuals 'fitting in' with group pressure. However, an important, but often underemphasised, finding in Asch's work is that the effect of social influence and conformity on behaviour is reduced by the presence of allies. Even if the majority make a particular decision, the conformity of the individual participant is dramatically reduced when even just one other individual agrees with them. Allen and Levine (1969) found that this was particularly the case if the ally was consistent in their variation from the majority. This finding is important because it calls into question an oft-repeated claim about the meaning of conformity research – that it suggests that group influence is necessarily bad, that it produces 'mindless mobs'. The impact of allies on the production of groupthink belies this point, suggesting rather that group influence can be both positive and negative – that camaraderie can challenge conformity as well as build it, and can help foster critical thought.

Minority influence

The extensive literature on conformity makes four major points.

1. The individuals in groups will be influenced by other group members.

2. As a consequence of conformity pressure, group similarity increases over time.

3. Our primary motivator in groups is to be liked, approved of and accepted, and we fear marginalisation and ostracisation. We do not want to be 'different'.

4. Logically, the direction of social influence moves from the majority to the minority – if most people think something, the chances are that individuals will conform to that majority view.

Moscovici (1980, 1985) was dissatisfied with this dominant story of how social influence worked. While he recognised that often, conformity pressure did work in the way that Asch and his followers predicted, nonetheless this account did not make sense of all human social behaviour. In particular, Moscovici noted that there would always be individuals or groups who stood against a crowd, who protested, refused and resisted the pressure of the larger social group. Furthermore, he pointed out that such minority voices could and did have an influence. Groups also are not as static as dominant ideas about conformity suggest. If conformity pressures were as simple as just the individual conforming to the pressure of the majority, group perspectives on issues would remain more or less the same over time. But think about any group you have belonged to, and you will recognise that this often is not true. Things do change. The dominant view in a group shifts over time. New ideas often come into groups as a minority view, but these minority views gradually take hold. Think, for example, about the way that fashion works. When you see a particularly outrageous style on the catwalk for the first time, the majority response is often 'wow, that's just too much'. But over time, the seemingly outrageous style becomes a fashion, a norm. (When the miniskirt was first introduced, it was seen as incredibly daring, and was only worn by a small minority of women. It is now ubiquitous.) Research on **minority influence** has emphasised the role of minorities and minority views in challenging received wisdom, changing norms and shifting the status quo (Mucchi-Faina et al., 2010).

To test how minorities might influence groups in an experimental context, Moscovici (1980, 1985) reversed Asch's social influence experiments. In each of his groups, he had six naive subjects, who did not know the purpose of the experiment, and one confederate. The seven group members were shown a series of slides of varying shades of blue, and were asked to state their colour. The confederate minority member consistently stated that the blue slides were green. A minority consistently said that the blue slides were green. In a control condition, there was no confederate, so participants were simply reporting their perception of the colour without manipulation of social interest. What Moscovici found was that, in the control condition, participants said that the slides were green in less than 1 per cent of the responses. This contrasted strongly with the experimental condition in which 10 per cent of all the responses said green, and 32 per cent of all subjects responded 'green' at least once. Moscovici suggested that this experiment documented the possible role of minority influence in gradually shifting majority perspectives.

In the real world, rather than the world of the laboratory, clearly not all minorities have an influence. For example, nudism or naturism has been a minority view in the UK for a very long time. However, the presence of this minority pressure group has not had a substantial influence on the majority's view that wearing clothes in public is generally a pretty good idea. What is it that makes some minority views more influential than others? How, for example, did the idea of 'rights for African Americans' in the civil rights movement in the US move from being a minority concern to an accepted majority position?

The key question, then, is 'what makes minority influence effective?' Generally, social psychological research suggests that its effectiveness is determined by the style of argument and how those styles are interpreted by the majority. First, minority influence is stronger if a view is expressed consistently (Moscovici, 1985). By consistently expressing the same view over a period of time, the minority appears confident (Moscovici and Faucheux, 1972), and may begin to get the majority to question their taken-for-granted assumptions. For example, in the case of the US civil liberties movement, the consistent, steady pressure and restatement of a belief that equality and rights for all fitted with the presumptions of the American constitution gradually won majority supporters over, to the point that this is now, broadly speaking, a majority view. Consistency highlights conflict between the minority message source and the majority view. By not abandoning, shifting or changing their position, the influencing minority is able to demonstrate a clear alternative view of social reality, forcing the majority to re-evaluate their point of view. Consistency makes individuals question whether the minority perhaps know or understand something they do not. It also garners visibility and legitimacy for the minority position. However, it is important that minority groups appear as consistent, not dogmatic (Maass and Clark, 1984). If reiterating their position makes them sound like a stuck record, they are unlikely to influence people. Rather, they need to be able to argue their position in a flexible way, with more than one counter-argument, taking other people's points on board, but maintaining a consistent viewpoint.

It has been suggested that people in a 'double minority' have less influence. A double minority is when an individual is in a minority group (for example, in the UK they might be Asian, or gay, or a Buddhist) and also holds minority views, e.g. pacifism). Festinger's (1954) social comparison theory would predict that we are more easily influenced by people we see as being similar to us. However, research on minority influence yields a more varied set of findings: out-group minority members who hold minority views can have a greater latent influence on attitudes than in-group minority members do. The social categorisation approach predicts that we are more likely to be influenced by minorities we see as being more 'like us'. So, for example, a black middle-class person is more likely to influence white middle-class views on institutional racism in the police force than a black working-class person. The route of influence here is presumed to be the perceived similarity between source and target (David and Turner, 1999). Essentially, majority members are understood here as 'recategorising' minority members as being 'one of us'. In contrast, Maass and Clark (1984) found that heterosexual participants were more inclined to be influenced by heterosexuals arguing for gay rights than they were by a homosexual group advancing this minority opinion. Rather than recategorising the minority group as 'one of us', participants were more likely to be swayed by the opinion of those who were already a part of their in-group. Out-group members were generally less effective as agents of minority influence.

The size of the group, and the relative size of the minority, has an impact on how influential the minority position might be. Moscovici and Nemeth (1974) found that a minority of one can be a more consistent influence, and therefore more influential, than a larger number of minorities representing slightly different points of view. However, if two or more minority individuals are consistent, their influence is stronger as their point of view is less likely to be dismissed as odd or unique to the one individual. In their social impact model, Latané and Wolf (1981) suggested that minority influence decreased as the size of the majority increased. Clark and Maass (1990) found that once the majority increased beyond a certain level, evidence of minority influence started to disappear.

Moscovici's (1976) original premise in advancing an idea of minority influence was that group processes are complex and interactional, and that the dialogical nature of group dynamics means that minorities, too, can shape group ideas. However, much research that has developed Moscovici's premise has focused on individual cognitive processes rather than group dynamics. So, for example, Levine and Kaarbo (2001) suggest that the dominant approach to studying minority influence involves looking at the individual cognitive responses of majority members to a (often anonymous) person who holds a minority view. These studies explore how this apparent 'minority' influences attitude change (for example, Alvaro and Crano, 1996; Martin and Hewstone, 2003), or other aspects of cognition like problem-solving (for example, Smith et al., 1996; Van Dyne and Saavedra, 1996).

For example, Martin et al. (2007) conducted experiments to explore the differential impact of majority and minority influence on attitude-consistent behavioural intentions. They set up experimental conditions to explore whether minority or majority influence would have a bigger impact on the likelihood of people expressing behavioural intentions that were consistent or inconsistent with their existing attitudes. For example, participants read a counter-attitudinal message (opposed to voluntary euthanasia), and were asked to indicate whether they would sign an advance directive or 'living will', which would be used to prevent them from being kept alive under particular medical circumstances. Participants were told that the statement they read had been written either by a minority or a majority member. They found that the impact of minority or majority influence was mediated in part by factors such as the personal relevance of the message itself.

While these kinds of studies may appear to focus on intergroup behaviour, or behaviour in small groups, in real terms the 'social' aspects of intergroup relationships (like group membership) is not the focus of this research – the understanding of groups is reduced to the influence of individuals on each other, to individual cognition and information processing.

Task — Imagine that you are the leader of a minority political party.

- How would you go about securing greater influence for your party?

- How would you gain influence from your minority position?

Social roles and social influence

Like Milgram, Zimbardo was interested in whether, in the right kind of situation, ordinary human beings would be subject to social influence in a manner that would make them likely to do terrible things. In the study known as the Stanford Prison Experiment, Zimbardo and his colleagues (Haney et al., 1973; Zimbardo et al., 1973) explored the place of social roles in influencing human behaviour. Social roles are patterns of behaviour associated with particular social positions. So, for example, the social role of lecturer has a particular behavioural set associated with it (teaching, supporting, maintaining appropriate social boundaries with students, etc.) as does the role of student (learning, being self-motivated, taking responsibility for your study, reading set work, being guided by the lecturer, etc.). These social roles have a significant impact on our social interactions. Think, for example, about the last time you were in a lecture situation. Your behaviour in this setting will have been guided by your understanding of your social role – you will not have jumped up to dance, or initiated a loud telephone conversation with a friend; rather, you will likely have engaged in note taking and listening, and perhaps asked appropriate questions in a polite way. Our social behaviour is guided by the situation we are in, and our understanding of what is expected of us socially in that particular context.

You will probably be familiar with Zimbardo's famous prison experiment, and so we will provide only a brief description of the study itself. Having screened 70 student volunteers to ensure that they were 'psychologically healthy', Zimbardo, Banks and Haney selected 24 of them, randomly assigning them to one of two conditions – prisoner or guard. Having secured consent to their participation in the study, the researchers arranged a rather life-like arrest of those in the prisoner category and their removal to a 'prison' set up in the basement of a building at Stanford University. In the prison, prisoners were subjected to conditions similar to a draconian prison context. Overseen by the 'guards' (who the researchers had kitted out with a guard uniform, khaki suit, sunglasses, etc.), they were stripped, deloused, given a prison uniform and assigned a prison number. With Zimbardo acting as 'warden', these research participants lived life for the next few days as prisoners and guards within this closed institution. As the study progressed, the guards took to their roles with increasing enthusiasm, with some becoming quite sadistic in their controlling behaviour (particularly at night, when they felt they were not being observed). One prisoner, seeking 'parole', was turned down by Zimbardo (raising rather significant concerns about the ethics of the study). He became acutely distressed, even developing a psychosomatic rash. 'Prisoners' demonstrated signs of what Zimbardo et al. (1973) termed pathological prisoner syndrome. Initially, they seemed to disbelieve their situation, then initiated a failed prison rebellion, followed by expressions of depressed mood, helplessness, apathy, rage and, in most cases, high levels of conformity and excessive obedience to the guards. These behaviours were seen by the researchers as evidence of **deindividuation** – a sense of loss of personal identity, loss of control, and identification with the prisoner role. The guards, in turn, demonstrated what the researchers termed a pathology of power. This was evidenced by their clear enjoyment of their role as guards (working overtime even, and expressing regret when the experiment came to an early end because researchers perceived it had gone out of control). They engaged fully with the guard role, and abused power by meting out minimally justified punishment, and engaging in unnecessarily cruel acts such as refusing prisoners food, bedding and toilet trips. While some participants became identified as good guards who did their job without abusing prisoners, they nonetheless turned a blind eye to the bad guards who did engage in behaviours that far exceeded the established routines of life in the fake prison. The behaviour of both guards and prisoners in this experiment has been attributed to conformity to social roles. The researchers suggested that people behaved in a way that fitted the social role they had been assigned and that the situation dictated people's behaviour.

Of course, there are significant ethical and methodological issues with this experiment. Ethically, the experiment caused great distress to participants, and Zimbardo's close involvement in the prison and his adoption of the role of warden has been subject to considerable criticism. He acknowledges that his involvement clouded his judgement, and he consequently allowed the experiment to 'go too far'. Methodologically, while prisoners and guards did take to their roles with great gusto and apparent full investment, nonetheless all participants knew that they were in an experiment, and the conditions of the experiment itself, with its very strong demand characteristics, might have had a significant impact on behaviour. Johnson and Downing (1979), in particular, suggested that participants were engaging in an elaborate role play, essentially an extended dressing-up session, and that this explained the high levels of role conformity better than Zimbardo et al.'s account of situational determinism and their emphasis on conformity to social roles per se.

In recent years, the findings of the Stanford Prison Experiment have been applied to an understanding of genocide (Browning, 1998; Hatzfeld, 2006) and events at Abu Ghraib prison in Iraq (Zimbardo, 2008). Essentially, this application of Zimbardo et al.'s work suggests that, under the right conditions, any individual is capable of human rights abuses – the situation draws people to conform to social roles of oppressor, captor, etc. This kind of argument opens a moral quagmire around the varying place of personal responsibility (agency) and situational determinism. For example, Crump (2008) questions whether the law *can prevent groups from making good people go bad*. This kind of literature represents groups and group influence as a force of evil in the world – a corrupting influence that brings out the worst in human beings.

Critical thinking activity

Passive recipients of social influence?

Critical thinking focus: analysing, evaluating, reflecting

Key question: *What role does agency have in our understanding of social influence?*

Read through the following account of the trial and sentencing of one of the American soldiers tried for human rights abuses in relation to the Abu Ghraib incidents.

> *During the court martial, Chief Warrant Officer Kevin Kramer, a military intelligence soldier called as a witness, referred to an email from the US command in Baghdad telling him to order his interrogators to be tough on prisoners. 'The gloves are coming off, gentlemen, regarding these detainees,' said the email. It added that the command 'wants the detainees broken'.*

> *Frederick, who was in charge of the night shift at the 'hard site' facility at Abu Ghraib, west of Baghdad, said military intelligence soldiers and civilian interrogators told guards how to treat detainees.*

> *That included stripping detainees, depriving them of sleep or taking away their cigarettes, Frederick said. Investigators wanted detainees 'stressed out, wanted them to talk more,' he added.*

Two psychologists who testified for the defence described Frederick as an introvert who depended heavily on others and had a strong desire to please, which they said helped explain why he did not discipline colleagues for abusing prisoners.

'Give me an image of the all-American boy, and it's this young man,' said a San Francisco-based doctor, Philip Zimbardo. 'He is a wonderful young man who did these horrible things.'

But Major Michael Holley, prosecuting, told the court Frederick was an adult who could tell right from wrong.

'This behaviour should not be subjected or imposed on any human being,' he said, showing a picture of prisoners, naked, bound and hooded.

He added: 'How much training do you need to learn that it's wrong to force a man to masturbate?'

(Reproduced from *The Guardian* newspaper with the permission of the Guardian Media Group plc (copyright Guardian Media Group plc))

Use the following prompts to guide your reading of the article and to form links between the theoretical material presented in this chapter, and this reported incident.

- To what degree do you think that Frederick, as an individual charged with human rights abuses, was responsible for his own behaviour?

- To what degree is his behaviour a reflection of social influence?

- What role do factors such as social roles, conformity, pressure etc. play in this kind of incident?

- Zimbardo acted as an expert witness in the defence of Frederick, arguing for leniency in sentencing as the individual was acting in response to situational pressures. Do you think his argument is correct?

Critical thinking review

This activity helps develop your skills of analysis and evaluation, and reflection, by applying theoretical material from the chapter to a newspaper report. You were also encouraged to think critically about social issues, and the important philosophical question of the relationship between agency (personal responsibility) and social influence.

> Applying theoretical knowledge in this way, and thinking critically about these knowledges, are important skills that will enable you to evaluate and make critical judgements about psychology research and its application to the real world.
>
> Other skills you may have used in this activity: recall of key principles and ideas, communication (literacy) skills if you write up the activity, independent learning.

Beyond small groups: understanding the psychology of the crowd

Most social psychological work on social influence has focused on the role of small groups in shaping individual behaviour. However, this is clearly not the only form social influence takes. In Chapter 3 we explored the role of larger societal groups, such as racial groups, on social behaviour (a theme we also return to in Chapter 10). Another possible way to study social influence is to consider how people behave in larger groups such as crowds. In 1895, Le Bon published a very influential book on crowd behaviour, which has had a potent influence on the way this phenomenon has been understood both in social psychology and in society at large (Moscovici, 1981).

While the 2011 student protests in London over the very large increase in tuition fees largely passed peaceably, the media and British public became particularly preoccupied with a small number of cases that illustrated the apparent influence of crowds on individual behaviour – the student who threw a fire extinguisher from a roof (whose subsequent court appearance suggested that he had felt pulled along by the activity of the crowd), Charlie Gilmour climbing the cenotaph and swinging from the Union Jack flag, and students 'mobbing' the royal car. Consider the following headlines.

Defacing the Cenotaph, urinating on Churchill . . . how young thugs at student protest broke every taboo

(*The Daily Mail*, 10 December 2010)

Cenotaph Yob is Son of Pink Floyd Star

(*The Sun*, 11 December 2010)

'They were lucky not to be shot': Police chief says armed officers showed 'enormous restraint' as mob attacked Charles and Camilla

(*The Daily Mail*, 10 December 2010)

Terms like 'thugs', 'yob' and 'mob attack' underscore a particular way in which crowds and crowd influence is conceptualised – the idea of deindividuation and 'mob' psychology. Le Bon (1895) suggested that people become 'submerged' into crowds, and that in that process they become less individual. He suggests that this moment of submergence marks the transition from individual to crowd psychology. Le Bon's ideas about the crowd portray it as a mindless mob, in which individuals lose a sense of their own individuality, their sense of selfhood. They lose the ability to control their own behaviour, as their individual will is subjected to the will of the crowd – they no longer make their own decisions, become a seething mass of emotionality, losing their capacity for individual thought. Le Bon characterises this aspect of crowd psychology as contagion. This contagion is a consequence of **suggestibility**. In crowds, according to Le Bon, rational responses are bypassed, and the primitive, emotional, racial unconscious is dominant as the vestiges of the rational conscious personality are swept away by the mob. He also notes that, in crowds, individuals are more likely to sacrifice their own self-interest to the interests of the group (Le Bon characterises this as further evidence of the irrationality of the crowd). Crowd psychology, according to Le Bon, is characterised by a perception of invincibility (power in numbers) and power (also represented as irrational).

Reicher (2008) suggests that Le Bon can be criticised at a theoretical, descriptive and ideological level. At the descriptive level, Reicher criticises the decontextualisation of the crowd, which is represented as a universal phenomenon, the same in nineteenth-century France, and twenty-first-century Britain, governed by a universal 'primitivism' and loss of contact with the 'rational individual'. He points out that Le Bon's description positions the crowd as if its actions were independent of state or police action, as if it were an isolated entity. At a theoretical level, Reicher indicates that the crowd is seen as activating an *off switch* (p188) on individual identity. This individual identity is understood as *a unique and sovereign construct which is the sole basis of controlled and rational action* (p188). The self here is understood as rational, individual, separate from social forces. In the form of the crowd, social influence here is only understood as that which deactivates individuality – our individuality itself is represented as basically asocial. Politically and ideologically, Le Bon's work ratifies the dismissal of collective action and silences the voice of the crowd by portraying it as deindividuated, irrational, primitive, pathological, less than human. In this sense, Le Bon's analysis props up the social order and the status quo by representing collective resistance to such a status quo as irrational. Look again at the headlines above, from news reporting of the student protests. The language of 'mobs', 'yobs' and 'thugs' clearly echoes Le Bon's reading of crowd psychology as primitive and irrational, and underscores the ongoing influence of Le Bon's thinking in popular contemporary understandings of crowd behaviour.

In relation to crowd behaviour, sociologists Turner and Killian (1987) suggest that crowds are not the irrational mob, swept away by emotion, that Le Bon's approach suggests. Emergent norm theory suggests that collective action takes a social coherence as a result of a range of interactive processes. Its proponents argue that crowd behaviour is governed by a set of norms that is not typical of everyday interaction, but that is not inherently irrational or pathological – the crowd, rather, has a logic of its own. Norms of social behaviour emerge within crowds as a result of negotiation within the large group context. Pointing to examples of extreme crowd behaviour, such as lynchings, or in the case of South African apartheid society, crowds immolating individuals who were perceived to be informants, Turner and Killian note that such events do not happen as suddenly or in the kind of isolation with which they are often reported. Rather, they note, there is often a prolonged period of milling around, of deliberation, before these extreme events take place. They are the product of a negotiation of dissenting voices and emotional reactions that are expressed within the group. Crowds are not the homogeneous masses of identical thought and feeling that Le Bon's approach to crowd psychology would suggest.

Reicher (2008) points out that these crowd norms do not emerge in complete isolation. People do bring their histories, their social context, their locatedness, to collective contexts, too. Our behaviour in crowds is a reflection of our social identity – how we see ourselves, our group membership, and our recategorisation of ourselves as part of the crowd. In his classic analysis of the 1980 St Paul's Riot, Reicher (1984) noted that first these events could not be understood as the isolated behaviour of a crowd. Rather, they were a reaction to a police raid on a black Bristol family's café in St Paul's, which produced five hours of collective action, including destruction of property. Reicher notes that, contrary to popular representations of mindless mobs, the actual activity of the crowd was very targeted – police, banks and 'outsider's' shops (not community property) – and also very bounded (the crowd did not move beyond the boundaries of the St Paul's area). He also notes that social identity was highly salient in these incidents – that people described themselves very clearly in terms of us (members of the St Paul's community) and them (outsiders, police, the state). Interactions on the day were strongly focused on a sense of community, conjoint identity and belonging. Finally, the targeted nature of the activity was an expression of an identification as an oppressed minority – as black, as poor – and a reaction against the agents of the state (the police), and the wealthy (banks and other property). Far from being a 'mindless mob', what emerges in Reicher's analysis is a clear representation of the events of St Paul's as a rational and co-ordinated response to perceived injustices, based on a coherent sense of a shared social identity. This runs quite strongly contra to popular media representations of the events, as well as to political rhetoric around what happened there.

Highlighting the importance of the social context within which crowds act, Stott et al. (2008) explored the impact of police practice on crowd behaviour. Using structured observations and questionnaire data, they determined that policing style had a potent impact on the norms that emerged within the crowd, and on the way that crowds behaved. Where police were non-paramilitary in their style, crowds appeared to respond with forms of non-violent collective psychology. This crowd response functioned to normalise non-violent behaviour and marginalise violent outbursts. In this sense, it might be argued that crowd behaviour is not simply an expression of the dynamics of the crowd itself, but exists within a social context that co-constitutes the activity of the crowd.

In contrast to the very negative representation of the action of the crowd that pervades social psychology, some contemporary psychologists have highlighted the positive aspects of collective behaviour, and the importance of cohesion in understanding this kind of collective action. For example, Cocking et al. (2007) explored crowd behaviour under emergency conditions. The dominant representation of crowd behaviour under these circumstances is of mass panic – disorder, irrationality, chaos. However, Cocking et al. found that, contrary to the popular images of panic and disorder that typify understandings of crowds, people in these circumstances tended to behave collectively, but in rational, orderly and considerate ways. They suggested that under emergency circumstances, people form a common identity in reaction to the threat, and behave in an altruistic and co-operative way (a finding later supported by their interview-based study with survivors of 11 different emergency events, Drury et al., 2009). While it may certainly be the case that there will be incidents of looting and violent competitive behaviour (think, for example, of some of the incidents that characterised the aftermath of Hurricane Katrina in New Orleans), these remain, nonetheless, minority behaviours in this kind of situation (Solnit, 2009). Indeed, in the recent crisis that followed the earthquake and tsunami in Japan (2011), it is remarkable how little negative behaviour was in evidence – generally, people co-operated and supported each other. This kind of work directly challenges the representation of social influence as a force for bad in society.

Skill builder activity

Communicating your ideas to an audience

Transferable skill focus: communication

Key question: *Are crowds unthinking, seething masses, irrational and primitive, or do they rationally express collective identities and political resistance?*

In class, divide into two groups, and construct a reasoned position to support each side of the debate around crowd behaviour. (If you are not studying psychology in a classroom-based setting, you might consider setting up a virtual debate.)

Use the following prompts to help prepare your presentation.

- In preparation for the debate, find an incident of recent collective crowd action (for example, the 2010 student protests over tuition fees, or the March against Cuts of 26 March 2011).

- Each team should develop a minimum of three substantive theoretical points to support their 'side' of the argument, supported by theory and research evidence.

- Each team should present a short presentation (maximum five minutes) on their key points.

- Using research and theory, opposing teams should deconstruct each other's arguments.

At the end of the debate, arrive at a group consensus as to the role of social influence, individuality, rationality, free will and social norms in constructing crowd behaviour.

Skill builder review

This activity helps develop your communication skills, focusing particularly on oral communication and presentation. These are important academic and life skills. The activity encourages you to reflect on what makes a good, well-reasoned argument, and how best to defend a theoretical position.

Other skills you may have used in this activity: critical thinking, comparison, independent learning, reflection, recall of key principles and ideas, information technology.

Assignments

1. Is social influence a force for good or bad in human behaviour? Critically discuss.

2. 'Our tendency to "group think" results in deindividuation and a lack of individual agency.' Critically evaluate this claim.

Summary: what you have learned

In this chapter, we have explored a range of theoretical attempts to understand the way that human beings are influenced by each other. We have considered ideas like obedience, compliance and conformity. We have explored the role of social norms, and particularly social roles, in encouraging conformity. We have considered how individual decision-making, judgements and behaviour are influenced by others in small groups, looking at ideas such as social facilitation and social loafing, which focus on how our effort in small groups is mediated by our perceptions of others' contributions and attributes. In exploring social psychological work on conformity, we have seen that often, in small groups, our decision making is influenced by what we perceive to be a majority view. We also noted Moscovici's caution that we should not neglect the important manner in which minority views are able to influence majority opinion. We concluded the chapter with a consideration of the behaviour of people in crowds, thinking critically about the traditional view that people become deindividuated in crowds. We considered alternative research that stresses the agency and directedness that people are able to demonstrate in groups, and which also focuses on the positive influence of crowds in, for example, emergency situations. To complete your critical thinking activity, you applied social psychological theory to an account of soldier's behaviour in Abu Ghraib. This activity helped develop your skills of analysis and evaluation, and reflection, by applying theoretical material from the chapter to a newspaper report. You were also encouraged to think critically about social issues, and the important philosophical question of the relationship between agency (personal responsibility) and social influence. This enabled you to evaluate and make critical judgements about psychology research and its application to the real world. In your skill builder activity, you developed your oral communication skills and your capacity to develop a reasoned argument, by participating in a debate around crowd behaviour.

Further reading

Mugny, G and Perez, JA (2009) *The Psychology of Minority Influence*. Cambridge: Cambridge University Press.

A clear overview of (mostly European) work on minority influence.

Zimbardo, PG (2007) *The Lucifer Effect*. New York: Random House.

This book offers an interesting and easy-to-read update to Zimbardo's thinking on social influence, with relevant contemporary examples. You may wish to read this book critically, considering, for instance, the political implications of conceptualising social influences as Zimbardo does.

Chapter 6

Prosocial behaviour

Learning outcomes

By the end of this chapter you should:

- have an overview of key research in the area of prosocial behaviour;

- understand the theoretical constructs of prosocial behaviour, altruism and empathy;

- understand mainstream models of prosocial behaviour: the evolutionary psychology approach and the notion of universal egoism, social exchange theory, and the notion of bystander apathy;

- understand the limitations of mainstream research on prosocial behaviour;

- understand the importance of seeing prosocial behaviour as a contextual and lived phenomenon.

What is prosocial behaviour?

How helpful are human beings? In a recent video posted on YouTube (www.youtube.com/watch?v=nNXG8AxqJuU), a man is featured absent-mindedly leaving a plastic bottle on the ground in a busy shopping mall, just next to a plastic recycling bin. We watch as person after person wanders past the bottle, looks at it but does nothing about it. Eventually, after a few minutes, a young woman stops, picks the bottle up and puts it in the recycling bin. As she does so, a flash mob responds, applauding her behaviour loudly, circling around her and congratulating her for this simple act before disappearing into the crowd. The woman looks embarrassed and confused at first, but warms to the crowd and takes a modest little bow as the crowd begins to disperse.

This little video tells us a few things about how **prosocial behaviour** is viewed in our society. It is seen as a special, but often rare, event. The expectation of the flash mob was that a large number of people would not pick up the bottle – if the first person who walked past had stopped and picked it up, there would have been little point to the video. Also contained in the video clip is the presumption that being prosocial is sufficiently unusual to warrant the attention and applause of a crowd. Social psychology's engagement with prosociality is rooted in similar assumptions. This area of research is concerned with the conditions under which people are likely to engage in prosocial behaviour, and also with understanding why so often people turn the other way when they see another human being in crisis or difficulty.

Prosocial behaviour is broadly concerned with acts that are seen as helpful, positive and promoting positive human relating. Eisenberg and Mussen (1989) define prosocial behaviour as *voluntary actions that are intended to help or benefit another individual or group of individuals* (p3). The idea of prosocial behaviour involving voluntary action is an important one, since it precludes any behaviour that is coerced in any way – for example, military personnel helping civilians would not be seen as engaging in prosocial behaviour unless their behaviour exceeded that which would be expected in the ordinary line of duty. Hogg and Vaughan (2008) argue that the study of prosocial behaviour *includes **altruism**, attraction, **bystander intervention** (helping a stranger in need), charity, cooperation, friendship, rescue, sacrifice, sharing, sympathy and trust* (p528).

The most frequently researched area of prosocial behaviour in social psychological work is **helping behaviour**. Helping is defined as a deliberate act intended to be of benefit to another person. So, for example, in the supermarket you may notice an elderly woman who appears to be distressed and having trouble breathing. You go over to her, and ask if you can get someone to help, or find her a place to sit and rest. If your intention is to be helpful, then the behaviour is a helping behaviour. In contrast, Gilbert and Silvera (1996) suggest that some behaviours that appear to be helpful are not – and that the distinction is often in our intention. For example, helping a colleague at work may appear to be a prosocial act. However, if your intention is to make them independent, and to draw attention to the contrast between your own competence and their incompetence, then this is not a helping behaviour.

Altruistic behaviour is helping behaviour that is motivated purely by a desire to help, with no expectation of personal gain and reward (for example, see Batson and Coke, 1981). Much ordinary, everyday caring behaviour is not strictly speaking altruistic. Think, for instance, of paramedics, nurses, teachers – they engage every day in caring behaviours that might be understood to make a positive contribution to society, but they are not seen as helping behaviours per se. This is because social psychologists tend to view this kind of vocational helping as part of a job – a strong, or perhaps even primary, motivator is not (just) to help the individual so much as to build a career, earn a living, etc.

The question of whether human beings are fundamentally selfish or selfless has preoccupied philosophers and social theorists for centuries. In psychology, this translates to a debate around the tension between egoism (helping behaviour motivated to reduce our own sense of discomfort) and altruism (helping behaviour motivated by a desire to benefit others).

Theories of prosocial behaviour

How has social psychology understood prosocial behaviour? Much of the focus on helping has sought to answer the question 'why do we help each other?' This question presumes that the idea of prosociality is puzzling in itself; that our tendency to help each other requires an explanation.

It is possible that this question contains within it the seeds of an answer because it sets up the question as if helping were an unnatural human behaviour that needs to be explained. Consider the following theoretical approaches, the assumptions that they make about human nature and the implications of those assumptions for an understanding of prosocial behaviour.

Evolutionary psychology (sociobiology)

Evolutionary psychology takes as its starting point the presumption that all human social behaviour can be understood in evolutionary terms – that we behave as we do because it is in the interests of our species. Evolutionary psychology predicts that natural selection operates to select traits that ensure the survival of the species and that, in reproductive terms, human beings are fundamentally self-interested – we behave as we do to ensure the survival of our own genetic endowment. If we understand the world in this way, it is easy to see that altruism as a phenomenon does become a bit of a puzzle to be solved. If human beings are motivated primarily by the idea of promoting reproductive fitness and the survival of their own genetic material through successful reproduction, then altruistic behaviour is a contradiction to the basic principles of evolutionary processes. Dovidio (1984) suggests that the **universal egoism** focus (i.e. the view that people are fundamentally selfish) is the dominant view in the social sciences, and that within this frame of reference altruism is rendered an impossibility. (We cannot be both fundamentally self-serving and altruistic.)

Social evolutionary theory argues that human beings are not truly altruistic, but that they merely appear to be so. So, for example, if you stop in the supermarket to help the woman who is out of breath, you are not doing so out of a genuinely selfless desire to help, but your selfish motives may not be entirely apparent. Can you think of selfish reasons why you might stop to help in this situation? According to the **selfish gene theory** (Dawkins, 1976, 2006), an animal might appear to sacrifice itself for another, but it is doing so from the selfish motive of ensuring the continuation of the species and, by extension, its own genes. This is called **kin selection**. For example, in wolf packs omega wolves might sacrifice themselves to protect the offspring of the alpha pair. This appears a selfless act, but on closer investigation, it is clear that the wolf is protecting its own genetic endowment, by proxy – it is related to the cubs it protects, and in securing their safety it is securing its own genetic future. Clearly, in many instances this is the case for human beings. We often go to extraordinary lengths for family, for example – giving our time, energy, resources, even our organs! But what about the adoptive parent, who will sacrifice as much, or even more, for the good of a child to whom they are not genetically related? We might extend this idea of looking after our own to tribes or even nation states. So this theory might explain why, for example, members of the military might sacrifice their lives for their country. However, this does seem a bit of a theoretical stretch. Is it not, perhaps, more parsimonious to accept that a level of altruism is as 'natural' to human beings as selfishness?

One possible social evolutionary explanation of what appears to be altruism is that we have evolved to be social and reciprocal beings. We depend on each other, and on a level of social harmony, as a species. As an extension of this, we have developed a tendency to engage in supportive and apparently altruistic behaviour in the assumption that, by behaving this way, we will receive altruistic behaviour back. So socially, rather than individually, our behaviour is not strictly altruistic.

A fundamental theoretical difficulty with this social evolutionary account of altruism is the way in which it treats both altruism and selfishness as real, static and unchanging phenomena, that are in some way essential to the nature of being human. In contrast, we would argue that both being altruistic and selfish are socially constituted, not absolute, taken-for-granted phenomena. We have never actually isolated a selfish (or unselfish) gene – although the term when used in the theory does seem to shore up a level of scientific certainty for the idea. But our ideas of what is selfish and what is altruistic are bound up in our social circumstances, point of view and understanding of social norms, and right and wrong behaviour. For example, a man who sacrifices his life in war for the good of his fellow soldiers might, in one context, be seen as heroic, self-sacrificing and necessarily good. However, from another point of view, this sacrifice has resulted in a family being left without a breadwinner and a dependent wife unable to make ends meet alone. Taken from this point of view, is his act entirely altruistic? We are not taking a stance either way here. Rather what we want to flag up is that our understanding of what is selfish, and what is self-less, will vary according to the lens through which it is viewed – and that lens is socially and politically constituted. Perhaps there is nothing essentially altruistic or selfish about any particular behaviour, but rather our understanding of its meaning shifts according to our particular context and value system?

Social learning and social norms

In contrast to the perspective of evolutionary psychology, a social learning approach to altruism does not look to our genetic endowment to explain apparently altruistic behaviour. Rather it suggests that we learn to be altruistic through our observations of our social environment and our understanding of which behaviours are reinforced and which are censored. As children, we learn to be altruistic through the direct instructions we receive about how we should behave, the rewards (or otherwise) that we receive for particular behaviours, and by watching the behaviour of others (modelling). In this way we adapt to social norms, and acquire particular kinds of social behaviour. Developmental psychology suggests that we learn empathy and kindness as children, and that these are transmitted to us as important social values within the first years of our lives (Coles, 1997, cited in Baron et al., 2008). Hogg and Vaughan (2008) suggest that we learn the key social norms of **reciprocity** and **social responsibility** in these early years. The principle of reciprocity implies that we should help those who help us, while the idea of social responsibility suggests that we should help those who are not in a position to help themselves or others (for example, due to poverty, disability, etc.).

Social exchange theory

Social exchange theory (Thibaut and Kelley, 1959) extends this idea of reciprocity, implying that *human interactions are transactions that aim to maximise one's rewards and minimise one's costs* (Myers, 2008, p429). Social exchange theory is an economic theory of human relating – it applies the principles of the market to human relationships. Basically, this perspective suggests that we will help others if the benefits of helping outweigh the costs (for example, Honeycutt, 1981). In this sense, this theory remains very clearly one that assumes that human beings are fundamentally selfish. When you are making the decision about whether to help the elderly woman in the supermarket, you weigh up the perceived costs (you might be made late for an appointment, you might have to deal with the unpleasant aspects of illness, she might need more help than you had originally judged, etc.) against the perceived benefits (you will feel good for having helped, you will look good in the eyes of others, etc.). We will help, ultimately, if we perceive it to be worth our while to do so.

Piliavin et al. (1981) offered a slightly more detailed analysis of prosocial behaviour, using the social exchange theory. They developed a bystander-calculus model, explaining that our decisions to help or not help develop through three stages. In the first phase, the bystander experiences physiological arousal in response to observing someone else in distress. This is, in itself, an empathic response, felt at a physical level. The more intense this response is, the more likely we are to help. In phase two, we label the physiological arousal we experience, a cognitive process that plays a central role in determining how we interpret and react to the situation itself. In the third phase, we run a cost-benefit analysis. This takes into account our own distress at the scene we are witnessing weighed up against the possible costs.

One of the difficulties with the social exchange theory in relation to altruism is the notion of 'what's in it for me?' that underpins the theory itself. By reducing human interaction to the economic values of social exchange (you scratch my back and I'll scratch yours), it already presumes, before it even begins to look at actual human instances of apparent altruistic behaviour, that such behaviour is fundamentally selfish. Self-interest is built into the theoretical framework. Consequently, almost any behavioural choice can be reframed and reread as a selfish one. The theory also understands our emotional experiences as costs and benefits – feeling guilty is a cost in the equation, feeling positive about yourself for having done something good is a benefit. Because of this, all behaviour that we do because it makes us feel good is recast as fundamentally self-interested. So, if you volunteer to help survivors of the Japanese earthquake and tsunami disaster and, in addition to all the positive impact this act has, you also feel good about yourself . . .

well, obviously that makes you selfish! This logic places us in the odd position where all positive action is reframed as selfish simply because of the internal rewards this offers.

Task

- Think about a recent incident when you were called upon to help another person.

- Write down the detail of the incident.

- List in as much detail as you can all your thoughts and feelings about the incident, when you decided whether to help, as you helped, and then afterwards as you reflected on the experience.

- List, too, all your possible motivations for helping, thinking through what the possible costs of helping were, and all the possible benefits.

- Now compare what you have written to the ideas suggested by social exchange theory. How full an account do they offer of your real-world experience of helping?

Empathy

In contrast to the point of view that human beings are fundamentally self-interested, some researchers suggest that we help purely for the good of the person being helped, and that is a part of human nature. **Empathy** is an important component of this kind of helping behaviour. What is empathy? Empathy is a sense of fellow feeling, the ability not just to feel sorry for someone in their plight, but to be able to put yourself in their shoes, and care about what happens to them. As Baron-Cohen (2011) has recently pointed out, social psychological research into empathy is quite limited.

Batson (1991) suggests that generally our desire to help is motivated by a genuine concern for people's welfare. He suggests that empathy – the capacity to put yourself in the position of the person in the situation – mediates our helping response. Whether people help or not is deter-mined by two factors – how much initial empathy they feel, and whether they have the option of psychological escape. If empathy is triggered as people watch others in distress or difficulty, they will help. Batson suggested that the cost-benefit analysis described in the previous section will only take place if empathy is not triggered in the first place, while empathy is the motivation for truly altruistic behaviour. What determines whether we respond empathically or not? According to Batson, our capacity to empathise is dependent on the perspective we take on the situation we observe. Batson et al. (1997) asked participants to read a story about a young woman university student, coping with life after the loss of her parents. In one condition, participants were instructed to put themselves in the young woman's shoes; in another they were asked to focus on the young woman's thoughts and feelings; in the third condition, they were instructed to remain detached and objective in their judgements about her situation. Participants in the first two conditions showed higher levels of distress than those instructed to take a detached perspective. They also demonstrated more empathic concern. Batson suggests that this distinction might explain the finding that simply observing a situation does not, in itself, yield prosocial behaviour – observers are more likely to notice the other person's experience and help, if the situation they observe evokes personal distress.

Batson was interested in distinguishing egoistic distress from altruistic empathy in human helping behaviour (Batson et al., 1981, 1991; Batson et al., 2003). He did this by setting up an experimental situation in which he aroused people's empathy, but allowed them two choice routes in their reaction to the situation they observed – on the one hand they could act to help, on the other they could simply avoid the situation. In other words, he allowed them to lessen their distress with no cost to themselves. He set up a complex experiment in which participants were asked to observe another participant, 'Elaine' (actually a confederate), complete an unpleasant task, which included her receiving electric shocks. At the beginning of the experiment, half the participants were told that they shared common values with Elaine (inducing greater empathy), while the other half believed they had very different values (low empathy condition). During the course of the experiment, Elaine disclosed to the participants that she had had a traumatic accident which involved electric shocks, and that she was finding the experiment very difficult, but that she wanted to continue. The experimenter intervened at this point, offering the participant the option of swapping places with Elaine. In half the cases, the experimenter tells participants that the experiment is nearly complete, while in the other half of cases, participants were told the experiment was far from finished. In this way, the experimenter offers half the participants an 'easy psychological escape'. Where empathy was high, the offer to exchange was accepted frequently, regardless of the other condition. Where empathy was low, and there was an easy escape route, participants tended to let Elaine continue to receive the shocks. The results of this experiment indicated that if empathy was high, then helping was high, even if escape was easy. It was only when empathy was low that ease of escape from the situation became an issue (such that if empathy was low and there was an easy rate of escape, then participants would choose not to switch with Elaine). Based on Batson's body of research, he concluded that feeling empathy for a person in need evokes motivation to help (that person) in which these benefits to self are not the ultimate goal of helping; they are unintended consequences (Batson and Shaw, 1991, p114) – in other words, pure altruism is possible, and we often help motivated by a desire to benefit others, not from fundamental self-interest.

A common feature of these models of prosocial behaviour is that they see it as a relatively disconnected, individual phenomenon. However, as we have already discussed above, our judgements about whether something is prosocial and helpful, or not, is shaped by the social context in which we read a behaviour. For example, if we see someone fighting in the street, we tend to interpret that as anti-social behaviour. However, if the person fighting is defending people they care about, or a cause they believe in, and with which they sympathise, they might see them as helping – as fighting the enemy for the common good. The maxim that 'one man's terrorist is another's freedom fighter' is another illustration of this – our interpretation of what is good and prosocial is shaped by our own social and political context and this, in turn, must have an impact on our choices to behave in a prosocial way.

Bystander apathy

In 1964, the murder of Kitty Genovese stimulated a significant increase in social psychological study of prosocial behaviour. Kitty Genovese was attacked on the streets of a New York suburb. She was approached by her attacker, Winston Moseley, and stabbed. Her cries for help were heard by several neighbours. Her distress was, according to *The New York Times*, ignored by 38 people who failed to respond to her cries. One shouted at her attacker to leave her alone, and Moseley ran off, only to return to attack her again shortly afterwards, and then a third time, as she made her way to the door of her apartment building, he stabbed her again and raped her. The attacks took place over a half-hour period, and, according to *The New York Times* report, it was only after the final attack that a witness called the police. Ms Genovese died on the way to the hospital. This incident became a motivator for social psychologists interested in the phenomenon of **bystander apathy**. It was seen in the popular press, and in social psychological research, as evidence of the failure of most people to intervene when others need help.

Perhaps of greater interest to us, as critical social psychologists, is the disconnect between the way that *The New York Times* and social psychological researchers have reported this story, and some of the detail of what actually happened, according to police reports. It is important to note here that, though this event has been consistently reported for years, a recent study showed that the actual facts do not match up to this particular version (Manning et al., 2007). In *The New York Times* it was reported that 38 silent witnesses did nothing to stop the attack – and this is the way that this incident has traditionally been taken up and reported in social psychological research. However, during the subsequent investigation, 12 people indicated that they had heard portions of the attack, but none had heard the entire incident, and many did not realise what they were hearing until after the fact. In other words, these were not quite the apathetic, cold, uncaring bystanders that we have read about in social psychology textbooks. One witness reported that his father did call the police – probably after the first attack (but the police did not respond). One 'bystander' did yell at Winston to leave Ms Genovese alone – and he did. For much of the attack she was not in public view – the worst aspects of the attack took place within the shelter of the apartment building where possible witnesses could not see what was going on. It is important to consider, when reading the literature on apparent 'bystander apathy', the degree to which researchers might be seeing what they want to see in human behaviour.

Latané and Darley (1969; 1970) were interested in understanding why bystanders did nothing, coining the phrase 'bystander apathy'. They were also interested in questions such as 'when will people help'? and 'how does the presence of other people influence behaviour in these kinds of situations?' Latané and Darley proposed a cognitive model to explain when people will help. They suggested that people go through five steps in deciding (consciously or unconsciously) whether to help. To engage in a prosocial act, the bystander must:

1. notice that something is happening;

2. interpret the event as an emergency;

3. take responsibility for providing help;

4. decide how to help;

5. provide help.

There are therefore five possible points at which a bystander may decide 'no' in this model, and no help will be given. To notice and interpret something as an emergency requires a cognitive process whereby the bystander defines the situation as an emergency – and what is defined as an emergency might vary from person to person (Hogg and Vaughan, 2008). To identify an event as an emergency requires that they see the event as unusual (it is not an everyday event), and understand that the event involves danger to people, animals or property. An emergency event is by its nature unanticipated, requiring instant attention. This means that the bystander cannot plan their reactions in advance, and often does not have time to think through all the possible available reactions. In emergency situations, the nature of the emergency is not always clear – in our woman in the supermarket example, you might fear you are intruding on a private moment, or misinterpreting her behaviour in some way. This ambiguity might make you hesitate in your reactions. When this happens we tend to look to each other for cues on how to behave – and if no one else is reacting, this may make us less likely to react ourselves. Latané and Darley (1969) found that bystanders were less likely to react the larger the group of other bystanders was: as the size of the group of witnesses increases, the likelihood of help being offered reduces. They tested this in an experimental situation where participants (all male university students) were asked to participate in a series of interviews about university life. Latané and Darley staged an 'emergency' while the young men were waiting to be interviewed: smoke started to stream out of a vent in the waiting area and participants' reactions were observed. Participants were observed in conditions where they were either alone, with two other participants they did not know, or sitting with two experimental confederates who ignored the smoke. They found that 75 per cent of participants who were seated alone reported the smoke, 38 per cent who were seated with other participants reported it, and only 10 per cent who were with confederates who ignored the smoke went to tell someone what was going on. This confirmed Latané and Darley's suspicion that being with others reduced helping reactions, and also suggested that in group situations how others respond will have a strong impact on how we interpret and respond to an emergency ourselves.

Latané and Darley (1976) suggest that three social processes affect helping behaviour, and explain the phenomenon described above. When bystanders are alone they typically do help. However, they suggest that the presence of others results in **diffusion of responsibility**. When we are by ourselves, we tend to see ourselves as solely responsible for what happens, but when there are others present our sense of responsibility is spread across everyone there. The presence of others can also make us feel self-conscious – we do not act because we worry that we are misinterpreting the situation and will be seen as silly or as overreacting. This is termed **audience inhibition**. This is particularly the case if, as we have noted above, the emergency itself is quite ambiguous. This is exacerbated by the effect of social influence on our judgement of the situation. As we have noted in Chapters 4 and 5 on social influence, the presence and behaviour of others will often have an impact on how we interpret and respond to the situations we are in. If there are other people present, and they do not seem to be responding to the emergency, we are less likely ourselves to interpret the situation as one in which help is needed. This produces **pluralistic ignorance**, where the emergency is not treated as an emergency because the group does not define it as one.

Latané and Darley suggested that, in the Kitty Genovese case, the bystanders noticed something was happening, but also paid attention to the reactions of other witnesses. Because other witnesses were not reacting, and not responding to the situation as an emergency (or were interpreting it as a domestic dispute), a sense of pluralistic ignorance had been constructed. With the second attack, as it became clear that there was an emergency situation, diffusion of responsibility meant that observers did not act because their expectation was that somebody else would.

Of course, one of the difficulties with this model of bystander apathy is that it is not applicable to all helping situations, and can only really account for one quite limited aspect of helping behaviour – helping in emergency situations. However, most helping does not take place under emergency conditions. While Latané and Darley's work has been held up as a clear example of prosocial behaviour research, it is describing a kind of helping situation that is far from typical.

What does social psychology tell us about other kinds of helping behaviour? First, there are clear individual characteristics that make us likely to help. However, individual differences only exert a limited effect (Dovidio et al., 1991), especially when the costs of helping or not helping are not seen as particularly high (Hogg and Vaughan, 2008). For example, our emotional state has an influence on whether we help or not. Perhaps unsurprisingly, we are more likely to help if we have the time, and if we are in a good mood, especially if the situation we are responding to is not an obvious emergency. So, for example, Isen (1970) found that teachers were more likely to give to a school fundraising effort if they had just succeeded on a task they did before being asked. If you are in a bad mood, angry or down, you are less likely to help. Negative moods tend to make us focus in on ourselves, and consequently we are less responsive to the needs of others (Aderman and Berkowitz, 1970). Guilt makes us more likely to help (for example, Isen et al., 1973).

We are also more likely to help when we are a part of a wider group with a sense of commitment or political investment in a particular social outcome. Our ideological commitments might make us more likely to intervene – for example, women who have a feminist commitment are more likely to intervene in a domestic dispute. If you are a member of a political or religious group that values a sense of responsibility for others, you are more likely to help generally.

Older people are more likely to help. In deciding whether to intervene, our motivation based on cognitive processing increases as we mature, while our self-serving and hedonistic motives decrease (Kahana et al., 1987). Documenting the Scrooge effect, Jonas et al. (2002) found that participants were more likely to intervene and help when there were clear reminders of their own mortality. For example, they interviewed people close to a funeral home, and found that they were more willing to donate to charity than those interviewed several blocks away.

Bystanders were also more likely to intervene if they felt they were competent to do so. Logically, a first-aid trained individual will feel more able to help with CPR than someone not trained, and consequently is more likely to help in a relevant emergency situation (Johnston et al., 2003). If you feel you are best equipped to help, you are likely to do so, regardless of the presence of other bystanders. For example, a nurse is more likely to help when there is an accident than someone without medical training (Cramer et al., 1988).

Gender plays an apparent role in determining prosocial behaviour. Intuitively, one might imagine that this is because women – the apparently gentle sex – would be more helpful, more empathic, more likely to care. However, social psychological research has largely demonstrated the opposite. Latané and Dabbs (1975), for example, found that men were more likely to intervene than women. This is likely, of course, as a result of the kinds of experimental situations that are set up to explore bystander intervention. As you have perhaps noticed when reading this chapter, prosocial behaviour is rarely studied in an everyday, ordinary interactive context. Much of the research focuses on rescuing type behaviour. In contrast, as Gilligan (1982) has suggested, women's ethic of care is rooted in a sense of belonging and communality. Research focuses less on the kind of everyday business of helping that involves undramatic gestures such as watering a plant, going round and listening to a friend, or helping out with a bit of babysitting. Eagly (1987) suggests it is not so much that women do not engage in prosocial behaviour as that social psychological research tends to focus on the kind of prosocial action men are more likely to take.

Characteristics of the victim also make a difference in our decisions to act. Perhaps, unsurprisingly, we are more likely to help if we like the victim – if they are a friend (for example, Bolger et al., 2000; Kiesler et al., 2000; Wellman and Gulia, 1999), or they look attractive (Athanasiou and Green, 1973; West and Brown, 1975; Harrell, 1978). The perception that the victim and bystander are similar and share common values increases the likelihood of bystander intervention (for example, Eagly & Crowley, 1986; Simon et al., 1998, 2000). Levine et al. (2005) suggest that this is an expression of social categorisation and in-group favouritism. However, bystander intervention reduces if witnesses see themselves as too similar to the victim – perhaps because they fear that if they intervene, bad things might happen to them, too. For example, often women do not help other women who are being harassed for fear that the harassment, or the stigma associated with the harassment, might be visited on them (for example, Bowes-Sperry and O'Leary-Kelly, 2005).

We are more likely to help if we see the victim as innocent in their suffering. Exploring helping behaviour in the aftermath of Hurricane Katrina, Fussell (2006) found that the likelihood of helping decreased if people perceived that victims were responsible for their own situation – particularly if they felt that people could and should have evacuated and were perceived to have chosen not to. Betancourt (1990) noted that bystanders are more likely to experience anger than empathy under these kinds of circumstances, and consequently will not act altruistically. If we see the victim as completely innocent, and in no way responsible for their behaviour, we are more likely to help them. This focus on the innocence of the victim may be an expression of defensiveness on the part of witnesses, since it functions to block our sense of responsibility to care or act in particular situations. I remember watching the film *The Accused* when I was younger, and being shocked when, at the most violent part of the gang rape scene, the woman sitting next to me in the cinema turned to her friend and said 'Well, she was asking for it really, wasn't she?' This kind of logic is often found in cases of sexual violence, where women are seen as complicit in their own attacks because they were dressed provocatively, or were out drinking, or acted irresponsibly (Gavey, 2005).

Understanding the value of research on prosocial behaviour

As with much mainstream psychological research, social psychological research on prosocial behaviour has been carried out in mostly Western societies, using mostly middle-class samples. Can we really conclude from this kind of research that people are naturally and inherently inclined to be selfish? Western middle-class contexts are known to be characterised by their placing of a strong premium on individualism and independence. Could what we are observing in these contexts be an expression of that cultural characteristic rather than an ultimate rule of human nature? As we have already noted, most of the early work on which models of prosocial behaviour have been based was conducted largely by men, on men, using experimental situations that favour masculine forms of helping. Can we really suggest that this is typical of human helping behaviour?

Like much social psychological experimental research, the work on prosocial behaviour suffers largely from the artificiality of the situations it sets up in order to explore how people help each other. Latané and Darley (1969, 1970, 1976), for example, did studies such as dropping pencils in lifts to see who would help pick them up. Do these kinds of studies really give us much insight into the broad range of human helping behaviour that we observe across so many different social settings? How we help is complex and located, not decontextualised in the kind of controlled experimental situations that such classical social psychology studies set up. Real-world prosocial behaviour is rarely about emergencies or picking up pencils – it is about lived relationships of care and support. Can a study that involves smoke coming out of a vent, or picking up someone's pencil for them in a lift, really help us to understand a sibling who cares for their severely disabled brother for 20 years after their parents died?

Nonetheless, if we want to build a society in which people are likely to help in emergencies, and to assist when there is a need, it is important to understand what sorts of conditions promote helping and prosocial behaviour. The more cynical and misanthropic egoist view, which suggests that people are fundamentally selfish, does not really offer much scope for helping us to better understand how and why people care and help. In contrast, understanding the operation of empathy, and the factors that make us more likely to step in and help, does offer opportunities for intervention. Interventions have been designed in recent years to reduce the bystander effect in order to increase community responses to particular kinds of emergency situations. For example, Banyard et al. (2007) designed a sexual violence prevention programme using a community of responsibility model. Rather than simply tutting disapprovingly about apathetic bystanders, this approach taught individuals in a university context how to help safely and effectively when they see an incidence of sexual violence. After participating in these community responsibility sessions, participants (compared to a control group) demonstrated clear positive outcomes in relation to their attitudes to helping, their knowledge about safe intervention, and their attitude towards helping at two-, four- and twelve-month follow-ups. This suggests that increasing perceived competence – helping people to understand how to positively, safely and effectively help – increases prosociality.

This finding is echoed in Avdeyeva et al.'s (2006) review of responses to the Hurricane Katrina disaster in New Orleans. They noted that if we want individuals to help under circumstances of disaster, it is important to ensure that communities are built to support such intervention in advance. They suggest that this requires clear, co-ordinated community leadership and activism, suggesting that programmes like Neighbourhood Watch can function to facilitate a sense in community members that they can intervene in such crises, and that such intervention is supported. Much social psychological work focuses on the negative impact of social and group influence on human behaviour – and the work on prosocial behaviour is no different, focusing on the way that the presence of others hinders prosocial action. In contrast, for example, Rodriguez et al. (2006) documented evidence of the positive social influence of community groups in the aftermath of Hurricane Katrina. A New Orleans group that styled itself as *The Robin Hood Looters* worked for a fortnight in its working-class suburb to search for and help rescue survivors in the neighbourhood, while another group co-ordinated its efforts to ensure safe and fair distribution of essential supplies, long before government aid was properly provided in the affected areas.

Critical thinking activity

Bystander behaviour

Critical thinking focus: analysing, evaluating, reflecting

Key question: *How do we understand bystander behaviour?*

Reread the sections above on bystander apathy.

The toddler Jamie Bulger was abducted and murdered by Jon Venables and Robert Thompson, who were both 10 years old at the time. As Venables and Thompson led Bulger through Liverpool, they were seen by 38 witnesses. While several questioned the children, none intervened to secure the safety of the toddler, though they noted that he was being treated roughly by the boys, had visible injuries and was extremely distressed. Read through the following extracts from a newspaper report on the incident.

> He (the barrister) *then described how witnesses had seen James with the two boys during the two-mile journey which lasted two hours and ended with his death. Many of them noticed that the boy was distressed, said Mr Henriques, but all seem to have assumed that he was in the care of an older brother or brothers.*

> *Some witnesses said James was crying and extremely distressed, some that he was laughing. Several noticed injuries to his head – a mark on the forehead and a bump on the right side, another bump on the top of the head, a graze on the face, a red mark on the cheek.*

> *Many reported that the little boy was held by the two older boys, one on each side, by his arms or his hands. One said they were dragging him and claimed that one of the boys kicked him in the ribs – 'not a full-blooded kick, but one of persuasion,' said Mr Henriques – and yet another said the two boys swung the child up as if in rough play. At one point, a woman saw a boy take hold of the little boy by the shoulders and shake him briskly.*

> *One woman who asked if the older boys knew the toddler was told they had just found him and were taking him to a police station. But later, approached by a school friend, one defendant said the little boy was the other's brother.*

> *A 14-year-old girl saw one boy run up the embankment leading to the railway line while the other followed, carrying the small boy, who was laughing. 'That may well be the last time anyone other than the two defendants saw James alive,' said Mr Henriques.*
>
> (From *The Guardian*, 2 November 1993) (Reproduced from *The Guardian* newspaper with the permission of the Guardian Media Group plc (copyright the Guardian Media Group plc))

Read over the following extracts from Levine's (1999) article on this case, which analysed witness testimony. These are extracts from witness testimony given in court.

Note: CT and CP are barristers; the witness is identified by B plus a number.

CT: Well, what you saw, you didn't feel that what was happening looked odd or unusual . . .

B7 (Mrs PM): I just thought it seemed a bit odd because they seemed too young to be looking after a young boy.

CT: That was why it was called to your mind?

B7: Yes

(Levine, 1999, p1137)

B13 (Mrs MD): Well, I thought they were going to the Post Office, because the baby was crying. I thought they were taking the baby to his mum at the Post Office, but they didn't. I overtook them and they turned left at the railings.

(Levine, 1999, p1137)

B11 (Mrs KR): I shouted on the bus sir, I shouted and all the people looked at me and looked to the window as I shouted, and I shouted, 'what kinds of friggin parents have they got, to let them out with a child like that?' to the man behind me. That's how disgusted I was with them swinging him.

(Levine, 1999, p1141)

CT: Can I ask you about the little boy? You noticed the graze? You didn't ask the little boy how he was and you didn't ask either of the boys how he had come by the graze?

B28 (Ms FS): No.

CT: It wasn't sufficiently bad, nor was there anything in the boys' demeanour to cause you to intervene?

B28: Yes, well I, when the three boys came in I automatically thought they were brothers.

CT: Did you? Why would you automatically think that? I'm sorry I don't want to be accused of interrupting you.

B28: It was just the way they were holding him, maybe he might have run out into the road or run off. I thought that the way they were holding him, they mightn't have wanted him to run around the shop.

(Levine, 1999, p1143)

Use the following prompts to guide your analysis of the text and to form links between the theoretical material reviewed and the adverts you have chosen.

- Summarise the various points in the texts where the boys were observed by witnesses. What did each witness see?

- How did the witness make sense of the incident?

- Does Latané and Darley's understanding of bystander apathy help us to understand why so many witnesses did not assist the child? Can you see evidence of diffusion of responsibility, audience inhibition, social influence and pluralistic ignorance in these accounts?

- Are there other, more contextually oriented issues that might better explain the failure of witnesses to act to prevent the crime?

Critical thinking review

This activity helps develop your skills of analysis and evaluation by applying theoretical material from the chapter to real-life examples. By analysing the material on the Bulger case, you were able to analyse textual data, and critically evaluate the usefulness of the notion of bystander apathy in understanding a real-life incident. You were also encouraged to consider alternative explanations for bystander behaviour.

Applying theoretical knowledge in this way, and thinking critically about these knowledges, are important skills that will enable you to evaluate and make critical judgements about psychology research and its application to the real world.

Other skills you may have used in this activity: recall of key principles and ideas, communication (literacy) skills if you write up the activity, independent learning.

Skill builder activity

Analysing and evaluating: benefits scroungers?

Transferable skill focus: textual analysis and written communication skills

Key question: *Is Britain prosocial? How do the British media represent individuals who draw 'benefits' in the UK?*

Prepare a written analysis of three newspaper articles, highlighting the application of a theoretical understanding of prosocial behaviour.

Use the following prompts to support your analysis.

– Find three recent newspaper articles that deal with issues relating to social welfare and benefit claimants. We suggest you look at disparate news sources – one left-leaning broadsheet, one right-leaning broadsheet, and one tabloid/red-top newspaper.

– Summarise the key points in each article, focusing particularly on how the relationship between the benefit claimant and the state is conceptualised in each.

– Analyse the articles for evidence of ideas about altruism, notions of reciprocity, social responsibility, empathy and social exchange.

– How useful are the theoretical models of prosocial behaviour in understanding social representations of those who make use of the British benefits system?

Write a 500-word report on this analysis.

Skill builder review

This activity helps develop your skills of textual analysis and written communication. These are important academic skills that can be drawn on in the work context when required to analysis the applicability and usefulness of theoretical ideas.

Other skills you may have used in this activity: critical and creative thinking, written communication, understanding and using textual data, information technology, reflection.

Assignments

1. It has been suggested that studies of prosocial behaviour are largely the studies of 'niceness' in white middle-class male contexts. Critically evaluate this claim.

2. 'The study of prosocial behaviour in social psychology is oriented to a view that human beings are essentially selfish beings.' Critically evaluate this claim and consider its implications for the study of prosociality.

Summary: what you have learned

In this chapter, we have outlined mainstream social psychological theories that seek to explain prosocial behaviour – or perhaps more accurately that attempt to describe and explain why people do or do not help each other. We have explored this in relation to evolutionary accounts, which focus on the idea that altruism is a logical impossibility since human beings are essentially selfish. We have also considered how the social exchange theory explains our decision to help (or not) in terms of a cost-benefit analysis (which, in itself, is ultimately self-interested). We have considered the role of empathy in mediating altruistic behaviour. We then explored Latané and Darley's focus on bystander apathy, exploring the strengths and limitations of this model. In particular, we have highlighted that much social psychological work has focused on isolated incidents of helping, or prosocial behaviour, often under 'emergency' conditions, and that this focus does not enable us to develop a sufficient understanding of the full range of human prosocial behaviour.

Further reading

Dovidio, JF (2006) *The Social Psychology of Prosocial Behaviour*. Mawah, NJ: Ehrlbaum.

This book provides an overview of mainstream social psychological work on prosocial behaviour, but also engages with critical perspectives, highlighting the importance of the role of contextual factors in understanding the way we help, and considering longer-term and more planned helping behaviours.

Learning outcomes

By the end of this chapter you should:

- *have an overview of mainstream perspectives on gender difference;*

- *have developed a critical position on the relative contribution of biology and society to the acquisition of gendered identities and behaviours;*

- *demonstrate a critical understanding of the limitations of essentialist models of gender;*

- *understand the importance of understanding and challenging gender inequalities;*

- *have an awareness of key challenges presented by feminism to mainstream psychology;*

- *have developed and used your skills in analysing data, communication of ideas, comparison, independent learning, reflection, recall of key principles and ideas, and information technology, by reflecting on the limitations of traditional theoretical views of gender for an understanding of transgender, and by thinking critically about the social phenomenon of baby beauty queens.*

Introduction

To include a chapter that is all about **gender** might seem odd in a social psychology textbook – gender is surely a matter of biology, so why on earth would it be of interest to a social psychologist? Social psychologists have, in fact, long been interested in gender, and questions about it have been asked under every topic studied in this field. These questions have usually focused on whether certain **sex differences** exist, the idea of gender roles, or why women are different from men in a range of social activities and behaviours (for example, aggression, leadership, managing emotions). In this chapter, we will consider the importance of gender in social life, and how gender is understood in social psychology. We ask questions like: What do we mean by the term 'gender'? How can we understand the role of gender in shaping aspects of our lives? Are there questions we can ask about gender besides ones which frame men and women as fundamentally different? Throughout this chapter, we will critically examine common-sense notions and 'truisms' about gender and gender differences to explore alternative understandings of this issue.

Why gender?

In everyday life, gender seems to be important to us and to our everyday activities. Popular books have been written about it (for example, *Men are from Mars, Women are from Venus*) and TV shows and films have been dedicated to exploring the differences between men and women (for example, *Sex and the City*). Gender seems to dictate simple aspects of our daily experiences – from the changing rooms we are 'allowed' to use in shops to how we divide up household chores. It is fair to say that gender can be understood as an important factor that seems to structure aspects of our lives – what one might describe as a key aspect of identity. This point has not been lost on social psychologists who have asked questions about gender in relation to a whole host of topics. For example, it has been claimed that:

- men are more aggressive than women, with men perpetrating more violent crimes than women (for example, Archer, 2004);

- men are more likely to demonstrate certain prosocial behaviours – such as helping a stranger in need – compared to women (for example, Latané and Dabbs, 1975);

- women's friendships tend to be more focused on emotional sharing and intimacy than men's friendships (Fehr, 2004).

As you can see, the focus in these studies is overwhelmingly on the issue of gender difference. A question that often preoccupies social scientists is: To what degree are the differences between men and women biological and to what degree are they social? Do the anatomical differences between men and women somehow influence how we structure and resond to the world socially? For example, what is the link between our physiology and how we divide everyday tasks, roles and responsibilities on the basis of gender?

Task — Make a list of between 10 and 15 typical household jobs (for example, doing the washing-up, putting water and oil in the car, DIY jobs, cleaning the toilet).

Now think of a household that you know of in which both men and women live (for example, this might be your own or a parent's home, a relative's house, a friend's house). Write down next to each item on your list who typically does each job (is it the woman of the house?, the man of the house?, both?)

From your list, are tasks equally shared between the men and women? Why do you think this might or might not be?

The 'nature' of gender?

Psychology (and the social sciences more generally) draw a clear distinction between sex and gender. This reflects an assumption that both biology and society have an impact on how we understand and experience ourselves and other people as gendered. The word 'sex' is often used to refer to the biological differences between women and men. The word 'gender', on the other hand, typically describes socially and culturally located understandings of these biological differences that attempt to make sense of and define what it means to be a man or a woman. This distinction between 'sex' (biological) and 'gender' (social) is often mapped on to understandings of biology as 'natural', fixed and unchanging, and of the social as mutable and in flux. These distinctions undoubtedly have intuitive appeal, resonating with popular claims that 'biology is destiny' as well as resonating with accounts of the nature/nurture debate. Are these distinctions as straightforward as they seem? To begin answering this question, we will take a look at the biological theorisations of sex differences.

Chromosomal sex

At a simple level, **chromosomes**, which are located in the nuclei of cells, can be thought of as the carriers of our hereditary characteristics. Humans have 46 chromosomes – 23 are contributed by the mother and 23 by the father. These chromosomes become organised into pairs (so 23 pairs of chromosomes = 46 chromosomes overall). One pair of chromosomes is distinctive from the rest because of its X shape or Y shape. If two X-shaped chromosomes become paired, the person will typically be female (XX), whereas males typically carry a pair containing an X- and a Y-shaped chromosome. These are the most typical patterns, but not the only ones possible – some individuals have different chromosomal patterns, which might include the following.

- Klinefelter's syndrome – this is when a man has an extra X chromosome which makes up the configuration XXY. This man will have male external and internal genitalia but he will tend to be infertile, and his outward appearance as he develops in puberty will be more feminine. Klinefelter's syndrome is also associated with the possibility of having learning disabilities.

- Turner's syndrome – this is when a woman only has one X chromosome (X0), not a pair of X chromosomes, which, as we have seen, is more typical in women. While this woman will have external female genitals, she does not develop breasts or public hair during puberty. Her ovaries do not develop and as a consequence she is infertile.

Chromosomal patterns are not the only biological process involved in sex differentiation – hormones have also been identified as playing a key role.

Sex hormones

A popular misconception is that men and women have different sets of **sex hormones**. Although it is true that, broadly speaking, we can divide hormones into two categories – **androgens** (which include testosterone) and **oestrogens** (which include oestradiol) – it is not true that androgens are only produced by men and oestrogens by women. Both men and women produce both kinds of hormones. The difference lies in hormone production, with men producing more androgens and fewer oestrogens and women producing the reverse of this pattern. A third kind of hormone is progesterone, which is produced by both men and women. In women, progesterone prepares the body for pregnancy. It is not clear what the function of this hormone is in men.

In adult women, one key function of hormones is the regulation of the (approximately) monthly fertility cycle – that is, the production of ovum or eggs, which basically ends in one of two ways: if the egg is unfertilised, menstruation will occur, but if the egg is fertilised then the uterus is prepared for pregnancy.

The female fertility cycle has long been characterised as presenting a very real problem for women as well as those around them. For example, in Plato's classic dialogue *Timaeus* (360 BC), it was claimed that when the womb was *left unfertilised long beyond the normal time, [it] causes extreme unrest* and *causes acute distress and disorders of all kinds* (cited in Philips, 2006, p64). In the nineteenth century, medical professionals similarly regarded it as a state of being 'unstable' mentally and physically. In the present day, some popular and professional understandings of the fertility cycle (including menstruation and pregnancy) often feature claims of women's moodiness, negative emotions (anger, depression, heightened irritability), irrationality and mental instability.

Is this a clear-cut case of biology influencing and directing women's emotional, psychological and behavioural responses? Is it the case that hormones make women mad? As an example, let's look at the process of menstruation. Studies looking at the link between hormone changes around the time of menstruation and emotional lability/mood have produced very mixed findings – some studies report a link, whereas others do not. Inconsistencies in findings were attributed in early studies to poor methodology. As Lahmeyer et al. (1982) point out: *Many early studies were criticized because they were retrospective in design, used too few subjects, mixed subjects of many different types, used infrequent ratings, did no physiological measurements to partition the menstrual cycle accurately, and did not accurately assess the psychological baseline of the groups studied* (p183).

Some studies have since reported that links between emotionality and hormone fluctuations are minor at best (Lahmeyer et al., 1982) and that mood changes are not necessarily particular to the menstrual cycle and may fluctuate from one day to the next or indeed across a single day (McFarlane et al., 1988). What's interesting is that although evidence for an actual link is mixed, both men and women tend to consistently attribute women's negative emotional responses to biology (when the woman was due to menstruate), but ascribed the same emotional responses to external factors at other points in the month. What this might point to is that social/cultural understandings of particular feminine biological processes (menstruation, pregnancy and so on) are so entrenched that they impact how we understand ourselves and others.

The idea that social/cultural understandings powerfully shape our experiences of biological processes does not mean, in any way, that women's experiences of premenstrual changes, distress, feelings of being out of control or not feeling themselves are not real. What it does mean is that experiences of premenstrual changes are not simply 'caused' by the body. It means that we can move away from the idea that it is a biological disorder that can be managed through medication but cannot be fundamentally changed – an assumption that could be seen to underpin many medical diagnoses of gendered experiences of distress, of which **premenstrual syndrome** is only one example (Ali et al., 2010).

The idea that biology is not destiny when it comes to premenstrual distress is demonstrated in a study by Ussher (2006) in which women who experienced premenstrual distress used an intervention called narrative therapy, which explores with clients different social understandings of premenstrual issues and related coping strategies. This intervention creates a space for women to rewrite their own personal story of mood and menstruation using culturally available under-standings. This intervention helped women to reframe their experiences more positively, with participants reporting a reduction of premenstrual symptoms and feeling more in control.

It is not only women who have often been portrayed as being at the mercy of their hormones. A popular view is that men are much more likely to be aggressive than women because of their higher levels of testosterone. In considering the evidence for this, Whitehead (2002) cites Clare's review of studies in 2000, which examined the relationship between male aggression and testosterone. Clare argues that while many studies show a correlation between levels of this hor-mone and aggressive behaviour, we need to be cautious about how we explain this relationship. We must remember that correlations do show cause-and-effect relationships, but that this does not mean that testosterone causes aggression. As Whitehead points out, if we assume that high levels of testosterone somehow causes aggression, *this leads to the question of how to explain aggression in individuals with very little testosterone such as prepubertal boys* (p12). We could also apply Whitehead's argument to women/girls with low testosterone levels.

However, we need to be very careful about making claims that particular problematic behaviour is based in biology. If we see behaviour as an expression of innate gender differences, then we assume it is fixed and cannot be changed. We can see how problematic this is when we look at how a biological argument might be used to justify antisocial behaviour. For example, if men have a 'naturally' higher sex drive than women, then perhaps criminal behaviours like rape, sexual assault and sexual harassment are simply an expression of an apparently natural male sexual aggression.

We are, of course, not arguing that biological processes are somehow unimportant in our everyday lives and experiences. However, what we are arguing is that a purely biological explanation can never give a full or truly useful account of gendered experiences and behaviours. If we reduce everything to biology, then we miss how these seemingly objective biological processes become enmeshed, shaped and understood within a very complex social/cultural context, which shifts across history as well as from culture to culture. While our bodies are certainly important, it is the cultural context within which we are located that render them meaningful, and the meanings of our embodiment are necessarily socially located.

Gendered brains

It is not just our hormones that have been implicated in making us different from the 'opposite sex'; our brain architecture has also been studied in an attempt to account for sex differences. For example, Baron-Cohen (2005) advanced the empathising–systemising theory, which basically suggests that the *female brain is predominantly hard-wired for empathy, and that the male brain is predominantly hard-wired for understanding and building systems* (p23). Essentially, Baron-Cohen is suggesting that human brains predispose women to be more emotionally sensitive and emotionally responsive, and men to be more rational. Since this fits with many dominant social common-sense ideas about men and women, this kind of argument can be compelling stuff. However, Cordelia Fine, in an interview with Jon Sutton (2010), cautions us about taking such evidence at face value and argues as follows.

> *Drawing a link between brain differences and psychological or social differences is no easy task. This is partly because the gender gap can close or even disappear depending on the social context, place and historical period . . . we are still at the beginning of the journey of understanding how the brain enables the mind. Even if we assume that a sex difference in the brain is reliable – generally not a safe assumption to make – what does it mean? The sheer complexity of the brain, together with our assumptions about gender, lend themselves beautifully to over-interpretation and precipitous conclusions.*

(Sutton, 2010, p900)

In other words, it is difficult to draw concrete conclusions about the links between brain structure and gender differences in thought and behaviour. The differences between men and women have shifted historically, a reality that belies a simple association of brain structure difference and difference in behaviour. (Surely differences in performance would be stable over time and place if it were this straightforward?) Furthermore, the brain itself is a developmentally plastic structure. Our brains continue to develop long after birth, such that it is possible that differences in brain structure, organisation and chemistry might be attributable, not just to innate biological propensity, but to the effect of learning and of differential gendered treatment of children on the developing brain.

Social understandings of gender

The work of anthropologist Margaret Mead is one of the most widely cited examples of how culture influences the meaning of gender, and how gender becomes expressed in different societies. In her famous book, *Sex and Temperament in Three Primitive Societies*, Mead (1935) described key differences in how gender roles were performed and played out in the Arapesh, Mundugumor and Tchambuli tribes of Papua New Guinea. A very basic description of Mead's key claims is outlined below.

- Arapesh society – men and women embodied what would be considered 'feminine' characteristics in Western culture. For example, they could be described as typically loving, caring, gentle and co-operative rather than competitive.

- Mundugumor society – both men and women adopted what could be described as masculine characteristics. For example, both men and women were said to display aggressive and assertive behaviours and were generally disengaged from child-rearing.

- Tchambuli society – women and men adopted what could be described as masculine and feminine characteristics respectively – that is, gendered roles seemed reversed in some ways. For example, men were considered too emotional and sentimental to make serious decisions; the women, on the other hand, took charge of economic and practical affairs.

While the detail of Mead's work has been criticised, nonetheless, one important implication of her research remains key: the idea that the gender differences with which we are familiar in the West – women as feminine, men as masculine – are perhaps not the result of biological processes but largely of the normative rules and rituals embedded in a culture. Mead's work suggests that it is through our location in a particular culture that we learn the meaning of gender and the rules around what is expected, and this becomes socialised into a particular gendered identity or way of being. While we are born biologically male or biologically female, the meaning of this distinction, and its implications for thought and behaviour, are largely social and cultural.

Social learning theory

Albert Bandura (1977) developed **social learning theory** as an explanation of how behaviours and characteristics are acquired by human beings through social interaction. He focused particularly (but not exclusively) on the importance of learning for the acquisition of gendered behaviour. Bandura argues that men and women acquire gendered social roles, and that these roles are produced largely as a consequence of social learning. Gender roles, he suggests, are primarily learned; they are not produced by biological differences. More specifically, Bandura argued that as children we learn what is considered typical or 'appropriate' behaviour for women and men through observational learning and modelling. Simply put, this means that we learn through observing and copying the behaviour of others, or model ourselves on the behaviour of others. **Observational learning** and modelling relies on a set of attentional processes that allow us to internalise the rules of behaviour. That said, just because someone observes normative gendered behaviour does not necessarily mean that they will perform them 'appropriately', for as Bussey and Bandura (1999) point out: *the extent to which they learn the details of the styles of behavior and become proficient at them depend on their perceived efficacy to master the modelled activities, opportunities to put them into practice, and the social reactions they produce* (p687).

How people react to our behaviour often functions to either reinforce or punish that behaviour. These reactions therefore have an impact on the likelihood that a behaviour will be repeated, or that it will be performed again in particular kinds of contacts. For example, a young lad who turns to a parent for comfort after falling and is told that 'big boys don't cry' is less likely to seek comfort in that way again.

Some studies provide evidence for the idea that children acquire gender-typed behaviour through learning and reinforcement (Fagot, 1978; Perry and Bussey, 1979). The Baby X experiment (Condry and Condry, 1976) certainly demonstrates that adults interpret behaviour differently for infants and children of different sexes. In this experiment, the researchers showed a video of a baby crying to 200 mixed gender adults. In one experimental condition, the baby was dressed in blue and named David. In the other, the infant was in pink and identified as Dana. The child was filmed engaged in identical crying behaviour, but for David, the viewing adults labelled this behaviour as anger, while for Dana they labelled it as fear. This difference in the perception of behaviour suggests that we view children through a gendered lens, and this does appear to have conse-quences for children. Fagot and Leinbach (1989) found that parents actively encouraged gender-appropriate behaviour, and discouraged gender transgressive activity, noting that the discouragement of transgressive behaviour for boys was particularly strong.

However, Greene (2003) argues that the evidence for observational learning is less clear-cut because of differences in childcare behaviour. A key assumption of social learning is that we are more likely to imitate the actions of those we perceive as similar – so boys are more likely to learn from men, girls from women. However, both boys and girls spend far more time in the presence of women in their early years because it is still the case that women tend to be positioned as primary caregivers as well as being in the majority in jobs as childminders, nursery nurses and primary school teachers. Despite this, and despite the greater availability for both sexes of female role models to observe and imitate, Greene suggests that both boys and girls display behaviours generally considered typical or appropriate for their sex.

Gender schema theory

While many scholars agreed with the broad idea that gender acquisition is learned, some were critical of the portrayal of the learner in social learning theory. Sandra Bem (1985), for example, argued that social learning theory suggests that children appear more or less passive in the process of learning when learning about gender roles. For Bem, *this view of a relatively passive child is inconsistent with the common observation that children themselves construct and enforce their own version of societies' gender rules* (p183). Bem proposed **gender schema theory** as an alternative to social learning theory to capture the ways in which learners actively use the information they receive about gender to organise and understand the world around them.

A **schema** can be thought of as a cognitive construct that organises information and knowledge that we glean from our experiences. It guides the processing and organising of new material, influences the retrieval of stored knowledge from memory and provides a basis for us to make interpretations about things in the world (for example, Fisk and Linville, 1980; Martin and Halverson, 1981). In short, it allows us to make sense of the world around us by drawing on information we already know. Bartlett (1932) first developed the concept of schema when trying to explain how people remember and retell the stories that they hear. Bartlett conducted a number of studies on this topic – the most frequently cited one featured the story called 'War of ghosts', which was a Native American folktale. Basically, he asked participants to read and recall stories over different time periods. What he found was that when recalling the original story, people tended to give a less detailed, distorted version. If aspects of the story were not familiar to participants, they would tend to gloss over them or reconstruct them to fit into knowledge/ information that was familiar to them. Bartlett used the idea of schemata to explain why participants produced distorted versions of original stories – familiar prior knowledge was being used to interpret, store and retrieve tales told.

Using the ideas formulated in broad schema theory, Bem (1985) proposed gender schema as the means through which children learn sex-typed or sex-appropriate behaviours. According to Bem, children learn about sex-typing from the culture they are located in, but this learning process is mediated by children's cognitive information-processing systems. The notion of gender schematic processing, that is, processing information that is broadly in accordance with a particular culture's rules for what is gender appropriate, appears to be well supported by studies that have tested this idea. For example, Giles and Heyman (2005) explored the role of gender schemas in children's understanding of aggression. They suggested that gender schemas around the dominant cultural idea that girls do relational aggression (for example, marginalise a person from activities, excluding an individual from a friendship group) and boys do physical aggression (for example, physical fighting or hurting one another) would impact how young children remembered stories about children's aggression. The results supported this idea: young children tended to distort or misremember information that contradicted dominant cultural ideas. For example, instances of girls doing physical aggression might be misremembered as relational aggression.

It is not the case that everyone uses strict gender schematic processing. For Bem, the use of gender schema is not inevitable; it is quite possible for people not to use gender as a central organising principle at all. If gender schematic processing is not used, individuals can develop and express identities and behaviours that are not sex-typed, that reflect aspects of both masculine and feminine characteristics. Bem used the term **androgyny** to refer to those whose characters seem to blend aspects of both masculinity and femininity. We will return to the notion of androgyny later in the chapter (see pages 149–50).

Evaluating mainstream social theories

Social learning theory and gender schema theory both seem to take into account the complex social milieu that intuitively seems to impact and shape our sense of our own gender identity and the identities of others. This, on the face of it, would seem like a welcome alternative to the reductionist biological explanations of gender discussed earlier in the chapter. Both social learning theory and gender schema theory emphasise the social nature of gender acquisition, and in this sense these accounts represent a more socially sensitive explanation of how we become men and women, masculine and feminine. However, Greene (2003) points out that these two theoretical approaches are still guilty of significant oversimplification of the complexity of gender acquisition. They also tend to see gender as something that, once acquired, is relatively fixed and stable – we will behave in a similarly gendered manner in all contexts and places. More specifically, Greene points out that social learning and some cognitive explanations focus very heavily on how we acquire gender-differentiated identities and behaviours in early childhood. While such theories accept that gender-typed behaviours and attitudes are acquired (i.e. are not natural or biologically given), they assume that once you have got them, you have got them for life and you do not lose them. As Greene suggests, these theories are, like many psychological theories, essentialist. The qualities and dispositions related to gender are posited as inherent to the person in the same way as personality traits are thought to be inherent. From this perspective, then, the social theories that we have reviewed so far can be seen as just as guilty of limiting possibilities for change as biological ones.

Task — Think about how you would describe your gender identity to another person. (For example, would you describe yourself as a new man, or a woman with old-fashioned values?) Is your gender identity the same across situations? If it is different, can you explain how?

Now think about how you might have developed a particular gendered identity – is it one that is common among your friends? Is it something you have seen in the media or in films?

> Can social learning theory explain how you developed this identity – in what ways does this theory help to explain your identity? In what ways does it not quite capture your sense of identity development?

Why change? Power, politics and psychology

For many people, gender simply is. People are men or women, masculine or feminine, and in this sense gender is an undisputed, taken-for-granted category. At this point, we would like to say a little more about why it has been important, historically, to challenge dominant notions of gender, and why some kind of change in our taken-for-granted understandings of gender might be considered important.

One of the difficulties with our tendency to categorise people into social groups, and to suggest that social groups are fundamentally different from each other, is that those variations in group characteristics are often valued differently socially. To make this clear, let us take the broad claim that men and women are different because, by and large, women embody feminine characteristics and men embody masculine ones. Characteristics that are typically regarded as 'feminine' – like being caring, emotional, subjective – have often been treated as of less value in Western culture compared to 'masculinised' characteristics such as competitiveness, rationality and 'objectivity'. We can see this very clearly in Weisstein's (1993) analysis of the characterisation of gender in psychological theory. She notes that the catalogue of 'feminine traits' that psychological research has tended to produce, characterises them implicitly or explicitly as:

> inconsistent, emotionally unstable, lacking in a strong conscience or superego, weaker, 'nurturant' rather than productive, 'intuitive' rather than intelligent . . . suited to the home and the family. In short, the list adds up to a typical minority group stereotype of inferiority.

> (Weisstein, 1993, p221)

Since feminine and masculine characteristics are often treated as having a one-to-one mapping with an individual's biological sex, the subordinate positioning of the feminine has been used to ratify unequal treatment of men and women in a variety of contexts. We do not have to look too far back in history to see examples of unequal treatment. For example, women activists successfully campaigned for women to have the same rights as men on a number of issues including property ownership rights, voting rights, the right to work in paid employment and the right to equal pay. Despite the legal right to equal pay, research in the UK, for example, continues to produce evidence of a clear pay gap between men and women (Office of National Statistics, 2010).

It is not just in the wider social world that men and women have been treated unequally. In psychology, unequal treatment can be seen in much classic psychological work, which was not only conducted by men but also on men. Women were not studied in their own right and because of this their experiences were largely ignored – or worse, pathologised – by psychology (you may remember the famous Kohlberg versus Gilligan debate from your studies in developmental psychology, for example). While this situation has improved in recent years, and while there are many female psychologists, and women are indeed studied in their own right, there are nonetheless still signs of a crude reductionism in place in psychological thinking about sex difference. Let us take a look at some recent claims about men and women.

- Men have higher IQs compared to women (Irwing and Lynn, 2005).

- Girls are more manipulative than boys (Björkqvist et al., 1992).

- Women might invite rape (for a review of this research, see Anderson and Doherty, 2008).

These research findings clearly reproduce traditionally stereotypical notions about men and women, and we would argue that the assumptions they make, and the methodology they use, need to be evaluated very carefully. To illustrate this point, let us take a look at a claim made in Chapter 6 that men are more helpful than women.

In gender stereotypical terms, we tend to consider women as more empathic, more in touch with the needs of others, more sensitive than men – and this stereotypical view would predict that women would be the more helpful sex. The idea that men are more helpful than women might seem counterintuitive. However, Eagly and Crowley (1986) argue that in their review of the literature, studies overall seem to suggest that men generally do the helping and women are generally the ones that are helped – in this sense, it is claimed, men are more prosocial than women. However, Eagly and Crowley took a closer look at studies that have made this claim, finding interesting evidence of a gender bias in the way that this research was set up in the first place. In particular, they were interested in the way that 'helping behaviour' itself was defined in social psychological research. Most of this research focuses on helping behaviour in short-term situations that involve helping a stranger – for example, helping a person who has collapsed on a train. Such experiments also tend to define helping as agentic – that is, acts involving active intervention in the situation. These two features of the experimental situation in research on prosocial behaviour position 'helping' in relatively heroic terms. The problem with narrowing down what helping is in this way is that it excludes other forms of providing support such as communal helping, which includes things like caring for relatives' needs, feeding your friend's cats when he or she is away or providing emotional support to those in your social network. For Eagly and Crowley (1986), it is not the case that women are less helpful than men; they are simply more likely to provide communal forms of help, whereas men are more likely to provide agentic forms of help (Eagly, 2009). The point here is that the way in which social psychological research is set up can often reflect the bias of the researcher, and that it is important to consider experimental set-ups and the assumptions that are built into research studies, when evaluating this kind of research.

The studies on helping behaviour served to create the impression that women were less helpful (and therefore less altruistic), but on closer inspection we can see that this is not the case. It seems important, then, to question studies that make claims that one group is better than or lesser than another group.

As soon as you make a group feel superior or inferior to another you run the risk of creating unnecessary divides between people, which can have very real consequences for those involved. For example, the idea generated in the helping studies that women are generally the ones that are helped may serve to create the impression that women are helpless, and that men are heroic. The idea that women are helpless might make them seem weak and dependent on men for help and protection. This might sound quite extreme, but some studies have suggested that women are often represented as 'the weaker sex' in our society, and that this representation can actually function to make women more open to victimisation. Logically, if women are portrayed as easy targets, then it is not surprising that they would be targeted as potential victims (see, for example, Lazard, 2009b). Given this, we would argue that it is always important to question both the foundations and the implications of research that focuses on gender differences. One strand of theorising that has challenged such mainstream findings is **feminist** social psychology, which we will look at next.

Challenging the mainstream: feminist psychology

It is fair to say that feminism is a contentious topic that often comes in for stringent criticism. Negative stereotypes about feminism abound. For example, Valenti (2007) suggests that:

> feminism is seen as super anti – anti men, anti sex, anti sexism, anti everything. And while some of those antis aren't bad things, it's not exactly exciting to get involved in something that's seen as so consistently negative. The good news is feminism isn't all about antis.

(Valenti, 2007, p6)

We would have to agree. Rather than focusing on feminism as anti-man, it is perhaps more helpful to see feminist work as primarily interested in power relationships and about transforming relationships where the power is unequal. There are many different forms of feminism. It is perhaps more accurate to talk of feminisms rather than feminism. We would suggest that what brings feminisms together is a broad political commitment to change unfair and unjust inequalities based on gender (Callaghan and Clark, 2006). In our writing, and for the purposes of this chapter, we focus on an approach to feminist research that is interested in the experiences of men and women, and that explores how gender might act to reinforce the operation of power in complicated ways.

As we saw above, when it comes to power differences between men and women, historically men have often fared better in some contexts than women (for example, they have been automatically entitled to voting rights, property rights, rights to a fair wage). However, contemporary feminism does not suggest that inequalities between men and women exist because men are somehow bad, or have conspired to do women out of their rights to things, or that men have always had it easy. What we would say is that a set of very complex social circumstances come together in certain contexts that work to constrain women's rights and/or choices in relation to men. Further, modern feminism is also often concerned with the way that dominant notions of masculinity constrain and regulate choices for men.

To identify and transform problematic gendered power relationships, feminist work has attempted to highlight how our common-sense or taken-for-granted assumptions about the world help to maintain unequal relationships between men and women. By presenting an alternative way of understanding these relationships, feminist challenges help us to think through how the practices we engage in might create unnecessary gender-based divisions between people as well help us think of ways we could change our practices. This is essentially what feminist challenges to some mainstream psychology have aimed to do. Wilkinson (1997) described five main challenges that feminist psychologists have put to mainstream psychology, which include:

- the poor science argument;

- women's 'internalisation' of oppression;

- celebrating difference;

- displacing difference;

- reconstructing difference.

We will briefly sum up each of these positions as described by Wilkinson in the following sections.

The poor science argument

As its name suggests, this challenge focuses on the idea that it is not the case that psychology has found proper evidence of women's inferiority to men because such studies are methodologically or theoretically flawed (for example, Hyde, 2005, 2007). Put simply, mainstream psychology is not doing 'good' science. We have seen examples of this earlier in social psychological research on gender differences in helping behaviour. As we have mentioned, the reason why studies suggested that men help and women are helpless is because of the way in which early studies defined helping behaviour. That is, they defined it in ways that are compatible with stereotypical male helping styles (Eagly and Crowley, 1986). It is perhaps not that surprising, then, that if you set up a situation that favours men – a situation that defines and focuses on the kinds of help that men are socially encouraged to do and are more practised at – men will more than likely come out of it looking favourable compared to women.

This challenge highlights how our assumptions about gender might impact how we define our subject matter, how we set up our studies and, ultimately, how we interpret our findings. It encourages researchers to think about, and reflect on, what we might end up creating when we design and run experiments. As Wilkinson points out, implied in this approach is the assumption that we can, if we try hard enough, do science better. This, in turn, implies that objective knowledge of gender is possible. As we have seen so far, both the notion of gender as well as the practice of science are grounded in social/cultural assumptions and practices. This raises the question of whether objective knowledge is attainable, and whether we should be looking to alternative methods of enquiry to answer the questions we have. We return to the question in our discussion of methodology in Chapter 9.

Women's internalisation of oppression

The idea of **internalisation of oppression** is grounded in the work of Horner (1972), which basically argued that women may well be inferior in some ways and that they may not do as well, or achieve as much, in comparison to men. The challenge presented by this argument lies in the idea that this inferiority is not an innate or intrinsic 'fault' in women but rather that women are positioned as inferior through gender socialisation processes. The idea starts with the position of the feminine as inferior and much less valued than the masculine, and that this is the outcome of women's historical, social and cultural oppression. In learning to be feminine, women learn and are socially encouraged to be inferior to superior masculine characteristics. Through this process of learning, women internalise the feminine and, concomitantly, notions of their lower status compared to men. This process may result in women fearing or avoiding success (in, for example, scholarly activity, the workplace) because women come to acknowledge that normative rules of behaviour place restrictions on what they should or should not do (Heilman et al., 2004).

While at face value this argument seems to locate the problem, at least in part, in gender socialisation, it still becomes the problem of women – women think they are inferior, women don't try to achieve the same as men because they 'fear success'. With this argument, the danger is that it is the victim who still gets the blame (Wilkinson, 1997).

Celebrating difference

This challenge starts from the position that women are different from men, but it is not the case that what makes women different is grounded in inferiority. Instead, women are seen as contributing something that is just as valid as the contributions of men, but simply different. This challenge is largely associated with the work of Gilligan, who noted in her 1982 book *In a different voice* that the social sciences tend to take the perspective of men as normative. This is not because men are somehow deliberately attempting to sideline women but because research work tends to be male dominated and therefore it is not surprising that research is carried out largely from a male perspective. As Wilkinson (1997) argues, *psychology, with its 'male voice', has described the world from its own male perspective, which it confused with the absolute truth* (p258). What those using this challenge would argue is that we need to listen to women's perspectives and create space for women's voices to be heard so that psychology can say something meaningful about women's lives as well as men's.

The problem with this challenge is that it can imply that women are a **homogeneous group** – that women are similar and that they have a shared perspective. This approach might skim over differences that exist between women. For example, women differ across age, social class, 'race', disability, sexuality as well as other social divisions. These differences between women not only mean that perspectives among them are likely to be quite diverse, but it also points to differences in power between women. Not all women are equal – for example, a teenage working-class mother might have less social power (for example, access to money, resources, support, social recognition and validation) compared to an adult middle-class mother. The point is that some caution needs to be expressed that one voice speaks for all (Wilkinson, 1997; Capdevila et al., 2006).

Wilkinson (1997) also points out that reinforcing the notion of women as different might well create the impression that women, because of their distinctly feminine characteristics (for example, being caring, empathic, focused on developing and maintaining relationships and relational connections), are better suited than men to certain caring roles that have traditionally been seen as women's work, such as childcare. Important to note is that feminists are not saying that women who want and enjoy caring work are somehow 'bad', but what is a problem is arguments that position women as better suited to that line of work. This is because these sorts of arguments can be used to restrict women's choices about what they can or cannot do.

Displacing difference

The focus on gender difference can sometimes distract attention away from the ways people behave that are *not* generally considered typical for their gender. For example, a man may be extremely caring – looking after his elderly relatives or wanting to do the majority of the childcare. Similarly, a woman might be extremely competitive and aggressively ambitious at work. If you think about it, acting in ways that are not gender-typical is more common than is implied in many of the psychological theories we have looked at so far in this chapter.

The idea that it is possible for a person to hold both feminine and masculine traits and characteristics is expressed in the notion of androgyny. Work around androgyny is popularly associated with the work of Bem (1972, 1974), who we discussed earlier when looking at gender schema theory (see page 142). A basic version of Bem's argument goes something like this: everyone holds masculine and feminine traits, and being able to express them is essential for good mental health and well-being. Androgyny was seen as a means to free people from restrictions placed on them by strict gender stereotypes and gender-typing. Androgynous people were represented as able to adapt to the demands of situations that require a more masculine response and those that require a more feminine response.

The concept of androgyny has been heavily criticised in various strands of feminist work. For example, Bem's work implies that gender inequalities could be countered simply by changing how men and women come to understand and engage with the world. This is a problem as the focus is on individual change rather than on wider social change. As we have seen throughout this chapter, there seems to be many practices that maintain gender difference and inequality, so focusing on individual change seems to oversimplify a complex social problem (see, for example, Hollway et al., 1989, for a more detailed critique).

Curiously, Bem's work on androgyny retains and uses the vocabulary of gender difference – that is, traits are referred to as either masculine or feminine rather than using gender-neutral terminology. By retaining the vocabulary of gender difference, this work seems to reinforce the strict gender stereotypes that it seeks to challenge (Wilkinson, 1997).

Reconstructing difference

This challenge emerges from the theoretical traditions of postmodernism and social constructionism (see also Chapter 9). As Wilkinson (1997) notes, it is probably the hardest to understand because ideas and notions emerging from this strand of thought are often counterintuitive.

Feminist work done in this area attempts to challenge essentialist notions of gender, gender identities and gender difference. What this means is that from this perspective, gender is seen as not fixed either by biological forces (for example, it challenges the idea of gendered identities/ differences as innate) or by social ones (for example, mainstream social theories that claim that once social forces have transmitted gendered traits or identities you are stuck with them and have them for life). Unlike mainstream social theories, work that attempts to reconstruct difference sees our social life, practices and relationships as historically and socially located, changeable and in flux. The gender identities that become available to us are likewise seen as fluid, shifting, fragmented and contested. Think about images of gender you see on a day-to-day basis. You will probably notice that there are lots of ways to 'do' femininity and masculinity, and that people may take on certain identities at particular times and/or on particular occasions. So, rather than arising intrinsically from us, gendered identities and gendered difference are produced (and reproduced) and reconstituted in our social practices and relationships, in situated and local contexts.

To say that gender is fluid and shifting does not mean we can change ourselves at will. This idea is explored by Butler in her influential books, *Gender Trouble* (1990) and *Bodies That Matter* (1993). Butler argues that gender is **performative**, that is to say, it is expressed through our actions, our relationships and our social practices. Importantly, though, Butler is not saying that doing gender is simply a case of performing a social role or acting the part. Performativity is much more than that – it is about an act that brings gender, a particular way of doing gender, into being. It is through the repetition of gendered acts, particular gender identities and particular gender differences that they take on the appearance of being 'natural', fixed and simply reflecting the way things are. This has important implications for how we understand sex and gender. At the beginning of this chapter, we said that sex was the term used to refer to biological differences and gender to social understandings of the difference between men and women. We assume that it is these biological differences between men's and women's bodies that give rise to social understandings of gender differences. That is, our social understandings are developed to make sense of these biological bodily differences. What Butler is suggesting is something altogether different. Butler suggests that actually it is the other way around – socially, gender matters. We use it as an organising principle to structure our lives and we divide up tasks and responsibilities according to it. Because we make gender matter, it makes biological sex salient and important. If it wasn't for gender, then sex wouldn't matter at all in the same way that other biological differences between people, such as eye colour or size of feet, are not considered all that important.

The challenge presented by this work is that rather than engaging with strategies that skim over gendered differences (for example, strategies that emphasise sameness, such as androgyny) or those that emphasise our differences and therefore run the risk of reinforcing problematic gendered stereotypes (for example, celebrating differences), we should rethink the notion of gender altogether by revisiting and questioning our assumptions about it. The radical stance taken up here, while being a strength, can also be seen as a weakness. As Wilkinson (1997) points out, this kind of work is often rejected as too radical or unintelligible, which may work to limit the impact or uptake of these ideas in mainstream psychology.

Learning from feminist challenges

As we have emphasised when outlining different kinds of feminist challenges, no one strategy is perfect. That does not mean to say that we should throw the baby out with the bathwater. All the challenges we have outlined here tell us something interesting about assumptions based solely on a person's gender. In doing so, they highlight shortcomings of current approaches used to study gender in social psychology. They raise questions such as: Why should the focus be on gender differences? Why not focus on similarities? Why are men and women treated as if they were homogeneous groups when common sense tells us that not all women are the same and not all men are the same? How can we transform problematic power relationships that are based around gender? It is questions such as these that help us reflect on our own assumptions about gender and, in doing so, help us think through the limits of current understandings of gender in mainstream psychology.

Critical thinking activity

Attitudes in context

Critical thinking focus: reflection

Key question: *How might different theories explain transgendered identities?*

Transgendered identity broadly refers to identities that are said not to match a person's biological 'sex'. Find a personal account of being transgendered (a magazine article, piece of fiction or online blog). Attempt to apply the theories and ideas from this chapter to this real-world example. Do the theories/ideas about gender we have looked at help to explain features of the text you have chosen?

Use the following prompts to help you identify links between theoretical ideas and the piece of text you have chosen.

- Summarise the key points of the account you have chosen.

- How is transgendered identity described? For example, does the person use a biological explanation to account for their experience?

- How might a social learning perspective, or a gender schema theoretical approach, make sense of this person's experience?

- What are the limitations of applying mainstream theories covered in this chapter to a case that does not easily fit into our common-sense understandings of gender difference?

Critical thinking review

This activity helps develop your skills of reflection, and application of theory, in relation to a range of theories covered in this chapter. To do this, you were encouraged to apply these theoretical ideas to a piece of text that described a person's experience of having a transgendered identity. This enabled you to think about the usefulness of these concepts in practice, and also to think critically about alternative understandings for common-sense ideas.

Applying theoretical knowledge in this way, and thinking critically about these knowledges, are important skills that will enable you to evaluate and make critical judgements about psychology research and its application to the real world. Other skills you may have used in this activity: evaluation, recall of key principles and ideas, independent learning.

Skill builder activity

Communicating your ideas to an audience

Transferable skill focus: understanding and analysing data

Key question: How are baby beauty queens represented in the media?

In groups, locate three different articles or sources that talk about baby beauty queens. We have chosen this topic for you to focus on because discussions around baby beauty queens raise interesting questions around gender in general, and femininity in particular. We would like you to think about how femininity is represented in each of these articles and prepare a short presentation for your class.

Use the following prompts to help you analyse your articles or sources.

- Think about how femininity for young girls is described in the article. Does the article draw differences between adult and child femininities? What does it imply is acceptable for young girls?

- Are beauty competitions seen as a good or bad thing for girls to participate in? According to your article, why is this?

- What similarities and differences are there across your articles? Is femininity represented similarly or differently? It might be helpful to draw up a list of key similarities and differences.

Use the following prompts to help you prepare your presentation.

- It might help to summarise key points of each article.

- Describe key femininities described in each article. What does this tell you about similarities and differences between adult and child gendered identities?

- Is your analysis of the articles grounded in the data? Return to the original article and use quotes to back up your points.

Skill builder review

This activity helps develop your ability to understand and analyse material and data. It has also helped your communication skills, focusing particularly on oral communication. These are important academic and life skills.

Other skills you may have used in this activity: critical thinking, comparison, independent learning, reflection, recall of key principles and ideas, information technology (if you chose to use computer-based presentation methods).

Assignments

1. 'Androgyny is the best of both worlds.' Discuss this statement in relation to psychological work on gender and gender difference.

2. Describe and critically discuss the contributions feminism has made on the topic of gender in psychology.

Summary: what you have learned

In this chapter, we have outlined mainstream social psychological theories of gender. We have explored mainstream efforts to theorise gender, which have included both 'nature- and nurture-based explanations. We have explored the limitations of such mainstream theories using the notion of essentialism and by highlighting the importance of changing gender inequalities. To explore the idea that change is needed, we discussed feminist challenges to mainstream ideas about gender, which draw attention to some of the problems with seeing men and women just in terms of difference.

To complete your critical thinking and skill builder activities, you have developed and used your skills in analysing data, communication of ideas, comparison, independent learning, reflection, recall of key principles and ideas, and information technology.

Further reading

McRobbie, A (2008) *The Aftermath of Feminism*. London: Sage.

Walter, N (2010) *Living Dolls*. London: Virago.

These two books offer an engaging and interesting exploration of the state of contemporary gender relations in the West, offering compelling arguments for the importance of a feminist analysis.

Chapter 8

Close relationships

Learning outcomes

By the end of this chapter you should:

- *have an overview of key research in the area of love and relationships, including concepts such as social exchange, prototypes of love, love styles and love stories;*

- *demonstrate a critical understanding of the reproductive and heteronormative assumptions of romance implicit in these models;*

- *demonstrate an understanding of the way that these models tend to focus on early adult and Western experiences of love and romance, and think critically about the implications of this;*

- *understand the core limitations of mainstream research on love and relationships;*

- *be aware of alternative trends in studies on this topic which focus on previously under-researched key issues, including love in adult life;*

- *have developed your oral communication skills and IT skills by preparing and delivering a presentation about theories of love and romance, and your critical and creative thinking skills by applying theoretical perspectives on love to a relevant film.*

Intimate relationships

Liking and loving is one of the most talked about topics in everyday life. Romantic relationships have been the subject matter of many 'pop psychology' books (such as *He's Just Not that Into You* and *Men are from Mars, Women are from Venus*) as well as films, daytime talk shows and many other forms of popular entertainment. Our conversations often revolve around making, keeping and breaking relationships as well as the trials and tribulations of being 'single'. In common-sense terms we recognise that the business of relationships is messy and complicated. Given this, one of the strangest things social psychology has attempted to do is to study in a scientific manner the nature of love and romance. The scientific method of investigating love, liking and intimate relationships involves trying to be rational and measure objectively those very things that are difficult to articulate and that are hard to pin down in an enduring and fixed sense. In this chapter, we trace a path through psychological understandings of intimate relationships, asking questions like: Why do we love each other? What is intimacy like? What counts as love, and how do we understand the differences between liking, loving and lusting?

Falling in love: young adult relationships

Most mainstream social psychological literature on relationships has started (and often ended!) with a focus on young adult relationships. A very large proportion of this research is conducted with American or other Western university students, and understanding youngsters in love has been a stalwart of personal relationship research. In this section we explore these mainstream ideas about liking and loving in these relationships.

Romance as social exchange

An influential theory in both academic and pop psychological representations of love and loving is **social exchange theory**. This approach to relationships uses an economic model to understand social interactions, understanding personal and intimate relationships in a kind of cost versus benefit model. Essentially, this reading of romance understands relationships as answering the question: What is in it for me?

Basically, a social exchange model suggests that people make decisions about their relationships based on their perception of the balance between the rewards or benefits of that relationship versus its costs. So Bertha is in a relationship with Johnny. Johnny is a tricky character, very bright, able and interesting, but at the same time, has a tendency to fly off the handle, and gets very clingy and needy when under stress. A social exchange model will predict that Bertha will consider the rewarding aspects of the relationship – that Johnny is a stimulating and interesting partner – against its costs to her – that his clinginess places her under considerable strain.

Thibaut and Kelley (1959) suggest that rewards are best understood as things that give pleasure and satisfaction to the people in the relationship (for example, feeling loved, physical affection, companionability etc.). Costs are the potential drains on our personal resources that emerge in relationships – the level of energy put into the relationship (the sense of giving to the relationship), punishments (passive aggressive behaviour, unpleasant remarks, physical or emotional aggression), and other kinds of negative interactions. This model uses a simple cost-accounting equation:

relationship satisfaction = rewards – costs

This way of thinking about relationships frames them as fundamentally selfish. Our understanding of the value of our personal exchanges is rooted in what is left in our metaphoric bank balance at the end of each week. But can relationships really be reduced to such simple equations of cost and benefit? For example, in the example of Johnny and Bertha above, Bertha's evaluation of the relationship may also depend on complex contextual factors. She might be having a particularly taxing time at work, or childcare responsibilities may be a particular strain. In this context, the demands of her relationship with Johnny may become overwhelming. Alternatively, she may be surrounded by supporting and loving friends, who are able to function as a buffer when things in the relationship with Johnny get hard. As you can see, when you put things in context, the reductionist approach, which distils human relationships to such simple, selfish and overly rational processes, falls apart somewhat. Life is more complex than the relational bottom line. Also notably absent in this theory is the experience of love and liking itself. Can we really see emotionality in such dry and dispassionate terms?

Task — Do you think that we can really understand close personal relationships using the economic metaphor of costs and benefits? Try applying this to your everyday experiences, thinking through some limitations of this model.

Liking and loving

So how does social psychology makes sense of the experience of liking and loving, and at what point does friendship become something more? An early social psychological attempt to theorise the nature of love was developed by Berscheid and Walster (1969; 1978). Their account focuses on a distinction between passion and companionability. Theirs is essentially a developmental model of loving relationships that suggests that the early experience of passion gradually gives way with time to a more enduring companionate love. **Passionate love** is seen as a kind of whirlwind of excitement, sexiness and sometimes pain. It is the agony and the ecstasy of early relationships. **Companionate love** is assumed to develop from this early passion, and is defined as a close relationship between two people whose lives are closely intertwined. It is characterised by close and steady affection and intimacy. This model suggests we settle into domestic happiness, reflecting common-sense assumptions that real love takes time to build, and that it is not the frivolous stuff of teen passions, puppy love or early dating. It is built on a foundation of friendship and is consequently assumed to be lasting, not ephemeral. Relationship satisfaction is more strongly linked to companionate love than passionate love (Sprecher and Regan, 1998).

Hendrick and Hendrick (2000) describe this model as the either/or theory of love – that you can either be passionate or be committed. They suggest that this is a rather narrow view of the nature of committed love, which can be both passionate and committed. Hatfield (1988) suggests that mature love is not exclusively about commitment and companionability, but rather that there is a difference in emphasis. Friendship is seen as a necessary condition for a stable relationship, but passion can be there, too. In their both/and take on companionate and passionate love, Hendrick and Hendrick (1993) suggest that both kinds of love can be present as important components of the same relationship, while Noller (1996) suggests that the combination of the two forms the basis for long-term relationships, commitment and marriage.

In young adults' accounts of romantic relationships, Hendrick and Hendrick (1993) found that friendship love emerged as a frequent theme in their understanding of love and romance. This suggests that the idea of companionate love is a powerful discourse in our understandings of romantic relationships: when we try to make sense of our own experiences of romantic love, the notion of companionability is a key element in our social understandings of this phenomenon.

There is an intuitive sense to the companionate/passionate love model – it fits with our Western folk wisdom about love and marriage. People settle together into a companionate relationship that is more real and substantial than the fleeting fire of early passion and lust. Romance in Western stories is supposed to end with happy ever after – with marriage and commitment. Built into the assumptions of this model is a clear, common-sense construction that suggests that real love is lasting and permanent, sensible, measured and committed. Real love forms the basis for long-term relationships. While this is not directly articulated, it is not difficult to see the **heteronormative** and reproductive assumptions that underpin this model. One form of love is privileged over all others in this model: essentially, Walster and Berscheid are suggesting that true love is that which forms a foundation for family life.

Prototypes

It might be argued that the simplified view of liking and loving represented in the passionate and companionate love model is, in fact, a reproduction of a social psychological **prototype**. As you have learned elsewhere in this book, prototypes are an important social psychological construct. In research on personal relationships, the prototype approach attempts to understand concepts such as love and romance in terms of some idealised notion of these phenomena. This work attempts to answer the questions: What is love like? and What is the most typical or ideal understanding of love? The assumption of this research is that if we have an ideal view of what romantic relations should be like, this will shape and influence our attitudes to our relationships, the kinds of relationships we seek out, and the way we evaluate the relationships we have. Gibbons and Gerrard (1997) suggest that we engage in social comparisons – comparing our actual romantic relationships with the idealised prototype – and that this influences and shapes our behaviour.

What does the Western prototype of love look like?

Early research in this area identified a number of features to the prototype of love (Fehr, 1988). Companionate love appears in these accounts as the most prominent aspect in the Western prototype of love. Following up this research, Fehr and Russell (1991) also found that student participants rated maternal love, parental love and friendship as the most prototypical. Interesting in the images this builds up of 'love' and 'intimacy' is the glaring absence of sex and passion. Is this in keeping with your understanding of what love is?

The Fehr and Russell study suggests that trust, care, honesty, friendship and respect are all prototypical features of love. When Regan et al. (1998) changed the research questions slightly to focus on romantic love (rather than just the prototype of love), they found that the ranking of passion increased slightly, but was still not ranked more highly than companionate love. In exploring the idea of whether companionate and passionate features of love figured highly in the prototype of love that was held by research participants, Aron and Westbay (1996) found that, in fact, the notion of **intimacy** was more central to the meaning of love than passion and acts of commitment.

This led Sternberg (1986) to develop his **triangular theory of love**, proposing that love had three components – intimacy, passion and commitment. These were mixed from eight types of love:

- non-love;
- liking (intimacy only);
- infatuated love (passion only);
- empty love (commitment only);
- romantic love (intimacy and passion);
- companionate love (intimacy and commitment);
- fatuous love (passion and commitment);
- consummate love (all three).

Hendrick and Hendrick (2004) suggest that this kind of social psychological knowledge can be usefully applied in couples therapy. They argue that these simple formulations are easy for individuals to recognise in themselves and can give couples a focus for working on their relationship. For example, if one partner in a relationship has high levels of passion and commitment, the other high levels of commitment and intimacy, it is easy to see where the commonalities lie, and also what areas are easily accessible for work and development.

However, it is also easy to identify the bias in Sternberg's theory towards a particular form of loving. Just looking at the language used to describe the different categories of love, it is easy to see that some forms are seen as correct ways of loving while others are viewed as much more problematic. The term 'infatuated love' almost dismisses as insignificant the kind of powerful passionate romantic connection that many people find quite exciting and fiery. In contrast, consummate love and companionate love are clearly positioned as right ways to love – the assumption that these are better that the other terms is written into the judgemental use of the language.

Task — Does our lived experience of love and romance really break down into simple components like 'loving' versus 'liking'?

Intimacy as interpersonal process

One of the absences in the prototype model of love is the idea of relationships as interaction. In contrast, Reis and Shaver (1988) suggested that intimacy functions as an **interpersonal process**, not merely as a component of a love prototype. Quality of relationship is understood to be dependent on our experience of intimacy. Laurenceau et al. (1998) used student participants to explore the interpersonal process model. They asked 89 students (51 women, 38 men) to complete a fixed format interaction record after every interaction they had with their partner that lasted more than ten minutes, collecting data on 3,955 **dyadic interactions**. They found that self-disclosure and partner self-disclosure were associated with reported experiences of intimacy. However, these behaviours alone were not enough to predict intimacy. Rather, *intimate interactions are those that are self-revealing and impart the feeling that one is known and validated and valued by one's partner* (Laurenceau et al., 1998, p208).

This analysis does focus on relationships as communicative and interpersonal. However, we need to look carefully at the over-simplification of complex dynamics in this model. It took these researchers 3,955 dyadic interactions, and a whole lot of statistical analysis, to work out that if partners talk to each other about intimate things and if they feel heard when they talk to each other, then they will feel close. Apart from the relative obviousness of this kind of conclusion, we have to question the formulaic nature of this kind of relationship research. Is it really possible to reduce the complexity of love and intimacy to an equation as simple as $(a + b) \times c = $ intimacy? Moreover, does this kind of formula really provide insight into the idea of intimacy as an interpersonal process?

Love ways

Extending the idea of relationship as an interpersonal process, Marston et al. (1987) suggest that love takes place in communication – that the way that we communicate love is key to understanding what love is like. They suggest that: *Communication is the fundamental action which both expresses and determines the subjective experience of romantic love* (p392). From a series of qualitative interviews, Marston et al. identified five themes around communicating love to a partner. These involve:

- saying 'I love you';

- doing things for your partner;

- being understanding and supportive;

- physical touch;

- being together.

From these themes, the authors developed categories of love ways – for example, active love, secure love, intuitive love. To understand personal relationships, it is argued that we need to understand love as a process, to understand how we love, and how that love is expressed as an interpersonal and communicative phenomenon.

Similarly, Marston et al. (1998) explored the experience of intimacy, passion and commitment, using qualitative, open-ended questions, which were then coded and factor analysed. From this analysis, the authors identified six different experiences of intimacy (openness, affection, sex, support, togetherness and quiet company); two experiences of passion (sexual intimacy and romance); and five experiences of commitment (supportiveness, expressions of love, fidelity, expressions of commitment, and consideration and devotion). Rather than a simple typology of passion versus companionship, their research suggests that our experiences are more nuanced and subtle, and far more subjective than these categorical notions of love allow. Marston et al. argue that to understand romantic relationships, we need to understand subjective experiences of love and romance.

Love styles

This focus on subjective experience is developed in Lee's (1976, 1988) notion of **love styles**. Lee suggested that love cannot be understood as a simple set of categories like passionate versus companionate. Rather our ways of loving are **heterogeneous** ways of being and feeling that he called love styles. He proposed a set of primary love styles that included Eros (passionate, intense, erotic love), Ludus (game-playing love, full of deception and ultimately quite shallow) and Storge (a blend of friendship and love, the kind of love that endures). Lee's secondary love styles included Mania (possessive and dependent; obsessive), Pragma (pragmatic, logical, committed, but lacking in excitement), and Agape (selfless love).

Lee had originally intended that these love styles be seen as a style of relating – something people could draw on differently in different relationships at different times. So, for example, in a more casual relationship, one might relate from the position of Eros love or Ludus, but in more committed relationships Storge or Agape might be more common. However, subsequent researchers have tended to treat these love styles as more enduring and linked to particular personality styles. So Hendrick and Hendrick (1986) developed standardised measures to enable a research exploration of these six love styles. For example, using the Eysenck Personality Questionnaire, Davies (1996) found a significant correlation between particular personality types and love styles. Extroversion (E) was associated with Eros and Ludus, neuroticism (N) was related to Pragma and Mania, and Psychoticism (P) was correlated positively with Ludus and negatively with Agape and Storge. This kind of research therefore suggests that there are links between personality type and love style.

In more recent research, Heaven et al. (2004) explored whether particular personality types and attachment patterns predicted the love styles of individuals' relationships. They found, for example, that neuroticism was associated with Mania, Ludus and Eros love styles, while extroversion predicted Eros. They also found correlations between Mania and Ludus love styles and anxious attachment patterns. They suggest that:

> emotionally unstable people tend to engage in possessive love and in game-playing and deception, but this link is mediated through an anxious attachment style (p111).

However, Watts and Stenner (2005) suggest that this kind of research takes something of a wrong turn. They argue that in looking at personality type and love style, there is an attempt to oversimplify love, seeing it as a property of individuals. The approach taken by authors like Hendrick and Hendrick and Davies suggests that as individuals, we have a particular love style that is a stable, inner aspect of our character. In contrast, Watts and Stenner suggest:

> We have failed to grasp love in the singular simply because love is not like that. It needs instead to be approached as a problem of competing ideologies each offering an alternative view of intimate adult partnering.

(Watts and Stenner, 2005, p86)

Our love style will shift over time, even within the same relationship. Rather than being a stable personality trait, we position ourselves relationally and contextually, in relation to the discourses of love that circulate in our particular culture. Watts and Stenner suggest that each love style, each discursive position on love:

> is a collection of beliefs, assumptions and expectations that are shared by a group and which work together to justify specific social arrangements and institutions. An individual person will simply buy into one (or more) of these ideologies in particular contexts and for certain periods of time.

(Watts and Stenner, 2005, p86)

Love is not an inner state, but a social psychological phenomenon.

This position is similar to Sternberg's (1995, 1996, 1998) suggestion that our experience of love is constituted in **love stories** – narratives that function as guiding metaphors in our understanding of love relationships. Sternberg had participants rate 100 narratives about love, and from these ratings, he distilled 25 key Western love stories, such as the horror story, the garden story, love as science, love as art, etc. These metaphoric stories of love help us to anticipate the plot in our own relationships and, if understood, might help us avoid painful repetitions of destructive patterns of relating.

Critical thinking activity

Love in context

Critical thinking focus: creative and critical thinking

Key question: How are love styles and love stories represented in popular media?

Reread the section above on love styles and love stories. Watch a film that might be regarded as a classic love story. (Examples you might want to consider are: *Gone with the Wind*; *Romeo and Juliet*; *When Harry Met Sally*; *Twilight*). As you watch the film, think about the kinds of 'love styles' and 'love stories' present in the plot.

Use the following prompts to guide your watching of the film and to form links between the theoretical material reviewed and the film you have chosen.

- Summarise the key plot points that are specifically to do with love, romance and intimate relationships.

- Do these reflect some of the love styles and love stories described by Lee and Sternberg?

- Find evidence of the following love styles in the movie plot: Eros, Ludus, Storge, Pragma, Mania and Agape.

- Can you find instances of specific 'love stories' in the film? For example, is it a fairy tale (the prince saved the princess, and they all lived happily ever after)? A horror story (Does she boil his bunny)? A garden story (love is nurtured over time and grows)? Love as science (having the right chemistry; thinking through the details)?

- Can you think of any other typical 'love stories' (dominant scripts about loving relationships)?

Now, try to think critically about the role of gender in our understanding of love and romance, and how this might be incorporated into Lee's and Sternberg's ideas.

– How are male and female characters depicted in the film?

– What kind of love styles do you see operating for female characters?

– What kinds of love styles are more typical for male characters?

– What does this tell us about the **gendered** nature of our social understandings of love stories and love styles?

Critical thinking review

This activity helps develop your skills of creative and critical thinking, and application of theory, in relation to Lee's love styles and Sternberg's love stories. To do this, you were encouraged to apply these theoretical models to a film. This enabled you to think about the usefulness of these concepts in practice, and also to think critically about our everyday understandings of the world, and our cultural scripts about love and romance. You were also encouraged to think critically about the role of gender in love and romance.

Applying theoretical knowledge in this way and thinking critically about these knowledges are important skills that will enable you to evaluate and make critical judgements about psychology research and its application to the real world.

Other skills you may have used in this activity: reflection, recall of key principles and ideas, communication (literacy) skills if you write up the activity, independent learning.

Understanding young lovers? Problems with relationship research

As we have seen so far, social psychological research on romance, and particularly on young adult romance, has its limitations. In attempting to develop parsimonious models of the complex social phenomenon of love and romance, much of this research is guilty of oversimplifying the lived experience of loving, using formulaic equations that reduce intimate relations to the interaction of simple factors (like the cost-benefit model). There is also a host of other criticisms that could be levelled at this work. Let us take a look at some of these problems.

It must be noted that this theoretical and research tradition is heavily rooted in middle-class American life. Can it be straightforwardly applied to other cultural contexts? Perhaps most concerning in most of this work, though, is its lack of a sustained gender analysis, and its heteronormative bias. Gender and sexuality are not really engaged with in this body of research, but surely intimate relationships are the one place where gender and sexuality are perhaps at their most significant?

To understand love and personal relationships, surely it is necessary to locate them in their social, cultural and historical context? Much of the research reviewed here purports to develop universal accounts of love and romance. But is it really possible to develop a universal story of such very personal and social phenomena? Our ideas about love have changed considerably, historically. For example, Simpson et al. (1986) point out that romantic love has only recently started to be valued as the main basis for marriage and marital choice in the West.

If the nature of romance in the West has changed this dramatically in the last century or so, then what does this tell us about how culturally and socially determined our experience of romance is? Research into personal relationships has tended to view Western versions of love as the norm, with other forms of love being seen as a variation on a theme. In common with other areas of psychological theorising, this kind of research tends to take an 'add culture and stir' reading of social experience. It is assumed that love is universal and that Western understandings of love embody that universality.

This point is well illustrated by Hendrick and Hendrick's (1990) study of Taiwanese love relationships. Their work starts with the presumption that Lee's original love styles have some universal applicability. They then add to this original model two further styles, which they feel adapts the model for use in a Taiwanese context. So, by blending Eros and Agape, they suggest there is a form of love that is both romantic and considerate, that captures a particularly Taiwanese form of loving. Similarly, a blend of Agape and Pragma produces the notion of 'obligatory love', which Hendrick and Hendrick see as being very typical of Taiwanese personal relationships.

Moving away from the issue of transcultural research and its problems, we need also to consider how age, gender and sexual orientation shape and frame our interpersonal relationships. The social psychological research reviewed above focuses very extensively on the experience of university students, and to a lesser extent on relatively new couples. We will return briefly to the issue of sexual orientation and sexualities in Chapter 10, but for now, we need to consider whether theory built on such experiences can be meaningfully applied to understanding long-term relationships, the experiences of middle-aged couples or older people re-entering the dating scene after a break-up. We will begin this exploration by considering adult romantic relationships.

Adult romance?

Like many young adults, social psychology seems to be rather uncomfortable with the notion that people 'of a certain age' still fall in love, have sex and enjoy romance. Romantic relationships in adult life, middle age and later life are substantially under-researched in personal relationships work. In this sense, research on intimate relationships tends to reproduce a dominant social construction about relationships – that the interesting part of the story ends when the happy couple ride off into the sunset. However, the story of relationships in middle age is a rather more complex one. While some couples do meet young and stay married till death do them part, divorce, remarriage, other new relationships and being single are all far more common now, in the West, than they were 60 years ago. To a large degree this sociological change is not reflected in our psychological thinking.

Gender plays an important role in mediating personal relationships in adulthood. For example, while Grote and Frieze (1994) found that marital satisfaction in middle-aged couples was predicted by passionate and companionate love (i.e. it fitted with the mainstream social psychological models of love and marriage), Grote et al. (1996) found that this experience of marital satisfaction was rather more mediated by gendered experiences. Family size, length of marriage and love styles were an important feature, but for men the presence of a traditional division of labour was more likely to make them happy in middle age. Perhaps unsurprisingly, for women, the opposite was true. In families where traditional gendered division of labour was in place – where women did all or most of the domestic work, had main responsibility for childcare etc. while men were the primary breadwinners – marital satisfaction tended to be lower for women.

Becoming a parent: intimate relationships and negotiating new identities as mother and father

The shift from being a child-free couple to becoming a 'family' is a substantial one. Becoming a mother or a father has implications not just for the relationship between mother and child or father and child, but also for the relationship between the couple who have the baby. Transition to parenthood is a vulnerable time for couple relationships, with high rates of divorce in the first five years post first birth. Cowan and Cowan (2000) suggest that this is because for the couple, old lifestyles and relationship arrangements no longer work once a baby is introduced into the mix, but that new ones take time to develop. Relationship satisfaction reduces after the birth of the first child (Belsky and Pensky, 1988; Twenge et al., 2003). This is perhaps because of reduced time for the primary relationship.

Using the concept of a relationship pie, Cowan et al. (1985) suggested that the parenting slice increases substantially for both parents from pregnancy through to two years post birth. However, they noted that this is significantly more the case for women than for men – that becoming a mother takes more physical and emotional energy for women than for men becoming a father. The shift from a two-person family to a three-person family shifts the 'exchange' balance in the relationship (Veroff et al., 2000). Becoming a parent results in less time for intimacy (Cowan and Cowan, 2003) and more 'juggling', tiredness and stress.

To try to understand how couples manage the time constraints in their lives when they become parents, and the competing demands of work, home and fun, Claxton and Perry-Jenkins (2008) looked at leisure in the transition to parenting for 147 heterosexual, working-class parents from two-income households. They found that when children are born there was a decline in leisure for both parents during the initial transition. This increases when women return to work, an experience that is reported as being associated with reports of more conflict and less love. What is clear from this kind of relationship research is that it is impossible to understand relationships in isolation from the context in which they take place. Work demands, varying ideas about gender, parenting etc. all shape the quality of intimate couple relationships.

Work, life and love

A key aspect of many relationships in adult life is the balance that couples need to strike between home and work, and between the demands of couple life and parenting life. This is often portrayed in terms of the idea of work–life balance. The problem of work–life balance is often portrayed as an issue for those in the higher socio-economic classes. The image of the power-suited mother juggling babies, nappies and legal briefs is the popular representation of working motherhood. In couples research, it is clear that there is greater marital dissatisfaction in higher socio-economic classes (Twenge et al., 2003), and that women in this class report high levels of role strain.

However, men and women of all classes report decreased marital satisfaction when working long hours and contributing to childcare. Perry-Jenkins et al. (2007) suggest that working-class parents are susceptible to role strain, too, and that this experience is worst for parents working shifts. The night shift, in particular, is associated with depressive symptoms, and women who work in shift patterns are more likely to experience relationship conflict. Role strain is not the preserve of the middle classes.

Hochschild (1997) suggests that modern work patterns produce increasing pressure on home life. Think about the metaphors that we use to describe our daily lives – as individuals we are expected to 'squeeze' things into our busy schedules, and 'juggle' with the competing demands of work, home and family.

Febbraro (2003) suggests that we can understand work–life balance in one of two ways: using either a scarcity hypothesis (our limited resources are overstretched across too many competing arenas) or an enhancement hypothesis (our multiple roles are complementary and our lives are enhanced by being able to function in both the domestic and work sphere). The scarcity hypothesis positions women as exhausted from juggling multiple roles. This is perhaps because women so frequently take primary responsibility for domestic and childcare arrangements. Baxter et al. (2008) point out that while men's contribution to housework remains stable across life changes, women's contribution increases dramatically with parenthood. Women are often positioned as responsible for the emotional well-being of their families, and this view of women as emotional labourers and as 'natural carers' has not been eroded by the increasing entry of women into the workplace (Arendell, 1999). Many women find they need to add the identity of competent and capable worker to their existing socially designated role as domestic goddess. This produces the ideology of the superwoman – the employed mother who does it all, *with aplomb, grace, and effectiveness* (Arendell, 1999, p1196) and is 'enhanced' by it. This construction of working as overburdening women, adding one more layer of strain to the domestic arena, is often presented as evidence that women 'cannot have it all'. For women, balancing high levels of domestic work, their location as emotional nurturers responsible for the psychological well-being of their families and the demands of work overstretches their resources (Daly, 1996; Hochschild, 1997). In contrast, the enhancement hypothesis suggests that multiple roles bring women considerable pleasure and enhance their lives.

What this representation of scarcity versus enhancement fails to take into account is the reality that women are drawing their lives and relationships against a complex social, political and economic backdrop. Duxbury and Higgins (1991) suggest that the ability to achieve work–life balance and avoid stress is a function of a combination of levels of work and family commitment and involvement, and expectations of work and family. Working mothers are thus firmly located as responsible for maintaining family life, maintaining the 'balance', with the result that institutions like 'the workplace' and 'the state' are relieved of responsibility for shifting to better accommodate families. Important for our argument in this chapter is the question of how we reconcile this complex social and political picture with our experiences of very intimate personal relationships.

In the socio-cognitive research on personal relationships reviewed in the first half of this chapter, the young romantic couple is rarely troubled by questions of who does the dishes or takes out the rubbish. However, for more mature couples, managing the complexity of work, parenting and romance, these are the central questions of everyday life, and their relationships are constituted within these contextual demands. Research needs to take seriously the question of what happens to 'love' once the credits have rolled, and our happily-ever-after couple has to deal with the mundane business of everyday living.

Understanding marriage as an institution

It is important to remember that personal relationships do not simply take place between two people – they are not merely interpersonal interactions. The happily-ever-after story of passionate and companionate love we considered at the beginning of the chapter is presumed to lead to a blissful wedded state. Heterosexual marriage is positioned as the natural and inevitable outcome of love. Is this always the case?

We would argue that gender plays an important role in mediating our desires for long-term relationships and marriage. In Blakemore et al.'s (2005) study of gender differences in the desire for marriage, the authors suggest that women's 'drive to marry' is stronger than men's. They suggest that this gender difference is stronger in women who have more traditional ideas about gender roles, who wanted to use the title 'Mrs', and who saw their destinies as linked to family life and their value in the domestic sphere. Women who were more career-oriented were less strongly motivated to find a long-term marriage partner. It is often women who choose to engage with the world of work rather than 'settling down' to become 'good wives and mothers' who need to negotiate one of our more stringent social norms: the idea that women want nothing so much as a good husband. To be happily married is still seen as the ultimate goal of womanhood.

Reynolds and Wetherell (2003) point out that these ideas about the 'compulsory' nature of marriage work as a **normative** process. By this, they mean that when we have social 'stories' about love and relationships that assume that one form of relationship is good and normal; this inevitably renders other ways of loving as deviant or problematic. In a qualitative study, in which they interviewed 30 middle-aged single women, Reynolds and Wetherell suggest that:

> Women in long-term relationships do not tend to be asked (in a concerned tone of voice), for example, 'how did you end up married?' . . . The single woman, in contrast, is expected to have an explanation for her 'condition', preferably a story of 'circumstances' and 'missed opportunities' or one that blames herself for being 'unable to hold on to her man'.
>
> (Reynolds and Wetherell, 2003, p490)

Is it the case that marriage is still seen as the 'right choice' for women in our society? Do terms such as 'spinster' still apply, and do they still have the same bite that they once did? It is suggested that this positioning of marriage as 'normal' for women marginalises single women. Given that marriage remains a heterosexual institution within our society, what does this mean for lesbian women? Essentially, this construction of marriage as the norm for women positions women who either choose to be single, or who are lesbian, as necessarily 'wrong', as not quite feminine, not 'proper women'.

Reynolds and Wetherell are arguing that neither 'single' nor 'married' are natural or taken-for-granted categories. Rather these constructs are best understood as regulative social practices within which women need to negotiate their identities as either married or single women. From their interviews, the researchers identified four discursive repertoires (or ways of making sense of the social world) that women deployed to express and make sense of their experiences of being single women.

1. Singleness as personal deficit: this is the familiar construct of the spinster on the shelf. This familiar story assumes that women who are single are in that 'condition' because they can't 'get a man'.

2. Singleness as social exclusion: this discourse represents single women as marginalised from the social world of couples, because they are viewed as a threat to marital harmony.

3. Singleness as independence and choice: this representation of singleness presents it as a privileged space – an opportunity to be yourself, and not have to answer to anyone else (inverting the power relation in the first two repertoires).

4. Singleness as self-development and achievement: this discourse links to the third, suggesting that singleness enables women to develop and grow as people, to focus on themselves and their careers. It is seen as an achievement in its own right.

These repertoires offer a range of social resources within which women are able to negotiate their identity as single. However, as Reynolds and Wetherell point out:

> What seems difficult to hold together in the current discursive climate is a positive construction of the category 'single' with the desire for relationship. One seems to obviate the other. The positive constructions of the idealized repertoires seem to render the desire for relationship difficult to admit.
>
> (Reynolds and Wetherell, 2003, p506)

In other words, within contemporary constructions of heterosexual relatedness, the degree to which we can be happily single is constrained.

Masculinity and intimacy

It is important to remember that women are not 'victims' of social practices like marriage. Femininity certainly functions to constrain women's choices, but masculinity as a construct is also limiting and constraining for men. Hollway (1998) theorised relationships between men and women as being about negotiating dominant notions of **masculinity** and of **femininity**. In a series of interviews about love, marriage and sex with British female and male partners in heterosexual couples, she suggests that three dominant ideas about sex and sexuality influence our understandings of relationships. Relevant here is the first discourse: the familiar male sex drive discourse positions men in terms of wild oats and testosterone. What she meant by this was that men are seen socially as driven by a desire for sex, almost as victims of their own hormones and biology. This discourse positions men as 'always up for it', permanently priapic and ready for anything with pretty much anybody. The phrase 'they'll chase anything in a skirt' typifies this discourse. It is easy to see how this both functions to enable men to 'get away with' sexual acting out, but also makes it very difficult for men to 'say no'. In other words, for example, men who are raped are often pathologised for that unwanted sexual encounter. The dominant discourse of male sexuality suggests that they should have wanted the sexual experience, and that 'normal' men would take advantage of the sex on offer rather than feeling victimised by it (Lazard, 2009a).

So what do we mean by masculinity? Connell (1987, 1995) and Carrigan et al. (1985) suggest that the cultural construct of masculinity in the West prescribes a set of characteristics, behaviours and social practices that men must negotiate in order to identify as men. Connell (1995) suggests that **hegemonic masculinity** refers to an idealised image of what it means to be a man in relation to representations of femininity, and also in relation to more marginalised masculine identities (for example, the 'geek' or the 'sissy boy'). Dominant characteristics of manliness involve being heterosexual, aggressive or assertive, being comfortable with taking (reasonable) risks and being rational.

Terry and Braun (2009) suggest that changes in our social understandings of masculinity have had significant implications for men's experiences of relationships, and their understanding of sex, romance and commitment. The fairly modern ideal of the 'new man' demands that men be both 'manly' and 'sensitive', and that to be a 'good man' in contemporary Western culture demands that men negotiate and reconcile these relatively contradictory demands in order to be both macho (but not too macho) and gentle. In their article 'When I was a bastard', Terry and Braun argue that men position themselves in long-term relationships as 'more mature' than their earlier selves. Playing the field, sleeping around and 'being a bastard' to women are constructed as a younger man's game, while a long-term committed relationship is a safe place in which to explore a more sensitive and mature self. This work around gender and relationships suggests that ideas about masculinities and feminities play a significant role in how we see ourselves in relationships, and how we view those relationships themselves.

Skill builder activity

Communicating your ideas to an audience

Transferable skill focus: communication

Key question: *What are the similarities and differences between three theories of love and romance?*

Choose three of the theories or models of love and romance covered in this chapter. Prepare a ten-minute presentation, comparing and contrasting these theories, and thinking through what notions of love and romance they convey.

Use the following prompts to help you prepare your presentation.

Summarise the key components of each of the three theories or models that you have chosen.

Ask yourself what the similarities in the models are? What are the differences?

Think about similarities and differences in the assumptions the theories make. For example, do they adopt a social cognitive frame of reference? Do they assume that love is universal, or that it is more culturally specific in its nature? How do the theories handle the issue of gender and sexuality?

Think about the audience for your presentation. How knowledgeable are they about the topic? What will they need to know about the material you are presenting?

Choose a method for your presentation. Will you simply speak about your ideas? Will you have notes? Will you use PowerPoint, overheads or smartboards?

If you choose PowerPoint (as many people do), think carefully about how you structure your presentation slides. Ensure that you convey one main point on each slide (you may have several sub-points). Ensure that your slides are not cluttered or over-full. Think about readability – ensure that the font size is large enough, that you choose a colour scheme that is aesthetically appealing, and that the slide is not too fussy or busy.

When presenting your work, remember to pace yourself. Ensure that you are not trying to squeeze a three-hour presentation into ten minutes, and don't rush when you speak.

Try to build in some interactive components, so that your audience feels they are part of your presentation.

It is always helpful to practise before you present to your formal audience.

Skill builder review

This activity helps develop your communication skills, focusing particularly on oral communication and presentation. These are important academic and life skills. The activity encourages you to reflect on what makes a good presentation, as well as reflecting on and critically thinking about theories of love and romance.

Other skills you may have used in this activity: critical thinking, comparison, independent learning, reflection, recall of key principles and ideas, information technology (if you chose to use computer-based presentation methods).

Assignments

1. 'True love is best understood as enduring companionate love.' Critically discuss this statement with reference to relevant psychological theory and research.

2. Is it possible to understand romantic love in the absence of an understanding of gender?

3. Imagine you have been asked to develop a therapeutic intervention for couples in crisis. Critically evaluate what social psychological theories would offer to such an endeavour.

Summary: what you have learned

In this chapter, we have outlined mainstream social psychological theories of love and romance. We have explored early adult relationships, considering psychological concepts such as social exchange, prototypes of love, love styles and love stories. We have highlighted how the focus on early adult life and Western models of romance in these approaches marginalises other ways of doing and being in love. To illustrate this point, we explored relationships in later life and highlighted the importance of contextualising factors such as work–life balance and gender in relational life.

To complete your critical thinking and skill builder activities, you have developed and used your skills in creative and critical thinking, communication of ideas, comparison, independent learning, reflection, recall of key principles and ideas, and information technology.

Further reading

Sternberg, RJ and Weiss, K (2006) *The New Psychology of Love*. London/New Haven: Yale University Press.

This book offers an up-to-date and detailed consideration of dominant Western psychological research on intimate relationships.

Chapter 9

Methodologies

Learning outcomes

By the end of this chapter you should:

- *have an understanding of the concepts of ontology, epistemology and methodology;*

- *have a critical understanding of the dominant postpositivist (or more accurately post postpositivist) assumptions that underpin most quantitative research;*

- *have an understanding of the strengths and weaknesses of quantitative approaches, particularly the experimental method;*

- *have an understanding of critical and qualitative alternatives to this paradigm;*

- *have a basic working knowledge of interpretative phenomenological analysis and discourse analysis.*

Introduction

In this book we have discussed a very large number of studies conducted by social psychologists to explore practical and theoretical questions. What we have hinted at is that psychologists have a range of techniques at their disposal for looking at possible answers to their questions, including popular methods such as experiments, attitude scales and interviews. In this chapter, we will provide an overview of the different methods available to social psychologists. We will also highlight some of the more complex issues that you need to consider when choosing which method(s) to use.

As we hoped to have shown you through the course of this book, doing social psychology often involves engaging with a whole host of complexities that were perhaps not obvious when you first started thinking about a topic or issue. We would argue that the same is true when it comes to choosing methods. In this chapter, we will ask the question: as social psychologists, how do we know what we know? To explore this, we will explore issues such as: what are quantitative and qualitative methodologies? Why are experiments one of the most popular methods used in psychology? In what ways do the methods we choose limit or constrain the kinds of questions we can ask? We will outline some of the social and historical context around methodological debates in the social sciences more generally, and in psychology in particular.

There are two broad approaches to research in social psychology – **quantitative** and **qualitative approaches**. These two broad approaches use very different types of techniques, collect different types of data and use different methods of analysis. However, do be aware that within each broad approach there are many different forms. There are numerous ways of doing quantitative and qualitative research, and these different ways of doing research are underpinned by different assumptions.

When considering the differences between various forms of research, it is important to remember that all approaches contain within them three basic intertwining assumptions:

1. Our **ontological assumptions** refer to our basic philosophical position on the nature of reality, and what can be known about reality (Guba and Lincoln, 1994). For example, how do we see the nature of our social world and the place of the human being within that social world (Bryman, 2001)?

2. Our **epistemology** refers to our assumptions about the relationship between the knower and the known; how the world might best be known. Epistemological questions are questions about the nature and construction of knowledge itself. These are questions to do with how we know what we know.

3. Our **methodology** emerges from our ontological and epistemological concerns. How can the enquirer go about finding out whatever he or she believes can be known? What are the best ways of finding out what we seek to know?

The ontological and epistemological assumptions we make together form our worldview. As social scientists, the main ontological issue that we must clarify is whether we think there is a single, objective real world. If we accept the view that there is just one social reality (realist ontology), then this determines the nature of our social science: our role is to uncover that objective reality. If, for example, we see intelligence as something 'real' and objective, then our role as social psychologists is to simply find better ways of measuring and knowing that reality. In contrast, if we do not accept a basic realist ontology, our question then becomes more complex. If there is not a single unitary world 'out there' for us to know, what is there that we might know? If we see truth as something more relative – that there are many possible versions of reality that could be known, depending on the perspective of the knower – then an approach to knowledge that is more sensitive to the contextual nature of our social world is needed. If we assume objective reality, seeking Truth with a capital T, then the best way to know this is through observation and measurement of that objective knowledge. As Campbell and Wasco (2000) suggest:

> if one accepts the premise of objective reality, then the goal of science is to discover the structure and function of that singular world. If one does not accept this premise, then the goal of science is to understand how we construct and interpret our realities.
>
> (Campbell and Wasco, 2000, p779)

There are many different social science worldviews, but for the purposes of clarity and simplicity in this chapter, we will distinguish postpositivism, critical realism and social constructionism. We will consider these in relation to methodologies and specific methods that are associated with each of these worldviews.

Positivist and realist approaches: quantitative methods

Quantitative methods are approaches that use numerical measurement and numerical quantities. This might involve counting up the number of instances of a particular behaviour (for example, in studies of prosocial behaviour, how often do men and women passers-by help people who seem to be in trouble?), measuring personality or traits by way of a psychometric test (for example, what scores do people obtain on Adorno et al.'s (1950) F-scale?), or quantifying attitudes through a survey-based questionnaire. Quantitative methods can be used (among other things) to make systematic comparisons between two groups (for example, what are the differences in men's and women's scores in intelligence tests?), or to compare the same group of people's responses at two points in time (for example, comparing racial attitudes before and after an intervention designed to reduce prejudice).

Most quantitative (and some qualitative) research takes a postpositivist or realist worldview. **Postpositivism** is based on a realist ontology – it presumes that there is a social world out there that might be directly known through objective observation of individuals and their behaviour and interactions. If you think back to your first-year psychology textbooks, you were probably told at some point that psychology was a science aiming to observe, explain, predict and control human behaviour. This is generally a goal of postpositivist science. The approach is associated with hypothesis-driven research. The postpositivist researcher is interested only in that which is testable, and the key principle in hypothesis testing is the principle of falsifiability. Karl Popper suggested that while we can never prove something to be unquestionably true, we can reject false beliefs by rigorously testing them (this is the principle that underpins the testing of the null hypothesis in psychological research). As we said above, all methodologies – including experimental ones – are underpinned by an epistemological position. The quantitative, and largely experimental, methods that characterise mainstream social psychology are rooted in this postpositivist approach, which broadly assumes the following about the way the world works and how we can find out about the world.

- The world (and all the things in it) exists independently from us and our observations of it. Things in the world are separate from us and have their own separate existence.

- We can find out and know the true nature of things in the world if we use methodologies that allow us to make objective, value-neutral observations.

For most people, the assumptions espoused by postpositivism seem so obvious that they are common sense – isn't it obvious that things exist separately from us? For some, the assertion that we are not separate from the things around us might seem positively ridiculous, unthinkable even. When trying to figure out or get to know something a little better, we often seek to find an unbiased view and encourage others to do the same. It might surprise you, then, to know that these assumptions about the way the world works and how we can find out about social phenomena have not always been so obvious, or considered common sense. Stainton Rogers et al. (1995) argue, for example, that such ideas only really started to predominate in the late 17th century when emphasis was placed on the importance of rationality and reason. In this social/historical moment, science as a rational method to obtain factual knowledge started to gain popularity over other ways of understanding and knowing the world (for example, through religion and so on).

In this approach, the researcher is cast as an objective observer of external realities. Any sources of researcher bias should be removed from the scientific endeavour. This objective, unbiased observation of social reality should, according to a postpositivist paradigm, be achieved through sound and proper application of good scientific methods. If we apply our methods properly, the postpositivist approach suggests, then it does not really matter who does the research, or what their motives, political views, emotional and other investments in the research might be. The purity of the scientific method should ensure the accuracy of the account the scientist produces. Unlike their **positivist** predecessors (who adhered to a principle of verifiability rather than Popper's falsifiability), postpositivist thinkers recognise that it is probably not possible to capture pure reality in our scientific endeavours because of the human flaws inherent in the research enterprise. However, they believe that good scientific methods enable us to control for such possible sources of bias.

The postpositivist paradigm also deploys a progressivist and cumulative model of science, assuming that new knowledges build on and exceed previous knowledges, as we move closer to a better and fuller understanding of an objectively knowable reality. In the social sciences, the emphasis on the social world as real and objectively knowable also often means that social psychological work that is postpositivist in its orientation assumes that we are looking for universal truths. In this sense, this kind of social psychology presumes that its knowledges are transcultural – true in all places and times, perhaps with a bit of cultural tweaking. Think, for example, about the relationship research that we looked at Chapter 8. Much of this research is concerned with the development of universal models of love and intimacy, with culture perhaps seen as an interesting addition to the overarching truth of love that social psychology uncovers.

How does all this work in practice? The postpositivist model of the social sciences will be the one that is most familiar to you, having spent a bit of time studying psychology. You will be familiar with its focus on hypothesis testing, falsifiability and objectivity, as this approach to research is the dominant one in psychology. The gold standard of research in social psychology is often suggested to be the **experimental method**.

Task — While watching TV, make a list of television adverts that use 'science claims' to sell their products. (The L'Oreal adverts are an obvious example of this with their *Here's the science bit*, but there are many others that claim that research has proved particular things related to their product.)

— How have the advertisers use science or ideas of science, and why? What scientific findings do they present?

— Imagine the same advert but without the science – would you say you more persuaded to buy the item because of their use of science? Why is that? What do you think is the appeal of the scientific explanation?

Experimental social psychology: the use of the scientific method

Modern social psychology (like psychology in general) most typically uses the quantitative experimental methods derived from the natural sciences to collect and analyse data. We have looked at different experiments throughout this book – for example, Zimbardo's prison experiment (page 106), Tajfel's minimal groups study (page 57), experiments to test Kelley's covariation model (page 30), etc. The experimental method is the foundation of much social psychological research. Experiments are situations that are deliberately set up by the experimenter; they are contrived situations that allow the experimenter to manipulate features of the experimental setting to see if these manipulations have an impact on people's behaviour.

Consider this basic example. Dr Jones is interested in the effect that observers have on memory. He hypothesises that the presence of observers will improve performance on a test of memory. To test this idea, he asks a group of participants chosen by **random selection** to learn a list of words and then recite them while being observed by a panel of judges. In a second condition, he has another group of randomly selected participants go through the same procedure, but instead of being watched by a panel of judges, they record their performance on a tape recorder. The participants in the condition with the judges perform better on memory test than those in tape recorder condition. Dr Jones finds that observation does improve performance on a test of memory.

In experimental research, researchers manipulate **independent variables** in order to see their effect on the **dependent variable**. In our example, the independent variable is 'observation', which is **operationalised** as the presence or absence of judges. The dependent variable is memory, which is operationalised through the word-list-based memory test. To be studied experimentally, all variables must be observable and measurable. Operationalisation is the process whereby something abstract like memory is turned into something tangible that can be measured, like a test of memory.

Can you think of any factors other than the independent variable (observation) in this experiment that might have produced the finding that observation improves memory? For example, what if one group of participants just happened to be better at memory tests than the other? The experimenter is able to introduce **controls** – ways of controlling the experimental conditions so that what is observed is just the effect of the independent variable on the dependent variable. The researcher might therefore control for the extraneous variable of greater competence on memory tasks by pre-screening participants to ensure that competence at memory tasks is reasonably distributed across the two experimental conditions. They could control for the possible influence of gender effects (gender of the observer, gender of the participant) and the effects of distracter variables (like noise outside the room) etc.

Experiments do allow the experimenter(s) to have a fair degree of control over everything that happens in the experimental situation. This is considered to be a highly desirable feature of experiments – if you can control and minimise the impact of all other factors (or, more precisely, variables) then you can be pretty confident that your experimental manipulation is the thing that is directly affecting people's behaviour – that is, that the independent variable is affecting the dependent variable. In experiments, experimenters can, to a large degree, control possible extraneous variables to minimise the possibility that they have an impact during the experiment. By controlling extraneous variables, they can be more sure that any change to people's behaviour is a direct result of their manipulations – that changes in the dependent variable are related to their manipulation of the independent variable. Through this element of being able to control for extraneous variables in the experimental context, this method appears to promise (or at the very least, have the potential for) valid and reliable results, which, in turn, suggest that the results can tell us something valid and reliable about the world in which we live. The experimental method is also valued for its replicability: by repeating experiments precisely, or by repeating the experiment with particular tweaks and changes to the conditions, it is assumed that researchers will be able to produce cleaner, more reliable and more valid results that increasingly accurately reflect the truths about human nature that the experimental method set out to uncover.

Other quantitative methods: surveys and psychometric tests

There are numerous other forms of quantitative research, and there is not sufficient space in this chapter to do justice to them all. Some of the most popular approaches to quantitative social psychological research involve the use of surveys, questionnaires and psychometric tests. Surveys typically sample opinions and attitudes to particular social events and phenomena. The intention is to build a profile of the population, based on a sample of responses. A good survey selects the sample carefully, using randomisation or (more commonly) some form of stratified random sampling. In addition to the quality of the survey questions, a good survey is determined by its sampling strategy and how well the sample enables the researcher to reliably generalise results to the larger population. This is achieved by asking a series of standardised questions, with a fixed response set (often presented as a Likert scale).

Psychometric tests are designed to measure particular psychological qualities. Examples of psychometric tests include IQ tests like the Weschler Intelligence Scales, personality tests like the Minnesota Multiphasic Personality Inventory, tests of specific abilities like the Rey Auditory Verbal Learning Test (a memory test), tests of aptitude, clinical tests like the Beck Depression Inventory etc. These tests help researchers to operationalise and measure abstract psychological states. So, for example, as social psychologists, we might hypothesise that membership of a low-status social group might have a negative impact on self-esteem. In order to test this hypothesis, we have to find a way of measuring the abstract, ephemeral notion of self-esteem. This is typically done by constructing a series of statements that are assumed to reflect various components of self-esteem, and then asking respondents to react to these statements (for example, by agreeing or dis-agreeing, by rating themselves on a scale of one to ten etc). In this sense, psychometric tests are not an approach to research in and of themselves, but are frequently used in quantitative research as a means of measuring the objects of study.

Task — Think of some of the famous experiments we have looked at in this book (for example, Tajfel, Festinger and Carlsmith, Zimbardo, Milgram).

How 'in control' of their experiments do you think these researchers were?

What 'extraneous variables' do you think slipped through to influence the outcomes of their research? How might they have controlled for these?

Do you think total control of research is possible? Do you think it is desirable?

Evaluating quantitative approaches to research

A key problem for social psychologists working within a postpositivist paradigm, using largely quantitative methods, is the issue of human beings as 'meaning-making' beings. A feature of being human is our capacity to reflect. However, the construct of human nature that is written into the assumptions of social psychological experiments and other quantitative approaches often underestimates this. Human beings are not passive recipients of social situations – they are sense-making beings. So, when they find themselves in strange situations, they will draw on their sense-making abilities to try to understand what is going on, second-guessing the researcher, trying to discern the purpose of research and work out what the researcher wants. For this reason, **demand characteristics** (our tendency to search for hints about how we are supposed to act in an experiment), evaluation apprehension (the anxiety that crops up from the sense of being observed in a study) and the issue of **social desirability** (our desire to do what seems socially 'right') become almost irresolvable problems for the social psychological experimenter. In questionnaire-based research, researchers introduce 'lie scales', and in experiments subjects are often deceived initially about the purpose of the research, or distractor tasks are used to fool subjects, or to take their focus away from trying to understand the nature of the research. However, even allowing for the possible success of these kinds of controls, this still does not really get researchers away from the problem that, while trying to second-guess the researchers, participants will necessarily be behaving somewhat differently from the way they would behave in more natural circumstances.

The control that researchers are able to exert over their work is both one of the greatest strengths of experimental research, and also its most significant weakness. As the task above hints, having complete control over the research endeavour is close to being an impossibility – there is always the risk of contagion of the research by factors that are beyond the control of the researcher. Many critics also express concerns that experimental research lacks **naturalistic validity** – that in an attempt to control the effect of extraneous variables, researchers create conditions that are too contrived to have applicability in the real world. Philosophers of science are also critical of the presumption, built into experimental research, of objective observation. Fox Keller (1985) pointed out that the mere act of observation changes the nature of that which is observed. She argues that, even within the natural world, at the atomic level, observing conditions can be demonstrated to change them. Since then, the observer effect has been well documented as a problem for social psychology. There is ample evidence, too, that the expectations and desires of researchers colour their interpretation of data. In early work by Rosenthal, it was found that experimenters would rate the performance of rats in a maze task, depending on whether they had been told that the rats they were observing had been bred to be clever or stupid (Rosenthal and Fode, 1963; Rosenthal and Lawson, 1964). Researchers' expectations colour the interpretation of what they observe (Rosnow and Rosenthal, 1997). This introduces a fundamental problem in experimental research – a tendency for evidence to be interpreted in a manner that confirms rather than disconfirms hypotheses.

Social psychologists also often use quasi-experimental design (or as Kazdin, 2003, terms it, queasy experimental design) rather than true experimental design. This follows a similar structure to experimental design, but lacks the key feature of randomisation. This kind of sampling strategy introduces significant problems in interpreting a lot of social psychology research. A frequent criticism levelled at social psychology is that it bases so much of its understanding of the world on research conducted on American university students – overwhelmingly white, middle class, and realistically not 'typical' of most people in the world. Think back to the chapter on personal relationships – so much of our psychological understanding of intimacy and intimate relationships is rooted in the experience of American university students. Can this kind of sampling practice really take into account the social complexity of our sexual relationships, our marriages and civil partnerships, our post-divorce re-engagements with the world of dating?

All quantitative research involves a level of operationalisation. The natural science paradigm that informs much quantitative social psychological research suggests that our study enables us to objectively view, measure and predict social behaviour. However, for example, tests and surveys cannot really purport to be direct measures of the reality of their objects, because the act of operationalisation itself involves a process of theoretical interpretation. Psychological constructs can rarely be observed directly – they must be 'turned into' something observable, that researchers presume to be a reflection of the object of interest, something that can be quantified and measured. For example, if you are studying depression using the Beck Depression Inventory, you are necessarily buying into Beck's particular theoretical view on what depression is and how it should be understood. Psychometric tests are necessarily framed by the worldview of those who constructed them. In this sense, they are already translating the real world out there for us.

Parker (1989), in his classic text *The Crisis In Modern Social Psychology – And How To End It*, suggests that the reliance on the experimental method in social psychology ignores and attempts to sidestep the way that social and psychological research is essentially research about power and ideology. By stripping away the social context within experimental research, by reducing our observations to the interaction of independent variables and dependent variables, we are editing out the complexity of our social world. As Tuffin (2005) suggests:

> *our social worlds include a vast complexity of variables, and it is the interplay of these that make the social aspects of our lives so fascinating, unexpected and at times unpredictable. In a sense it is this complexity that defines social life. So why then has it become so popular for social psychologists to adopt methods that strip social life of much of its meaning in order to study it?*
>
> (Tuffin, 2005, p21)

For example, can we really understand the social and political complexity of modern racism in the context of minimal groups studies? Or do we lose something of the reality of a social phenomenon by stripping it down to its composite interacting parts? Westland (1978) suggests that what happens in a laboratory context can never really have direct value in the real social world. In the real world, the variables observed in laboratory contexts intersect so wildly, so unpredictably, with other aspects of the social context that they simply do not behave as they do in the 'pure' conditions of the experimental set-up.

Horkheimer (1995) was critical of the postpositivist understanding of the social sciences in general. His suggestion that postpositivism does not take adequate account of the way knowledges are mediated by the (socially and historically constructed) personhood of the researcher remains a valid one for much social psychological work. Social psychological researchers tend to under-estimate the degree to which their work is coloured by the social positioning of the researcher. In effect, this reifies social reality as something that exists 'out there' to be known, rather than under-standing social reality as produced through the interpretative lens of the scientist. Many post-positivists do accept that research always contains within it an element of bias that is produced by the researcher's investments, but suggest that by being scientific and maintaining intellectual rigor and scepticism, we nonetheless have the best chance of producing good quality research that is useful and applicable to real-world social problems.

Critical thinking activity

Exploring experimental research

Critical thinking focus: critical thinking; evaluation

Key question: *How do psychologists know what they know?*

Read this classic social psychology article:

Ross, L, Greene, D and House, P (1977). The false consensus phenomenon: An attributional bias in self-perception and social perception processes. *Journal of Experimental Social Psychology*, 13(3), 279–301.

Use the following prompts to guide you through an analysis of these extracts.

Summarise the research questions posed by the article.

Summarise the methodology used.

Summarise the main reported findings and conclusions.

Can you think of other ways of understanding the outcomes of the research? For example, consider:

- the sampling strategy;

- the 'naturalness' or 'artificiality' of the study;

- ways the experiment might call into effect issues of social desirability, expectancy etc.

From your reading and reflection, what do you see as the advantages and disadvantages of the experimental method in social psychology?

Critical thinking review

In this exercise, you have developed your skills in critical thinking and evaluation. To do this, you have summarised the article and have reflected critically on the method used. You have used your critical understanding of the experimental method and have considered the limitations of this method in research practice.

> Thinking critically about research in this way enables you to consider the basis on which knowledge claims are made.
>
> Other skills you may have used in this activity: reflection, independent learning, understanding data.

Critical and constructionist approaches: qualitative methods

While quantitative methods tend to ask 'how' questions that focus on quantity (how much? what's the amount?), qualitative methodologies ask 'what', 'how' and 'why' questions. For example, qualitative psychologists might be interested in questions such as: What is the experience of depression like? How are young mothers popularly portrayed in the current cultural context? Why might convicted offenders struggle to get work? These questions require methods that allow researchers to explore the range and complexity of responses that could be made in relation to them. For this reason, techniques such as interviews or focus groups are often used in qualitative studies.

The distinction between qualitative and quantitative techniques not only describes some differences in the method used to collect and analyse data, but may also flag up differences in the overall methodology employed in a study. You might well be thinking that surely methods and methodology mean the same thing. Well, not quite. While the words 'method' and 'methodology' are often used interchangeably, there are some important conceptual and practical distinctions between them. The term 'methodology' can be thought of as encapsulating not just a method of data collection or way of doing analysis (for example, doing an interview, giving people a questionnaire etc.), but the broader philosophical assumptions that shape the research process. All researchers adopt a philosophical or, more accurately, an epistemological position, when they study a topic hoping to generate some further knowledge about it. All researchers make assumptions about what counts as valid knowledge. These include the theories they subscribe to for making sense of social phenomena as well as which methods can be used and how they should be used to collect data. The knowledge produced through a piece of research will be shaped by the researcher's epistemological position. The postpositivist assumptions that underpin quantitative research are so taken for granted, so much a part of scientific orthodoxy, that they are often not very clearly articulated.

In contrast, qualitative approaches tend to make the philosophical orientations of their methodology rather more explicit. Much qualitative methodology is rooted in either critical theory, or constructionist understandings of the social world. Critical theory suggests that 'reality' is not a transparent objective externality, but rather it is always located in and interpreted through our social, cultural and historical values – our gender, ethnicity, economic and social position all contribute to our interpretation of this 'reality'. This is such that it is not useful in social scientific argument to refer to an objective external reality. Knowledge can never be 'pure' or 'factual' – it is always located, always contextual. Research within this tradition is understood as a co-construction between research participants and the researcher. The researcher cannot be objective about, or external to, the process since their desires and interests shape the research from the start.

To illustrate this, think about some of the interests you are considering exploring for your third-year dissertation. Where does your sense of 'interest' come from? Why are you interested in pursuing the topics that intrigue you? The research questions you have are shaped by your history – personal, academic, social and political. From the very start, the moment you say 'I am interested in studying conformity', there is an 'I' at the centre of the research enterprise, constructing the question, being interested. The identity of that I, that knower, is very important in qualitative research. In quantitative research, this I is seen as bias, and various attempts are made to control it or edit it out, in the interest of producing value-neutral, objective research. Qualitative research, on the other hand, suggests that getting rid of the I at the heart of research is impossible, and that instead of trying to remove bias, what we need to do is fully understand how knowledge emerges as a co-construction within the **hermeneutic** field.

Interpretative phenomenological analysis

A good example of a qualitative methodology that is shaped by some of the assumptions of critical theory is interpretative phenomenological analysis, or IPA (Smith, 1996). Smith developed IPA from the well-established tradition of phenomenology – a philosophical and methodological tradition concerned with the study of experience. Influenced by philosophers like Husserl and Heidegger, phenomenology is concerned with individuals' subjective experiences, their personal accounts and perceptions of a particular event or experience, not with attempting to produce universal, objective accounts of psychological reality.

IPA has five key characteristics. It is:

1. **phenomenological** – it is concerned with the subtle nuances and textures of people's experiences;

2. **subjective** – the approach is concerned with the worldview of the participant, with developing an insider perspective on a particular phenomenon (Conrad, 1987);

3. **ideographic** – most quantitative research takes a **nomothetic** approach. Kant suggested that a nomothetic approach refers to the tendency to generalise, while an ideographic approach aims to specify. IPA attempts to capture the quality and texture of individual experience;

4. **interpretative** – IPA is interpretative in two senses. On the one hand, it attempts to understand how people make sense of their own experiences – how we interpret and make meaning of the

things we do, think, feel and live. To understand this also requires a level of interpretation from the researcher, too. To access the individual participants' lifeworld requires that the researcher attempts to understand that lifeworld – an act that itself necessarily involves interpretation. In this sense, the researcher becomes the *primary analytical instrument* (Fade, 2004, p2), making sense of the participant's sense-making.

5. **reflexive** – when we use IPA, we are trying to understand the participant's personal world, but this interpretative aspect means we can never know this directly or completely. For this reason, researchers must reflect on their own position in the research, how their own view of the world is embedded within and constructs the research.

Phenomenology has a broad, critical-realist orientation, assuming that what people say reflects their inner world, but that the research that we build on these accounts is necessarily partial and located through the interpretative activity of the researcher. It is also influenced strongly by symbolic interactionism, an approach that suggests that how we make meaning of our lives is negotiated within a social and cultural context – that our meanings are built up interactionally (in our relationships, social context and relationships with social institutions). For example, if you want to understand the experience of being an alcoholic in the Western world, this needs to be understood by considering the experience against a social context in which social drinking, binge drinking etc. are viewed in a particular way. It also needs to be understood within an under-standing, say, of dominant models of rehabilitation – AA's 12 steps and abstinence-only model, for instance (Denzin, 2002). Our experience of alcoholism (or any other experience we might have) is necessarily a social experience.

How does IPA work? First, IPA is generally based on very detailed qualitative data – usually derived from interviews, daily diaries or other personal accounts of experiences. This data is converted to a verbatim written transcript, which is then subject to a very detailed and careful analysis. IPA involves looking for patterns and connections in participants' accounts of a particular experience. The themes must be grounded in data, and IPA generally involves quoting from interviews to support themes when the data is written up. We do not have space to give a very full account of the way that IPA works in practice (fuller accounts of this method can be found in Smith and Eatough, 2006; Smith and Osborn, 2003; Willig, 2001), but the basic steps of an IPA are as follows.

- As you interview and transcribe data, keep detailed notes on your thoughts, feelings and ideas, including, for example, notes on participants' non-verbal communication, the tone of the interview, your reactions to participants across the interviews or at particular moments in the interview, your ideas about potential themes.

- Once you have transcribed the interviews, read the transcripts several times. In the left margin, comment on interesting points, ideas and assumptions. On the right side, note any interpreta-tive ideas you have, coding what participants have said into units of meaning.

- In this first level of coding, pay attention to the experiences of your participants, to evocative phrases, to the subtleties and textures of the language that they use to convey that experience. Note, too, similarities and tensions both within accounts and across accounts. How is one point that they make similar to, or different from, a point they made earlier? For example, in a series of interviews about alcoholism, regret emerges as a clear theme across all of the interviews. In one account, towards the end of an interview, a participant might say *I have no regrets,* while earlier in the interview, they said *I regret hurting the people I loved. I feel awful about the time I wasted when I could have been building a real relationship with our son.* Our interpretative job here is to use the material in the interview to make sense of this apparent contradiction.

- List your initial codes from each participant on a separate piece of paper, looking again for connections between the codes you have identified, organising them into clusters based on similarities and tensions in the account. Keep checking back to the data to ensure that the categories you are building here still resonate with what the participants have said.

- From these sheets, you can start to build a list of superordinate themes and subthemes that emerge from the data.

- This cycle is repeated for all the interviews you have conducted, with a sense of regularly comparing emerging themes from each interview with each other, until you have an overarching set of themes that give a vigorous account of the data that you have.

- Once you have completed this cycle with all your interviews, you will be able to build a master table of your superordinate and subthemes, with relevant quotes to support each of these analytic categories. You can then begin the process of writing this analysis up.

Skill builder activity

Analysis of qualitative data

Transferable skill focus: textual analysis; understanding and using data

Key question: *How do we use IPA in practice?*

Read the interview extract below. The extract is from an interview with Millie, a woman doing a professional degree. She is talking about the experience of having to leave her daughter some distance away with her parents while she pursued her studies. This arrangement is necessary because of the great geographic distances in the country where she lives (South Africa) and the fact that urban centres and universities can be very distant from rural villages.

Using the stages of IPA data analysis described above, code the interview extract and develop some initial ideas of how these codes might become themes.

I left my girl at home. But we both do very well, but even so, I miss her. Well, that's the hard part, knowing that you have to miss it, you can't see them as often as you want. That you don't know ((unclear)). You know that my daughter is physically disabled. My father tells me, first my father tells me that she's very naughty, she opens things that she shouldn't, and I think how is that possible, she's disabled? But when I come there, I see she's very mobile, and erm, when she started to try to walk with her stumps, when they told me, I couldn't really see how could she do that, but when I go home, and I see that, yes, she's moving around.

(From Callaghan, 2008, pp141–142)

Use the following prompts to help conduct your analysis.

– Read through the extract twice. Jot down any first thoughts you have about it.

– Code the extract, looking for units of meanings in the text, and paying particular attention to how the participant experiences being a mother, being a student, being far from her child, and how she makes sense of this experience.

– Look at any connections or contradictions in the text.

– What do you think some emerging interpretative or thematic concerns might be? What would you guess might be some of the themes that would emerge from this kind of data? What would you be looking for in other interviews on the same topic?

Skill builder review

This activity helps develop your textual analysis skills. Being able to analyse qualitative data is a key academic skill for psychologists.

Other skills you may have used in this activity: critical thinking, comparison, reflection.

Social constructionism: discourse analysis

Social constructionists develop the themes of critical theory further, suggesting that what we understand as reality, and particularly our social reality, is itself socially constituted, as is our knowledge of that social reality. Our social context does not simply offer a lens through which reality is viewed (with reality still being seen as something objective out there that is known in this partial manner), rather our individual and social realities are constituted within the social locations of gender, class, race, culture, economics, politics, etc. The social constructionist perspective suggests that there is no objective external reality, no Truth with a big T, but rather that there are multiple truths that are socially constituted. Both researcher and researched are actively engaged in the production of this social reality, and therefore again, critical reflexivity is a key component of a social constructionist approach to research. Research can never be 'objective'. Rather, from a social constructionist point of view, research is radically subjective, always interrogating how it is produced.

Social constructionism is anti-essentialist. While most psychological work presumes an inner world, with a core sense of self that drives our social interaction, our development, etc., social constructionism suggests that our sense of self is built in language – in the ways that we talk about ourselves. Shotter (1989) suggested: *Most of us feel that there must be something, some 'thing' within us which functions as the causal centre of all our activities, that 'I' that wills our actions. But must there be?* (p133)

A common social constructionist alternative to the idea of a stable core organising ego is the idea of selfhood or subjectivity – a sense of self that is constituted in **narratives** – in the stories we tell about ourselves. For example, if somebody asks me the scary question 'Who are you?', I will generally articulate my sense of self-identity in two ways. One way is by telling a series of stories about myself (for example, when I was five, I fell down a flight of stairs, and since then I've always been scared of heights; when I was 11, I moved to South Africa. I'm the first person in my family to go to university). Another is to identify myself through a range of subject positions (I'm a woman, a mother, a university lecturer, a dog-owner, etc.). Both strategies – and we tend to use both to describe who we are – involve positioning our sense of self in relation to social context, history and narrative. In this way, we weave a coherent sense of self. However, these stories of the self are always themselves socially located. For example, you would probably tell a different story of who you are if you were in a job interview from the one you would tell when out on a first date. This is not generally because you are lying or because you are being inaccurate in one account, but rather because our sense of self is contextual and it is performative. We enact our sense of self in a social context.

Social constructionism is also anti-naturalist. It resists naturalising accounts of human experiences, challenging biologically reductionist explanations of complex human experiences. Bruner (1990) suggested *it is culture, not biology, that shapes human life and the human mind, that gives meaning to action by situating its underlying intentional states in an interpretive system* (p35).

Social constructionists are not naive relativists – they do not suggest that we somehow do not have bodies, or that our bodies do not have a certain physical reality to them. However, in social scientific terms, they suggest that what matters is not so much the physicality of our bodies as the sense we make of that. Think back to Chapter 7 on gender. When understanding how gender works socially and historically, is it really meaningful to understand it as a basically biological phenomenon? Or is it more useful to consider how we make sense of our gendered bodies in social interactions, in discursive networks etc.?

Discourse analysis is a good example of a social constructionist qualitative methodology. In this chapter, we will outline a Foucauldian approach to discourse analysis, following Parker, (1992, 2002), but it is useful to note that there are several other forms. All discursive forms take as their starting point a view that language is not merely representative, but that it is constructive and productive. As Wetherell and Maybin (1996) note: *Language is not a transparent medium for conveying thought, but actually constructs the world and the self through the course of its use* (p220).

Think about the differences between describing a woman as a 'woman', a 'lady', a 'girl' or a 'chick'. What are the differences in your associations to these terms? Describing a woman as a 'girl' could serve numerous functions. It could be teasing, insulting, a compliment, a put-down, a reference to 'girl power'. In this sense, language has both a context and a function; it is a kind of action. It produces an impression; it constructs a particular social reality. It isn't just representing some objective reality of girlhood – it serves a particular purpose. As Foucault (1972) suggests, discourses are *practices that systematically form the objects of which they speak* (p49). In other words, the way we talk about gender, for example, is not only limited by the language that forms gendered talk, but our talk about gender also forms gender itself. When we draw on the language of heteronormative masculinity to talk about men, we are simultaneously drawing on dominant discourses of masculinity (talking about men as aggressive, as predatory, as promiscuous, for instance, in a way that men have been described many times before) and reproduce masculinity in that form. Discourse analysis is characterised by a focus on the textually mediated nature of experience and action (Parker, 1992). A discourse analytic perspective sees language as a social practice, not just an individual activity (Fairclough, 1992). Further, language is no longer seen as a vehicle for the expression of experience. Rather language is seen as both producing social practices, and as produced by such practices. These discursive practices are seen as constructing our sense of self-identity. Henriques et al. (1998) suggest: *Furthermore, the subject itself is the effect of a production, caught in the mutually constitutive web of social practices, discourses, and subjectivity: its reality is the tissue of social relations* (p117).

Discourses and narratives position social actors – for example, a discourse of femininity positions men and women in a particular network of social relationships. So within discursive constructions of masculinity and femininity we take up the subject position of man or woman.

Within a Foucauldian frame of reference, discourses are also understood to have a regulative effect. Foucault (1975, 1976) analyses the ways in which the Western notion of the individual, and Western practices of the self such as psychology, discipline and control people through confession, observation and regulation. This occurs, not through overt oppressive practice, but in the way that the Western concept of self is constructed in social and linguistic practice. In *Discipline and Punish*, Foucault (1975) makes the point that the nature of power has shifted in Western society, from overt control and oppression to what he calls disciplinary power. He uses the example of punishment for crimes to illustrate this point. In medieval times, for example, power was exerted on people in a very direct and observable way. An individual who had committed a serious crime could expect a public, and very physical retribution – public hanging, flogging or, in the case of crimes like treason, being hanged, drawn and quartered was a particularly brutal and bloody way to meet your end. Foucault contrasts this with modern systems of punishment, using the example of Bentham's panopticon (see Foucault, 1975). The panopticon is an observation tower in the centre of a prison complex, from which all activity within the prison might be observed. The effect of this sense of being watched is that, over time, prisoners do not require overt punishment – rather they begin to regulate themselves. (Our British preoccupation with CCTV cameras is another example of this kind of panoptical process.) Extending this metaphor of crime and punishment to daily living, Foucault suggests that in constructing a set of regulative norms, we discursively constitute some things as acceptable and others as deviant, and construct within that linguistic distinction the incitement to self-regulate, to fit in, to be normal. Discursive approaches regard power not as a force that resides in the hands of the powerful, and oppresses the masses, but rather *as a multiplicity of discursive practices that fabricates and positions subjects* (Levett et al., 1997, p3). Seen in this way, power and ideology are no longer separated from and operating on individuals, but are interwoven into the subject positions that the person takes up, and are mediated by language.

Task — Look at the example, below, of an extract from a conversation between Kate and a friend.

> *You're just being a bit too serious Kate. You need to lighten up a bit. If you don't loosen up and have some fun, you're going to end up on the shelf. Men don't want to spend time with a girl who never smiles!*

What representations of masculinity and femininity can you see in the text?

What are some of the 'shoulds' here? What does the speaker think women should be like? What language is used to describe women? What should women want and need? What are men like, what do men want and need?

How might these assumptions about gender, constructed discursively in this kind of everyday talk about masculinity and femininity, function to regulate men and women?

Assignments

1. Critically compare (post)postpositivist and critical perspectives on social psychological problems. What are the advantages and disadvantages of each approach?

2. What are some of the differences between interpretative phenomenological analysis and discourse analysis? What kinds of research questions do you think you would want to answer using each method?

Summary: what you have learned

This chapter pulls together key strands underpinning both mainstream and critical psychological research reviewed in previous chapters, by focusing on the philosophical assumptions that inform social psychological research. We have explored the philosophical bases for much social psychological knowledge, critiquing the notion of psychology as 'science' and querying the ontological, epistemological and methodological foundations of the discipline. This sets the backdrop to an articulation of alternative, more critically oriented paradigm, and to a consideration of qualitative methodologies in social psychology. Specifically, we have looked at two qualitative methodologies – IPA and discourse analysis.

Further reading

Denzin, NK and Lincoln, YS (2005) *The Sage Handbook of Qualitative Methods*. London: Sage.

This excellent handbook of qualitative research offers both a breadth of coverage on different methodologies, and a depth of understanding of the philosophical underpinnings of various approaches.

Van Der Stoep, SW and Johnson, DD (2009) *Research Methods for Everyday Life: Blending Qualitative and Quantitative Approaches*. London: Wiley.

This book offers a clear overview of both quantitative and qualitative research approaches.

Chapter 10

Keeping the social in social psychology: the importance of context

Learning outcomes

In this chapter, we will draw together the main themes of the book, giving particular consideration to the appearance and disappearance of 'the social' in social psychology. By the end of this chapter, you should:

- *have an understanding of the way that psychology tends to theorise the individual as a relatively asocial being;*

- *be able to demonstrate a critical understanding of key social issues like hetero-normativity, class, ethnicities and disabilities;*

- *have a critical understanding of the way in which key social issues are largely excluded from mainstream social psychology, and the implications of these exclusions;*

- *have a critical understanding of the context specific and ideological nature of social psychology.*

Introduction

Throughout this book we have explored various ways of understanding social/psychological experience, behaviour and interaction. What we have tried to bring to the fore is the ways in which it is sometimes easy to lose sight of the social when looking at what individuals do. To a degree, the 'social' aspect of social psychology is often obscured by the focus of psychology on the individual. But who is this individual? How can we understand what it means to be human, without understanding the person-in-context (Ingleby 1986)? To understand, for example, the break-up of an intimate relationship, you would need to understand the break-up in the context of the whole relationship, your interactions with other friends, your understandings of gender – what it means to be a man or a woman in an intimate relationship, your understandings of what a relationship means (are 'relationships' typically heterosexual in your worldview?), your understandings of love and sex itself, and how this fits with dominant social ideas of love and sex. In other words, your relationship needs to be understood within the larger context within which it is nested.

What do we mean by context? Context is a term that is often bandied around in psychology, to refer to the 'stuff' that influences behaviour, feelings and personality that is not individual. The nature of this context often remains poorly articulated. In this chapter, to draw together the themes of this book, we will explore in greater detail what the context of social psychological work might be.

Individual?

To understand the importance of context in social psychology, we need to unpack the artificial distinction that is often drawn between the individual and the social. As we have seen, in traditional social psychology the individual is often posited as the primary unit of analysis. This means that social psychology has tended to focus on individual functioning within social and interpersonal contexts. But what is this 'individual'? In most modern social psychology, the individual is framed as primarily a cognitive being. The individual is seen as a rational, sense-making unit. At the same time cognitive processes also render the individual open to cognitive distortion. For example, our tendency to categorise the physical and social world leaves us open to the development of prejudice, which is understood within dominant social psychological models as a kind of cognitive distortion. In the social cognitive approach, the social is positioned as external to the individual; it is conceptualised as a set of variables that influence a relatively independent, unitary individual. The individual is seen as relatively independent, self-directing and in control. Within this frame of reference, traditional social psychology positions the social as that which influences us, but we remain separate from those social forces. So, for example, in research on stereotyping, stereotypes are understood as cognitive schema held by the individual. These are seen as basic cognitive units, the building blocks of our mental processes. The social within this model becomes the filler material, added to the individual cognitive process, not the focus of study. The social is effectively marginalised within dominant social cognitive models of human behaviour and experience.

It is our argument that this model positions the individual and the social as dichotomous, and that this dichotomy is artificial. What do we mean by this? A **dichotomy** can be thought of as a pair of ideas that are set in conceptual opposition. You will be familiar with these kinds of dichotomous oppositions from your first-year work in psychology. For example, think about the famous nature versus nurture debate, or free choice versus determinism. In everyday social interactions, think about ideas like masculinity and femininity, reason and irrationality, ability and disability, black and white. These binaries appear to be opposite to each other. However, they are logically intimately connected – you cannot define one half of the term without reference to the other. So, for example, it is very difficult to talk about femininity without talking about masculinity. Often these terms are described by virtue of that which they are not. In relation to formal social psychological thinking, if we retain this dichotomous thinking about the individual and the social, we run the risk of over-focusing on the individual at the expense of fuller articulation of the role of social context. This problem also perhaps results in a misunderstanding of the nature of the human being we are trying to understand. As human beings, we do not exist as biological entities, separate from but interacting with our social worlds. As Bennington and Derrida (1999) suggest, humans are ***always-already social*** (p231), permeated with sociality. We are born fully social and fully biological beings. In understanding human beings as fully social, we need to critically consider the maintenance of these artificial dichotomies in our understanding of social psychological phenomena, and to challenge the factors in academic writing that maintain them. We suggest that a key project for social psychology in the future is to dissolve this artificial dualism between the individual and the social.

Rather than seeing the social as something that influences the individual, we would argue that the social is inherently productive. In other words, the social makes up or constitutes the personal, it constructs who we are, how our identities and relationships take shape and become constituted through a complex web of social interactions. We can see this quite clearly if we think about our early experiences of playing. It is not uncommon for children to be given 'gender-appropriate' toys. Through our engagement with this kind of play, what is being communicated are normative assumptions about what is appropriate for certain genders, and this impacts and shapes in various ways our sense of who we are, our gendered identities. We may choose to reject strict gender-typed behaviours, but in doing so we nonetheless make that rejection in relation to dominant constructions of masculinity and femininity. We remain engaged with a complex social process that produces us as a particular kind of gendered being. In this sense, the social is productive: we do not passively receive social information in the manner that social learning theory suggests. We build our gendered identities within a social context made up of relations between ourselves, between ourselves and institutions, and between ourselves and dominant ideologies.

It is important to note that we are not suggesting that we are determined by social forces that exist 'out there'. Our argument is much more complicated than that, and our notion of what it means to be human is not this passive. We are not reproducing here the assumptions of social learning theory that human beings are blank slates who acquire social characteristics from an external environment. Rather, what we want to explore is how our personhood, our individuality, our biological experiences become meaningful in human terms through the complex symbolic and representational frameworks that function in social spaces. Of course, in understanding ourselves as men and women, it is important to take biology into account. But the meaning of that embodiment, how we make sense of our embodiment and live embodied lives, is embedded within a network of social meanings. To further develop these ideas, we will consider the ways that several contextual issues might be seen as constituting human subjectivity.

Political contexts and dominant cultural frameworks

Most social psychological work either does not engage with what are sometimes termed macro levels of analysis, or engages with them very superficially. The macro level of analysis might be considered those aspects of human life that function in a broad-brush manner, forming the framing context in which we live our lives – our larger social, political, economic and cultural milieu. Because social psychology has tended to focus on the individual in society, and because the work of social psychology has largely studied that society in either intrapsychic or inter-personal ways, the political, cultural and economic context is typically either excluded from analysis or touched on in a very tangential manner. So, for example, if you consider the way that social psychology has studied social influence and social norms, largely this has been by focusing on small group experiments such as Asch's conformity studies or Zimbardo's prison study. In these studies, the broader social and political context within which our ideas about conformity and our understanding of social norms exist is left at the laboratory door. Culture, political life and economic concerns slip away in the apparently value-neutral space of the experimental study. The effect of this is that the predominantly Western, liberal and capitalist assumptions of much social psychology evade analysis.

To illustrate the importance of this broader social and political context, let us take a look at a dominant social ideology in the West. For example, a dominant cultural concern in the West is the notion of **liberal humanism**, and its implication in capitalist economics and social arrangements. **Capitalism** is the dominant economic system in the world today. It is a system in which the means of production (for example, natural resources, energy, factories, etc.) are privately owned (for example, by individuals, local companies, multinational corporations), and where production is geared to making a profit (Tormey, 2004). In this system, profit is held by the owners of the means of production, but is shared with workers (usually in the form of wages). In the free market ideal of capitalism, the logic of supply and demand is allowed to moderate the market in a relatively unfettered way. There is a strong emphasis in capitalism on private ownership (Scott, 2005), and the owners of property are seen as the individuals who have the right to determine what happens to it, with minimal state (or other) intervention (Case, 2004). This emphasis on privacy and on the right to determine what happens to our own 'stuff' underscores the links between capitalism as an economic system, and liberal humanism as both a set of cultural values and as a political ideology.

Liberal humanism, too, is a dominant value system globally, and is particularly pervasive in Western culture. Perhaps best characterised as the idea that underpins the American Dream, liberal humanism values individual rights and responsibilities, the notion of free choice and the ideals of freedom and equality. Generally, in Western societies, these characteristics of liberal humanism are presumed to be unquestioned forces of good, and are seen as natural, inevitable features of a 'civilised society'. Who has rights and responsibilities? Who is seen as able to make free choices? Who strives for personal meaning and who wishes to live free and equal? The individual does. In order to be able to make choices, to have rights etc., the individual of the liberal humanist political system must be rational and independent.

But why does all this matter to a study of social psychology? Essentially, because the individual that most traditional, mainstream social psychology studies is the unitary subject that is characterised by liberal humanist ideology (Henriques et al., 1998)

To illustrate the ideological (rather than taken-for-granted and apparently true) nature of the ideas of liberal humanism, let us look at one of its key principles – the idea that we are free to choose. To suggest that choice is free is to suggest it is unfettered – that the individual is free to choose. However, is any choice truly free? From our choice of breakfast in the morning, through to our choice of partner, political party or country of residence, our choices are neither completely free nor completely determined by social or other factors. Rather our choices are both enabled and constrained by social, economic, political and other contextual concerns. For example, on the completely trivial matter of our choice of breakfast – this is shaped by our experiences of breakfast, by the resources we have available to purchase food, by our gender (what is regarded as a 'good breakfast' for a woman in contemporary Western society?), by our location in a place where breakfast cereals are pre-manufactured and readily available, and where there is a labour force to produce them etc. Our choice of breakfast food is certainly there – we are not forced to eat a particular substance – but it is not entirely free.

Applied to breakfast foods, this consideration of the importance of discourses of free choice may not seem particularly important. However, consider the importance of the doctrine of free choice when applied to a more controversial social issue, such as the question of women's place in pornography. The pornography debate has historically been divided into a few camps. The radical feminist view is that pornography is an exploitative industry that uses and exploits vulnerable women who are positioned by it as objects of a male gaze, and as oppressed victims of sexual violence, abuse and exploitation (e.g. Mackinnon, 1989). In contrast, liberal feminist and pro-pornography discourses suggest that the radical feminist view patronises women by positioning them as victims who have no say in their own lives (e.g. Strassen, 1995). This focus on apparently free choice obscures the operation of a broad range of social factors that function to constrain women's choices in these kinds of circumstances, suggesting instead that women have chosen freely to engage with pornography, and that that choice should be respected. This apparently liberal concern with freedom, and particularly with the freedom to choose, overemphasises the capacity of the individual to act freely from the influence of social factors. Ultimately, it can offer very conservative readings of people's actions in their social world. If free will is presumed in the absence of actual free will, by neglecting the role of social factors you run the risk of entrenching socio-economic inequities and perpetuating an American-Dream ideology that hides the nature of a social reality in which some people's choices are really very constrained indeed. The construct of free choice appears on the surface to be in everyone's interests, but by placing a premium on it in our culture, we slide past the 'real' social and economic conditions of our world, producing a cosy illusion that enables the privileged to secure their position, safe in the knowledge that everyone is 'free' to choose to be what they are.

These kinds of taken-for-granted aspects of culture – the everyday workings of ideology – have implications for human identity and for human relationships. In this case, we have explored how liberal ideology, and specifically the notion of free choice, becomes implicated in the construction of people's sense of self (the construction of the agentic individual). We have considered the importance of acknowledging the ideological nature of the individual that social psychology tends to take as its basic unit of analysis. In this way, we can understand better the kind of social psychologies we are producing.

Heteronormativity

Some people are gay – get over it! was the slogan used in the 2009 UK campaign tackling homophobic bullying. The need for this campaign reflects the continuation of various forms of unequal treatment of the Lesbian, Gay, Bisexual and Trans (LGBT) community in society (Collins, 2010). To understand this kind of discrimination, some researchers have suggested that contemporary culture functions in a way that presumes reproductive heterosexuality, and that this heteronormativity is a context that may shape, support and maintain anti-LGBT sentiment. Put simply, heteronormativity describes predominant assumptions that heterosexuality is normal and 'natural' – the way sex 'should' be (Robinson, 2005). This ideology functions to normalise heterosexuality and marginalise gay, lesbian, bisexual and other 'queer' sexualities (for example, Butler, 1990; Green, 2010). (In the context of Queer Theory, the term 'queer' is used in a positive and affirmative manner, reclaiming a term previously used to insult, humiliate and degrade.) Ideas around gender are important to heteronormativity. Cultural ideals about what it is to be a proper feminine girl/woman or a proper masculine boy/man are tied to heterosexuality. To make this clear, many of the practices associated with femininity and masculinity are tied up with attracting a member of the opposite sex (Epstein, 1997). For example, displaying an interest in wanting sex with women is one way in which men can display an acceptable masculine identity in line with culturally normative ideas about what it means to be a proper man (Hollway et al., 1989).

Of course, in practice, many people (including those who identify as heterosexual) deviate from these ideas and do so quite frequently. When people deviate from normative notions of heterosexual masculinity and femininity, we tend to notice – this points to how powerful these ideas are. It is also common practice when people deviate from normative ways of being to try to bring them back in line and/or punish them for their behaviour. Discrimination, harassment and bullying have been thought of as one way in which people who deviate from normative heterosexual behaviours are 'punished'. For example, calling someone 'gay' only works as an insult because it implies that they are not living up to normative expectations of femininity or masculinity, and because of this being gay becomes positioned as 'not normal' and as deviant (see Renold, 2005).

Heteronormativity functions as a context that shapes people's sexual/gendered identities, practices and interactions. This can be seen in Epstein's (1997) study of retrospective accounts of gay men's experiences of harassment at school. In interviews, these men discussed how they were routinely bullied and harassed for doing things that did not match expectations of appropriate heterosexual and masculine behaviour, such as being 'effeminate' or holding hands with another boy. To try to deflect bullying, these men performed heterosexual masculinity by:

* harassing other gay or effeminate boys – this provided a means of presenting themselves as heterosexual and masculine because a display of aggressively rejecting gay sexuality can work to communicate one's masculine heterosexuality;

* harassing girls – by treating girls as sex objects, boys are able to constitute themselves as 'properly' heterosexual and masculine.

While heteronormativity can be seen as powerfully shaping particular discriminatory behaviours, it is important to remember that what is considered acceptable or appropriate is not set in stone. As we have said earlier, there are lots of ways of doing femininity and masculinity (and indeed heterosexuality), which points to how these identities, practices and behaviours are provisional, socially located and open to change.

Disabilities

Take a moment to think about what disability means to you. What images and words spring to mind when you think about disability? For many, the archetypal representation of disability is the wheelchair, and our understanding of what constitutes a disability is fairly narrow (for example, many people focus on physical disabilities, but will not necessarily consider mental health difficulties when first asked to think about what disabilities might mean). A number of researchers have highlighted how predominant social representations of disabilities tend to be negative rather than positive. As Hodgkins and Baility (2009) note, in contemporary representations disability is typically read as inability, impairment and incapacity. In short, what is made more or less explicit is the idea that disability is a flaw. They argue that this language of impairment is currently used in laws against disability discrimination. For example, in the Disability Discrimination Act (1995) – recently repealed by the Equality Act (2010) – disability is described as *a physical or mental impairment, which has a substantial and long-term adverse effect on a person's ability to carry out normal day-to-day activities.* Hodgkins and Baility suggest that such representations work to invalidate or make inferior those with disabilities in relation to normative understandings of those who are 'able'. Indeed, they point out that many representations position those with disabilities as dependent and vulnerable. Such social understandings of what constitutes normative abilities provide a context that supports or enables the marginalisation, social exclusion and discrimination of those with disabilities (Bell and Heitmueller 2009; Goodley and Lawthom, 2008; Sayce and Boardman, 2008).

As with other points of difference and discrimination that we have looked at so far, which bodies become constituted as deficient or valued is very much embedded within the historical and cultural context in which they are situated; the meaning attributed to various kinds of bodies/ (dis)abilities is variable, changeable and contextual. This opens up the possibility of social change. Hodgkins and Baility (2009) argue that for social change around current forms of disability discrimination:

> It is necessary to recognize disablism as a significant issue and foster zero tolerance toward it. This requires vigilance and action to make active challenge at each and every moment it appears. So that all bodies are valued, their diverse relativity must be embraced and celebrated; when rejected, critical responses must be made. However, it needs to be remembered that this requires effort, commitment, and reflexivity, for often the normative is so dominant in its expression that it represses acknowledgment and acceptance of diversity, thus legitimating its oppression.
>
> (Hodgkins and Baility, 2009, p227)

To challenge the insidious exclusionary practices of our culture, we need to recognise and counter its presumptions around 'normal' bodies, 'normal' ability, destabilising the taken-for-granted nature of particular ways of being human.

Ethnicities, race and belonging

In Chapter 3, we unpacked some key issues in relation to the significance of race in social psychological thought. However, we also highlighted the way that social psychological work in this field typically neglects the complexity of the social context within which racial identities are constituted. In other words, our understanding of race and racism is often seen in cognitive terms. The intergroup aspect of most intergroup psychology sees the group as relatively abstracted from its social context. Race and racism therefore are understood in social psychology more or less separately from economic, local, national and global politics. We would like to suggest that the experience and social reality of race and racism simply cannot be adequately understood this way. Rather, race is intimately connected to the social, political and economic conditions that constructed it in the first place.

In the twenty-first century, race and ethnicity have become far more complex and difficult to define and understand theoretically. We cannot understand them separately from, for example, issues of migration, globalisation, post-colonialism, nationhood, or from cultural norms such as multiculturalism or xenophobia. Anthias (2002) has suggested that, rather than seeing race as a property of individuals or of groups of individuals in contemporary society, it is useful to think of race and ethnicity as related to location and positionality. In other words, ethnicity and race become more salient, and significant in different ways, in different contexts. For example, white Britishness takes on a largely invisible, unarticulated but hegemonic character in Britain (as we saw in Chapter 3), where it functions as the 'norm' against which the racialised 'other' is drawn. In this sense, we might refer to British culture as characterised by an unarticulated, largely invisible **hegemonic whiteness**. In contrast, a white British person living in Saudi Arabia is positioned differently in that context, by virtue of their current location. However, in a globalising and post-colonial world, this situation is not quite as simple as it might sound. The 'Britishness' of the white subject is also influenced by the historic position of Britain, by histories of empire and colonisation, by its current economic position (as a G8 member, for instance). Also, their racial and ethnic position is further shaped by its intersections with other subject positions – such as their gender, sexuality, ability/disability etc. Anthias suggests that we need to acknowledge:

> that identification is an enactment that does not entail fixity or permanence, as well as the role of the local and the contextual in the processes involved. It becomes possible to pay attention to spatial and contextual dimensions, treating the issues involved in terms of processes rather than possessive properties of individuals.

> (Anthias, 2002, p277)

For social psychologists, the implication of this is that we need to move beyond a view of individuals who interact in and form groups and away from a view of identity as static and fixed, to a more complex understanding of the interaction of people with their social, political and historic context.

Class

It is popular in media representations, political discourse and, to a lesser degree, academic writing to dismiss **class** as insignificant in contemporary British culture. In 1999, the then UK Prime Minister Tony Blair pledged to create:

> a classless society, a New Britain where the extraordinary talent of the British people is liberated from the forces of conservatism that so long have held them back, to create a model 21st-century nation, based not on privilege, class or background, but on the equal worth of all.

However, social inequities prevail, despite the expressed intentions of politicians. Such inequities continue to have a significant impact on human social experience, despite the popular reluctance to talk seriously about class.

What do we mean by class? In *Capital*, Marx suggested that the key to understanding social class is the idea of property ownership. He suggested there were three social classes: landowners, who owned land, and drew income largely from rent; the bourgeoisie, who owned the means of production (factories, machinery etc.) and earned income from profit; and the proletariat/workers who sold their labour for a wage. Owning the means of production is a source of power for the bourgeoisie since it works to shut certain people out from the means of production. A Marxist analysis locates class in property, not income or social status. Modern capitalist economics suggest that class relates to income – we are regarded as working class if we earn, for instance, less than £20,000 per year. Dialectical materialism also suggests that class emerges as an aspect of a collective class-consciousness – a sense of commonality and solidarity based on a common social position within the class struggle.

Much modern literature refers to the idea of socio-economic status rather than class. Socio-economic status focuses on the interacting domains of income, occupation and prestige – not property or identity (Demarest et al., 1993; Krieger et al., 1997). Higher levels on each of these indices of relative wealth are seen as an index of purchasing power (Gallo and Matthews, 2003). Socio-economic status has been linked, for example, with health inequalities and difficulties with educational access and attainment. A low socio-economic status has negative consequences for social mobility. The construct of socio-economic status has been useful in the sense that it enables a consideration of relative wealth and its impact on social experience, using a more complex measure than simple property ownership. However, within this analysis a focus on consciousness – on class identity – is lost through a focus on objectively measurable indices such as occupation, education, income etc. It is this understanding of how our class identity is constituted and shifts over time that has largely been absent from social psychological theorising.

In social psychological work, class or socio-economic status is largely neglected. However, where present it is included largely as an independent variable on which social cognitive measures are compared. For example, Bowman et al. (2009) explored the impact of social class on attributional processes, anticipating that American working-class individuals would provide causal attributions that valued self-reliance, while middle-class individuals, who had greater material resources and more material choice would value personal control. They also found that working-class university students were more likely to attribute situationally than their middle-class counterparts. Stephens et al. (2007) studied the interaction of class with choice, finding that working-class participants tended to make choices based on similarity to others, while middle-class participants chose objects that made them stand out from the crowd.

The difficulty with these kinds of approaches to class is that they tend to position it as a property of individuals – as an individual, I bear a particular social class. Class is also positioned here as a static individual property, one that does not change over time and context. It is also understood as homogeneous, as if there were a solid 'thing' called middle class or working class that means the same thing to everyone. This is largely a result of fixing class as linked to observables such as job, income and education level, and not taking into account the full complexity of class identifications.

Consider, for example, the complexity of identification involved in being a working-class young person moving into an academic environment. It has been suggested that, for working-class women, getting an education, particularly a higher education, is a contradictory and often difficult experience (Lynch and O'Neill, 1994; Reay, 1998). Reay notes that *higher education is both hazardous and uncertain for working class women: an experience in which there are potential losses and gains* (Reay, 1998, p12). Education has a powerful impact on identity. Higher education is characterised by a series of practices and assumptions that are middle class in nature, and the process of gaining a degree necessarily implies class mobility and a shedding of key aspects of working-class identity. Hey (2003) suggests that working-class individuals moving into the academy experience an identity conflict: on the one hand, they feel the positive aspects of their new-found social mobility, but on the other hand they often feeling compelled to *fight back* in the *class competition*. She argues that, in gaining education and associated status, the connection to working-class origins is both intensely felt and irrevocably severed. Furthermore, the identity of 'working-class intellectual' is one that troubles everyday assumptions about both the academy and about class (Smith, 1988). The effect of these contradictory positions is to set working-class women adrift in academia, belonging neither in the new position of the academy nor in the old class background of childhood (Walkerdine, 1990). Hey (2003) argues that a politicised reading of class and academy requires attention to subjectivity.

> What I am suggesting here is that we need more than ever to recognise that it is the capacity of capital to simultaneously disorganise and permeate us that meets up with feminist theoretical/ political persistence in positioning the private, personal, local and intersectional as crucial.
>
> (Hey, 2003, p339)

In other words, to understand the complexity of class experience we cannot simply reduce it to an independent variable, or an individual trait. Rather, we need to understand the complexity of the way that it intersects with other aspects of social life (like gender, race, culture, etc.), the way that it shifts over time, how it functions as an aspect of lived social experience, and as an aspect of broader social and political life.

Where are we going to?

In this closing chapter of the book, we have sought to explore some of the aspects of social life that are often neglected and under-theorised in mainstream social psychology. We argue that for a coherently *social* social psychology to emerge, we need to attend to the preoccupation of social psychology with the individual as a relatively asocial entity. We need to explore more fully how complex social, economic and political phenomena function to constitute personal subjectivities – to understand how the person exists as a fully social being.

Critical thinking activity

Socialising social psychology

Transferable skill focus: analysis and evaluation

Key question: *How social are our social psychological knowledges?*

Choose one chapter from Chapters 1 to 8 of this book. Reread the chapter, and consider the following questions.

To what degree do the theoretical perspectives and research studies presented in this chapter make clear and explicit their own cultural locatedness and political and socioeconomic investments?

To what degree do they make clear and explicit issues around:

- class;

- sexualities;

- ethnicities;

- culture;

- political ideology.

Does the absence of an engagement with these issues mean that they are irrelevant to the issues covered in the chapter you are focusing on?

If not, what is the effect of their absence? What is obscured when they are not made explicit?

Critical thinking review

This activity helps synthesise your understanding of the key themes of this book by focusing on the analysis and evaluation of the content of one chapter of the book from a critical social perspective.

Other skills you may have used in this activity: critical thinking, reflection, recall of key principles and ideas.

Assignments

1. Can we understand social psychology without understanding the prevailing culture in which it is constructed?

2. To what degree does social psychology adequately theorise 'the social'?

Summary: what you have learned

In this chapter we have drawn together the critical threads of the book to develop a clearer understanding of the nature of the 'social' in social psychology. We have considered the nature of the individual that is at the heart of mainstream social psychological thinking, and have critically considered how this individual is a socially, culturally and economically located phenomenon. To develop this critical understanding, we have examined some of social psychology's absences and exclusions. We have considered the failure of much social psychology to engage with the cultural and ideological assumptions that characterise Western society, and have also explored the absence from mainstream social psychology of concerns around sexuality and particularly heteronormativity, the failure to engage with hegemonic whiteness, with disabilities, and with class. To complete your skill builder activity, you have explored in detail the nature of the social as conceptualised in the theory and research reviewed in one chapter of the book. In this way, you were able to draw together the critical themes of the book, and to understand the importance of keeping the social in social psychology.

Glossary

actor-observer effect	the tendency for actors to attribute their own behaviours to situational or external causes.
affirmative action	a process intended to combat discrimination by increasing representation of minority groups in certain arenas such as employment, education and so on.
altruism	the capacity to put the needs of others ahead of our own; the ability to self-sacrifice.
altruistic behaviour	behaviour that is intended to benefit others, with no particular concern for benefit to oneself.
always-already social	the idea that human beings are not born as encapsulated individuals, separate from but influenced by, the societies in which we live. Rather, we are understood to be permeated with sociality.
androgens	the male sex hormones, responsible for the development of male sex characteristics.
androgyny	a tendency to hold both masculine and feminine traits.
apartheid	an Afrikaans term that literally means 'separateness'. It refers to the legislated form of racial segregation that characterised South African society pre-1992.
attitude	a hypothetical mental construct that evaluates objects, people and events.
attribution theory	the theory of how people make causal explanations to make sense of other people and events.
audience inhibition	the tendency to be inhibited from taking action because of the presence of others. For example, we do not act because we worry that we are misinterpreting the situation and will be seen as silly or as overreacting.
authoritarian personality	a personality associated with a particular kind of oppressive family history and childhood, characterised by stringent and authoritarian parenting practice. The authoritarian personality is characterised by traditional, conventional values and attitudes and a tendency to place faith in a strong leader. It has been suggested that authoritarianism is linked with the form of racism associated with fascist ideology.
behaviourism	an approach that posits all behaviour as learned through experience.
bogus pipeline	a fake lie detector test that is used to encourage participant honesty.

bystander apathy	the tendency for witnesses to events not to intervene in emergency situations.
bystander intervention	helping activity by those witnessing an event where help is needed.
capitalism	the dominant economic system in the world today. It is a system in which the means of production (for example, natural resources, energy, factories etc.) are privately owned (for example, by individuals, local companies, multi-national corporations), and where production is geared to making a profit (Tormey, 2004).
chromosomes	the strand of DNA that carries genetic material and forms the basis for the transmission of inherited traits.
class	society's social strata, based on economic divisions (including income, property ownership, access to and control over the means of production) and also on a sense of identity or class consciousness. Typically, we refer to working, middle, upper middle and the upper classes.
co-constructed	refers to the manner in which interdependent terms are implied by each other. So, for example, the construct of marriage must necessarily imply the contrary state of singleness. The two terms co-construct one another. In relation to knowledge production, co-construction refers to the way that researchers and research participants build knowledge together.
cognitive dissonance	a state of disequilibrium produced when our attitudes and behaviour are not in harmony.
common-sense psychology	attempts to explain how laypeople develop their own ideas or theories about people and events; also referred to as naive psychology.
community reparation	a scheme in which offenders are ordered to do work that benefits the community.
companionate love	assumed to be a stable and enduring form of love, based primarily on shared intimacy, friendship and mutual respect.
compliance	changing your behaviour on the instruction or under the influence of another. Compliance also involves a response to a direct instruction from another person. It differs from persuasion in the sense that it targets behaviour change (regardless of shift in attitude), while persuasion is intended to change people's attitudes.

conformity	changing your attitudes or opinions as a result of social pressure. This can include conformity to the behaviour of a group, conformity in large groups (crowd behaviour, or what is sometimes termed 'mob psychology') and conformity to social norms.
controls	the various strategies and mechanisms used by researchers to ensure that their results in an experiment are a result of the manipulation of the independent variable(s) and not of extraneous or chance factors.
correspondence bias	see *fundamental attribution error*
correspondent inference	focuses on whether we attribute causes to a person's disposition (internal factors) or to external circumstances (external factors).
covariation model	suggests that we ascribe causes to people and events by running a complex cognitive analysis of possible causal factors.
crowd behaviour	crowds are seen as having their own social norms, which shape the behaviour of individuals within the crowd.
deindividuation	the loss of personal responsibility within social groups, often resulting in an erosion of social norms and values.
demand characteristics	our tendency to search for hints about how we are supposed to act in an experiment and (often unconsciously) change our behaviour to fit what we perceive to be the purpose of the experiment.
dependent variable	the variable in a study that is measured in order to see the impact of the manipulation of the *independent variable*.
deviance	behaviours that exceed or violate cultural norms.
dichotomy	a pair of ideas that are set in conceptual opposition, as complementary or mutually exclusive terms. Examples include masculine and feminine, white and black, self and other, nature and nurture.
diffusion of responsibility	the tendency in a group situation to see responsibility for action as shared, distributed among all members in a group. In relation to the question of bystander involvement, the tendency is to assume that someone else will take responsibility for taking action.
discourse analysis	a particular approach to the analysis of qualitative data that emphasises the productive effect of language (i.e. the idea that language does not (just)

represent the social world, but also has consequences for the way that we understand that world and our position within it).

dyadic interaction	an interaction between two people. A dyad, a group of two, is the smallest possible social group.
elaboration likelihood model	a model devised by Petty and Cacioppo (1986) that suggests that there are both direct and peripheral routes to persuasion. The persuasiveness of a communication may depend on factors relating to source, message and receiver, as well as emotional and contextual factors and heuristics. The most persuasive thing about a communication is not necessarily the message itself.
empathy	the emotional capacity to put yourself in the position of the person in the situation, and to understand the situation (both emotionally and intellectually) from their point of view.
epistemology	our assumptions about the relationship between the knower and the known, how the world might best be known. Epistemological questions are those about the nature and construction of knowledge itself. These are questions to do with how we know what we know.
ethnocentrism	a tendency to value your own ethnic group above others, and to see the world largely from within your own cultural value system.
evaluation apprehension	the anxiety that crops up from the sense of being observed in a study, which can confound research.
evolutionary psychology	a psychological approach that explores how human behaviour has emerged to ensure the biological survival of the species.
experimental method	in psychology, the use of the experimental method involves setting up contexts in which the researcher is able to control for extraneous variables, and manipulate the independent variable in order to observe its effect on the dependent variable. Participants in experimental research are randomly selected.
F scale	a personality test designed to measure the *authoritarian personality*.
false consensus effect	the tendency to overestimate how similar other people will be to us.
femininity	the culturally constructed qualities that constitute 'being a woman'. Often referred to in the plural as 'femininities'.

feminist	belonging to a diverse grouping of theoretical and ideological approaches, broadly united in a concern around power relations and gender inequality.
fundamental attribution error	the tendency to explain people's behaviour by ascribing dispositional or internal causes rather than situational or external ones; this idea has also been referred to as *over attribution* and *correspondence bias*.
gender	the culturally and socially constructed and historically located roles, behaviours and characteristics that are seen as appropriate for men and women. This is understood as different from sex, which refers to the biological properties of being male or female.
gender schema theory	a theory developed by Sandra Bem as an explanation of how an individual become gendered. She suggested that gendered information is transmitted through cognitive gender schemata.
gendered	having the characteristics of gender, or constructing gender differences.
hegemonic masculinity	the dominant form of masculinity within a culture – what Connell terms the 'winning styles' of masculinity.
hegemonic whiteness	the way that whiteness is positioned as a taken-for-granted 'norm' in Western culture, while other racial categories are positioned to articulate and define themselves against this presumed norm as 'different'.
helping behaviour	behaviour that is oriented towards helping others.
hermeneutic	concerned with interpretation and meaning.
heterogeneous	varied. For example, a heterogeneous group is one that is made up of people from a broad range of backgrounds and with a range of abilities etc.
heteronormative	refers to the pervasive cultural value that presumes heterosexuality is the norm, or the typical form of human relationship. It tends to be implicitly assumed, rather than explicitly expressed.
homogeneous group	a group in which all members are more or less the same, and share similar backgrounds, experiences and characteristics.
ideographic	refers to approaches that focus on the specific (in contrast to the generalising trend of nomothetic research); is concerned with the quality and texture of individual experience.
impersonal causality	the idea that the outcomes of a particular behaviour or choice were not necessarily intended by the actor; rather the effects of the action are understood to be unintentional or accidental.

in-group	a category of people presumed to be 'like me' in some way; the social group to which I see myself as belonging.
independent variable	the independent variable is the variable whose levels are manipulated in order to examine the impact of these changes on the dependent variable.
individual mobility	the ability to distance ourselves psychologically from low-status social groups with which we might be identified.
informational social influence	the assumption that other people's behaviour reflects an accurate interpretation of a particular situation. For example, in an emergency, we will often take our cue from other bystanders to decide how to act, as we assume that if they do not interpret the situation as an emergency, it probably isn't.
institutionally racist	practising racially based discrimination that is integral to the functioning of particular institutions or organisations.
interdependence	a quality of mutual dependency.
intergroup behaviour	the behaviours associated with the formation of social groups.
internalisation of oppression	suggests that members of oppressed groups adopt the negative stereotypes and internalise the negative treatment that is associated with their group membership, and may as a consequence begin to act in a manner that is consistent with this.
interpersonal process	a model of intimacy that suggests it is constructed from self-disclosure and partner responsiveness. We feel close to people when we reveal material about ourselves, and when we feel understood by our partner.
interpretative	an approach to research that values the subjective and interpretative work of the researcher.
intimacy	the subjective experience of closeness; characterised by a sense of close association and affiliation.
kin selection	an evolutionary mechanism that selects for traits and behaviours that increase the inclusive fitness of the donor. This refers to the selection of traits that increase the likelihood of survival of the genetic material of the individual animal and its genetic relatives. Animals may 'sacrifice' themselves for the good of the greater herd, as this is the best way to ensure the continuation of their own genetic material.
liberal humanism	an ideology that entrenches the value of individual rights and responsibilities, the notion of free choice, and the ideals of freedom and equality.

love stories	Sternberg suggested that our understanding of love is shaped by love stories – narrative structures that function as guiding metaphors for our romantic involvements.
love styles	Lee's six models of love (Eros, Pragma, Agape, Storge, Mania and Ludus).
masculinity	the culturally constructed qualities that constitute 'being a man'. Masculinity should not be conflated with male individuals – it functions as a discourse. As Connell and Messerschmidt (2005) note, *hegemonic masculinities can be constructed that do not correspond closely to the lives of any actual men*. Often referred to in the plural as 'masculinities'.
methodology	a theoretically guided set of methods and principles that guide the way we set about studying phenomena.
minority influence	the way that minority groups and minority group members influence the attitudes and behaviour of the majority group.
modern or symbolic racism	in the second half of the twentieth century, and the beginning of the twenty-first century, it is suggested that most racist practice is more subtle and covert. Racism is less frequently expressed in a direct and obvious way, but instead is embedded in institutional practices and in social arrangements that discriminate racially.
mundane realism	the extent to which an experimental situation is similar to real life.
naive psychology	see *common-sense psychology*
narratives	in psychology and social theory, narratives refer to the stories we tell about ourselves, to knit together a coherent self-identity.
naturalistic validity	the quality of being sufficiently true to life to have real-life applicability, thus making the study valid. Some experimental conditions are too artificial, too controlled, and consequently lack naturalistic validity.
nomethetic	the tendency to generalise.
normative	refers to the shared norms that shape social structure and social relationships.
normative social influence	how the behaviour and expressed attitudes of social groups influence us to conform to group norms.
obedience	compliance with the instructions of an authority figure.
observational learning	the process whereby behaviour is learned from the observation of a model.

observer effect	the idea that the mere act of observing conditions can act to change them.
oestrogens	the female sex hormones, responsible for the development of female sex characteristics.
ontological assumptions	our basic philosophical position on the nature of reality, and what can be known about reality.
operationalise	whereby the researcher renders the object of their study observable and measurable. (For example, in a study of depression, operationalisation might involve construction of a depression scale, which provides an observable and quantifiable measure of the relatively abstract and ephemeral construct 'depression'.)
out-group	a category of people presumed to be 'not like me' or 'other' in some way; the social group to which I do not see myself as belonging.
over attribution	see *fundamental attribution error*
passionate love	the kind of love that is primarily sexual, lust-based and exciting.
performative	not a pre-existing state that is 'real', but rather continually and variably enacted or 'performed' (for example, Judith Butler suggests that gender is performative).
personal causality	the idea that a person intended to cause an event, action or set of circumstances.
persuasion	a form of social influence that involves moving yourself or someone else towards a shift in attitude or behaviour.
phenomenal causality	the notion developed by Heider, which centres on the perception of causality.
phenomenological	refers to approaches that are concerned with an understanding of the subtle nuances and textures of people's experiences.
pluralistic ignorance	where the emergency is not treated as an emergency because the group does not define it as one.
positivism	(or more correctly in modern psychology, neopositivism) a philosophical orientation to knowledge production, based on a realist ontology, concerned with observation, prediction and control. The positivist researcher is interested only in that which is observable and testable.
postpositivism	an approach to scientific enquiry rooted in the principles of falsifiability.

prejudice	a general term for any negative attitude towards a social group, as in racial prejudice, gendered prejudice, anti-gay prejudice etc. Prejudice includes emotional, cognitive and behavioural components.
premenstrual syndrome	a set of physical and emotional responses characteristic of the phase just before the onset of menstruation.
prosocial behaviour	behaviour that is in the interests of others, or that is intended for the good of society.
prototype	a social cognitive term that refers to the most typical example of a phenomenon.
psychodynamic	based on the work of Freud, this approach suggests that human behaviour is produced through a complex interaction of unconscious and conscious processes.
psychometric tests	tests designed to measure particular psychological qualities, enabling researchers to operationalise and measure abstract psychological states.
psychopathology	diagnosable, individual mental health difficulties.
qualitative approaches	approaches that are oriented to an understanding of meanings, experiences and understandings of our social worlds, and are rooted in primarily textual and interpretative data.
quantitative approaches	approaches that use numerical measurement and numerical quantities.
random selection	the process of drawing research participants from the population in such a way that all members of the population have an equal chance of inclusion in the sample, and each individual's inclusion in the sample in no way precludes the inclusion of another member of the population.
realistic conflict theory	a theory developed by Muzafer Sherif, Carolyn Sherif and their colleagues to explore the possibility that intergroup phenomena, like racial conflict, might be linked to conflict over limited material resources.
reciprocity	responding to behaviour in kind: so responding with a positive behaviour to a positive behaviour, and reacting to a negative behaviour with a negative one. This kind of reciprocity is understood to be the basis for social exchange.
reflexive	engaged in the process in qualitative research whereby researchers attempt to make clear the way that their own stance, positionalities, investments and desires shape the knowledges they produce. Researchers must reflect on their

own position in the research, how their own view of the world is embedded within and constructs the research.

restorative justice	a legal process in which dialogue is opened up between the victim and offender, which gives the offender an opportunity to put right the harm they have done to the victim.
schema	cognitive structures that draw together the information individuals hold on specific subjects. They are akin to files within a filing cabinet. We hold schema, for example, on gender and shopping, or gender and mathematics.
segregation	practices of racial separation, usually legislated (for example, the rule that African Americans had to sit at the back of the bus in the US in the 1950s).
self-efficacy	an individual's belief in their own capacity to do something.
selfish gene theory	an approach to understanding evolutionary processes as driven by genetic processes. Species behaviour is seen as being oriented to the survival of a particular genetic endowment. Because of this, evolutionary psychology suggests that all behaviour is ultimately 'selfish' (not at the personal or individual level – this is not a self-conscious process) in that it is oriented towards species survival.
sex differences	in psychology, this tends to refer to the presumption that the biological differences between men and women are directly associated with consistent differences in cognitive, social, emotional and behavioural traits and abilities.
sex hormones	the hormones that trigger the development of both primary and secondary sex characteristics.
social categorisation	categorising people into groups on the basis of the perception of common attributes.
social change	the ability to change the social conditions that structure social categorisation or that inform social comparisons.
social comparison	the process whereby individuals compare their perceived in-groups and perceived out-groups on key indices.
social constructionism	a philosophical approach to knowledge production that suggests that what we understand as 'reality' and particularly our 'social reality' is itself socially constituted, as is our knowledge of that social reality.
social creativity	a strategy that involves redefining the characteristics of the derogated social group as positive.

social desirability	research participants' desire to be seen as socially appropriate, and the accompanying tendency to fit our behaviour to our perception of what is seen as socially desirable.
social exchange theory	a theory that suggests that we make decisions about how to behave in our relationships on the basis of a cost-benefit analysis. On the basis of this analysis, human beings tend to behave in the way that has the optimal predicted outcome for them.
social facilitation	when task performance is improved by the presence of others.
social identity	an aspect of self derived from our perceived membership of social groups.
social identity theory	a theory that attempts to explain the psychological processes that underpin intergroup discrimination. In particular, the theory is concerned with the minimal conditions under which intergroup discrimination will be observed.
social influence	the process whereby individual behaviour is influenced by the actions, statements and beliefs of other individuals. This process can take place as a consequence of both individual action and group process.
social learning theory	a theory developed by Bandura as an explanation of how young people acquire behaviour. The theory suggests that this takes place primarily through observational learning and role models.
social loafing	our tendency to put less effort into group activity, based on the perception that 'someone else will do it' if we don't.
social mobility	the ability to move from one social group to another.
social representations	collective, shared knowledge that people use to understand their social world.
social responsibility	suggests that we should help those who are not in a position to help themselves or others.
social roles	socially defined and prescribed sets of behaviours and attitudes that are seen to 'fit' a particular social position.
stereotype	an over-generalised belief about the characteristics of people, based on their group membership.
subjective	taking a particular stance that is perspectival in its nature, that is shaped by the location and understandings of the viewer.

suggestibility	the tendency to be influenced by others.
theory of planned behaviour	makes similar assumptions to the *theory of reasoned action*, but also factors into the decision-making process the individuals' perceived behavioural control – how much say they feel they have in their ability to perform a particular behaviour.
theory of reasoned action	offers a theoretical explanation of the relationship between attitudes and behaviour. The approach suggests that, before we choose to behave in a particular way, we consider the possible outcomes and implications of our actions, and that this is done in a rational way.
triangular theory of love	Sternberg's model, which suggests that love is composed of three intersecting parts – intimacy, passion and commitment.
universal egoism	the idea that human beings are fundamentally selfish, and that human behaviour is oriented to looking after oneself.
validity	the extent to which a study or research situation reflects the idea or concept that the researcher is attempting to measure.
vignette	a hypothetical scenario(s) or set of stories that are presented to participants in research studies as a method to elicit and collect responses, which will form part of a data set.
Yale model of persuasive communication	a model that suggests that persuasive communications are composed of three variables: the source, the message and the receiver.

References

Aderman, D and Berkowitz, L (1970) Observational set, empathy, and helping. *Journal of Personality and Social Psychology*, 14(2), 141–8.

Adler, A (1917) *The Neurotic Constitution*. New York: Moffat, Yard and Company.

Adorno, TW, Frenkel-Brunswik, E, Levinson, DJ and Sanford, RN (1950) *The Authoritarian Personality*. New York: Harper.

Ahn, W-K, Kalish, CW, Medin, DL and Gelman, SA (1995) The role of covariation versus mechanism information in causal attribution. *Cognition*, 54, 299–352.

Ajzen, I (1988) *Attitudes, Personality and Behaviour*. Milton Keynes: Open University Press.

Ajzen, I (2005) *Attitudes, Personality, and Behaviour*. 2nd edition. Milton Keynes: Open University Press (McGraw-Hill).

Ajzen, I and Albarracín, D (2007) Predicting and changing behavior: a reasoned action approach, in Ajzen, I, Albarracín, D, Hornik, R (eds) *Prediction and Change of Health Behavior*. Mahwah, NJ: Lawrence Erlbaum Associates.

Ajzen, I and Fishbein, M (1980) *Understanding Attitudes and Predicting Social Behaviour*. Englewood Cliffs, NJ: Prentice Hall.

Ajzen, I and Fishbein, M (2005) The influence of attitudes on behaviour, in Albarracín, D, Johnson, BT and Zanna, MP (eds) *The Handbook of Attitudes* (pp173–221). Mahwah, NJ: Erlbaum.

Ali, A, Caplan, PJ and Fagnant, R (2010) Gender stereotypes in diagnostic criteria, in Chrisler, J and McCreary, D (eds) *Handbook of Gender Research in Psychology*. New York: Springer Publishing.

Allan HT, Larsen, JA, Bryan, K and Smith, P (2004) The social reproduction of institutional racism: Internationally recruited nurses' experiences of the British health services. *Diversity in Health and Social Care*, 1(2), 117–26.

Allen, VL and Levine, JM (1969) Consensus and conformity. *Journal of Experimental Social Psychology*, 5, 389–99.

Allport, GW (1935) Attitudes, in Murchison, CM (ed) *Handbook of Social Psychology* (pp789–844). Worcester, MA: Clark University Press.

Allport, GW (1954) *The Nature of Prejudice*. Cambridge, MA: Perseus.

Alnuaimi, O, Robert, LP and Maruping, LM (2010) Team size, dispersion, and social loafing in technology-supported teams: A theory of moral disengagement perspective. *Journal of Management Information Systems*, 27(1), 203–30.

Altemeyer, B (1981) *Right-wing Authoritarianism*. Winnipeg: University of Manitoba Press.

Altemeyer, B (1998) The other 'authoritarian personality', in Zanna, M (ed) *Advances in Experimental Social Psychology* (pp47–92). San Diego, CA: Academic Press.

Alvaro, EM and Crano, WD (1996) Cognitive responses to minority- or majority-based communications: factors that underlie minority influence. *British Journal of Social Psychology*, 35(1), 105–21.

Anderson, I and Doherty, K (2008) *Accounting for Rape: Psychology, Feminism and Discourse Analysis in the Study of Sexual Violence*. London: Routledge.

Antaki, C (1994) *Explaining and Arguing: The Social Organisation of Accounts*. London: Sage.

Anthias, F (2002) Where do I belong? Narrating collective identity and translocational positionality. *Ethnicities*, 2, 277–85.

Archer, J (2004) Sex differences in aggression in real world settings: a meta analytic review. *Review of General Psychology*, 8, 291–322.

Arendell, T (1999) Hegemonic motherhood: deviancy discourses and employed mothers' accounts of out-of school time issues, Working Paper 9. Berkeley, CA: Center for Working Families.

Aron, A and Westbay, L (1996) Dimensions of the prototype of love. *Journal of Personality and Social Psychology*, 70(3), 535–51.

Aronson, E (1969) The theory of cognitive dissonance: a current perspective. *Advances in Experimental Social Psychology*, 4, 1–34.

Aronson, E and Carlsmith, JM (1963) Effects of severity of threat in the devaluation of forbidden behavior. *Journal of Abnormal and Social Psychology,* 66, 584–8.

Aronson, E and Mills, J (1959) The effect of severity of initiation on liking for a group. *Journal of Abnormal and Social Psychology,* 59, 177–81.

Asch, SE (1955a) Opinions and social pressure. *Scientific American*, 193, 31–5.

Asch, SE (1955b) Studies of independence and conformity: a minority of one against a unanimous majority. *Psychological Monographs,* 70 (416).

Astana, A (2010) Britain's divided schools, *The Observer,* 10 October. Downloaded from www.guardian.co.uk/education/2010/oct/10/britains-divided-school-system-report (accessed 30 December 2010).

Athanasiou, R and Green, P (1973) Physical attractiveness and helping behavior. *Proceedings of the 81st Annual Convention of the American Psychological Association*, 8, 289–90.

Augoustinos, M and Walker, I (*1995*) *Social Cognition: An Integrated Introduction*. London: Sage.

Avdeyeva, TV, Burgetova, K and Welch, ID (2006) To help or not to help? Factors that determined helping responses to Katrina victims. *Analyses of Social Issues and Public Policy*, 6(1), 159–73.

Baddeley, A (2007) *Working Memory: Thought and Action*. Oxford: Oxford University Press.

Bandura, A (1977) *Social Learning Theory*. Englewood Cliffs, NJ: Prentice Hall.

Banyard, V, Moynihan, MM, and Plante, E (2007) Sexual violence prevention through bystander intervention: an experimental evaluation. *Journal of Community Psychology*, 35, 463–81.

Bartlett, FC (1932) *Remembering: A Study of Experimental and Social Psychology*. Cambridge: Cambridge University Press.

Baron-Cohen, S (2005) The essential difference: the male and female brain. *Phi Kappa Phi Forum*, 85(1), 23–27.

Baron-Cohen, S (2011) *Zero Degrees of Empathy: A New Theory of Human Cruelty*. London: Penguin/Allen Lane.

Baron, R, Branscombe, NR and Byrne, D (2008) *Social Psychology*. 12th edition. London: Pearson.

Batson, CD (1991) *The Altruism Question: Toward a Social-Psychological Answer*. Hillsdale, NJ: Erlbaum.

Batson, CD and Coke, JS (1981) Empathy: a source of altruistic motivation for helping?, in Rushton, JP and Sorrentino, RM (eds) *Altruism and Helping Behavior* (pp167–87). Hillsdale, NJ: Erlbaum.

Batson, CD and Shaw, LL (1991) Evidence for altruism: toward a pluralism of prosocial motives. *Psychological Inquiry* 2(2), 107–22.

Batson, CD, Early, S and Salvarini, G (1997) Perspective taking: imagining how another feels versus imagining how you would feel. *Personality and Social Personality Bulletin*, 23, 751–8.

Batson, CD, van Lange, PAM, Ahmad, N and Lishner, DA (2003) Altruism and helping behaviour, in Hogg, MA and Cooper, J (eds) *The Sage Handbook of Social Psychology* (pp279–95). London: Sage.

Baxter, J, Hewitt, B and Haynes, M (2008) Lifecourse transitions and housework: marriage, parenthood and time on housework. *Journal of Marriage and Family*, 70(2), 259–272.

Bell, D and Heitmueller, A (2009) The Disability Discrimination Act in the UK: helping or hindering employment among the disabled. *Journal of Health Economics*, 28(2), 465–80.

Belsky, J and Pensky, E (1988) Marital change across the transition to parenthood. *Marriage and Family Review*, 12, 133–56.

Bem, SL (1972) *Psychology Looks at Sex Roles: Where Have all the Androgynous People Gone?* Paper presented at the UCLA Symposium on Sex Roles.

Bem, SL (1974) The measurement of psychological androgyny. *Journal of Consulting and Clinical Psychology,* 42, 155–62.

Bem, SL (1985) Androgyny and gender schema theory: a conceptual and empirical integration, in Sonderegger, TB and Anatasi, A (eds) *Psychology and Gender* (pp179–226). Lincoln: University of Nebraska Press.

Ben-Ner, A, McCall, BP, Stephane, M and Wang, H (2009) Identity and in-group and out-group differentiation in work and giving behaviors: experimental evidence. *Journal of Economic Behavior and Organization*, 72, 153–70.

Ben-Zeev, T, Carrasquillo, CM, Ching, A, Kliengklom, TJ, McDonald, KL, Newhall, DC, Patton, GE, Stewart, TD, Stoddard, T, Inzlicht, M and Fein, S (2005) "Math is hard!" (Barbie, 1994): Responses of threat vs. challenge mediated arousal to stereotypes alleging intellectual inferiority, in Gallagher, AM and Kaufman, JC (eds) *Gender Differences in Mathematics* (pp189–206). Cambridge: Cambridge University Press.

Bennington, G and Derrida, J (1999) *Jacques Derrida*. Chicago: University of Chicago Press.

Bentler, PM and Speckart, G (*1979*) Models of attitude-behavior relations. *Psychological Review*, 86, 452–64.

Berkowitz, L (ed) *Advances in Experimental Social Psychology* (vol 19, pp123–205). New York: Academic Press.

Berscheid, E, and Walster, EH (1969) *Interpersonal Attraction*. 1st edition. Reading, MA: Addison-Wesley.

Berscheid, E and Walster, EH (1978) *Interpersonal Attraction*. 2nd edition. Reading, MA: Addison-Wesley.

Betancourt, H (1990) An attribution-empathy model of helping behavior: behavioral interventions and judgments of help-giving. *Personality and Social Psychology Bulletin*, 16, 573–91.

Billig, M (1982) *Ideology and Social Psychology*. Oxford: Blackwell.

Billig, M (1987) *Arguing and Thinking: A Rhetorical Approach to Social Psychology*. Cambridge: Cambridge University Press.

Billig, M (1988) The notion of 'prejudice': some rhetorical and ideological aspects. *Interdisciplinary Journal for the Study of Discourse*, 8(1–2), 91–110.

Billig, M (1995) *Banal Nationalism*. London: Sage.

Björkqvist, K, Lagerspetz, KMJ and Kaukiainen, A (1992) Do girls manipulate and boys fight? Developmental trends in regards to direct and indirect aggression. *Aggressive Behaviour*, 18(2), 117–27.

Blair, T (1999) Speech to the Labour Party Conference, Brighton, 28 September. Available at http://news.bbc.co.uk/1/hi/uk_politics/460009.stm

Blakemore, JEO, Lawton, CA and Vartanian, LR (2005) I can't wait to get married: gender differences in drive to marry. *Sex Roles*, 53, 327–335.

Blass, T (2004) *The Man Who Shocked the World: The Life and Legacy of Stanley Milgram*. New York: Basic Books.

Bolger, N, Zuckerman, A and Kessler, RC (2000) Invisible support and adjustment to stress. *Journal of Personality and Social Psychology*, 79, 953–61.

Boninger, DS, Krosnick, JA, Berent, MK and Fabrigar, LR (1995) The causes and consequences of attitude importance, in Petty, RE and Krosnick, JA (eds) *Attitude Strength: Antecedents and Consequences*. Hillsdale, NJ: Erlbaum.

Bowes-Sperry, L and O'Leary-Kelly, AZ (2005) To act or not to act: the dilemma faced by sexual harassment observers. *Academy of Management Review*, 30(2), 288–306.

Bowman, NA, Kitiyama, S and Nesbitt, RA (2009) Social class differences in self, attribution, and attention: socially expansive individualism of middle-class Americans. *Personality and Social Psychology Bulletin*, 35(7), 880–93.

BPS (2009) *Ethical Code of Conduct*. Available at www.bps.org.uk/what-we-do/ethics-standards/ethics-standards

Brannigan, A (2004) *The Rise and Fall of Social Psychology: The Use and Misuse of the Experimental Method*. New Jersey: Aldine Transaction.

Breckler, SJ (1984) Empirical validation of affect, behavior, and cognition as distinct components of attitude. *Journal of Personality and Social Psychology*, 47, 1191–205.

Brehm, JW (1956) Postdecision changes in the desirability of alternatives. *Journal of Abnormal and Social Psychology*, 52, 384–9.

Brewer, MB (2001) In-group identification and intergroup conflict: when does in-group love become out-group hate?, in Ashmore, R, Jussim, L and Wilder, D (eds) *Social Identity, Intergroup Conflict and Conflict Reduction*. New York: Oxford University Press.

Brown, RJ (1996) *Prejudice*. Oxford: Blackwell.

Brown, R and Hewstone, M (2005) An integrative theory of intergroup contact, in Zanna, M (ed) *Advances in Experimental Social Psychology*, 37, 255–343.

Browning, CR (1998) *Ordinary Men: Reserve Police Battalion 101 and the Final Solution in Poland*. New York: Harper Perennial.

Bruner, J (1990) *Acts of Meaning*. Cambridge, MA: Harvard University Press.

Bryman, A (2001) *Social Research Methods*. Oxford: Oxford University Press.

Burger, JM (2009) Replicating Milgram: would people still obey today? *American Psychologist*, 64, 1–11.

Burgoon, M (1995) Language expectancy theory: elaboration, explication and extension, in Berger, CR and Burgoon, M (eds) *Communication and Social Influence Processes* (pp29–51). East Lansing, MI: Michigan State University Press.

Burman, E (2003) Discourse analysis means doing discourse. *Discourse Analysis Online*. www.shu. ac.uk/daol/articles/open/2003/003/burman2003003.html (retrieved 10 January 2011.)

Bussey, K and Bandura, A (*1999*) Social cognitive theory of gender development and differentiation. *Psychological Review*, 106, 676–713.

Butler, J (1990) *Gender Trouble*. London: Routledge.

Butler, J (1993) *Bodies that Matter: On the Discursive Limits of 'Sex'*. London: Routledge.

Cadinu, MR and Rothbart, M (1996) Self-anchoring and differentiation processes in the minimal group setting. *Journal of Personality and Social Psychology*, 70(4), 661–77.

Calhoun, LG, Selby, JW and Warring, LJ (1976) Social perception of the victim's causal role in rape: an exploratory examination of four factors. *Human Relations*, 29(6), 517–26.

Callaghan, J (2008) *Becoming Professionals: South African Women Students' Accounts of Applied Psychology Training*. Manchester: Unpublished doctoral thesis.

Callaghan, J and Clark, J (2006) Feminist theory and conflict, in Shefer, T, Boonzaier, F and Kiquwa, P (2006) *The Gender of Psychology*. Cape Town: Juta.

Campbell, R and Wasco, S (2000) Feminist approaches to social science: epistemological and methodological tenets. *American Journal of Community Psychology,* 28(6), 773–91.

Capdevila, R and Callaghan, JEM (2008) It's not racist, it's common sense: a discursive analysis of political discourse around asylum and immigration in the UK. *Journal of Community and Applied Social Psychology*, 18: 1–16.

Capdevila, C, Ciclitira, K, Lazard, L and Marzano, L (2006) 'If I am woman, who are they?' The construction of 'other' feminisms. *Psychology of Women Section Review*, 8(2), 23–31.

Carrigan, T, Connell, R and Lee, J (1985) Toward a new sociology of masculinity. *Theory and Society,* 14(5), 551–604.

Case, KE (2004) *Principles of Macroeconomics*. London: Prentice Hall.

Ceci, SJ and Bruck, M (1993) Suggestibility of the child witness: a historical review and synthesis. *Psychological Bulletin*, 113, 403–39.

Chaiken, S (1979) Communicator physical attractiveness and persuasion. *Journal of Personality and Social Psychology*, 37, 1387–97.

Chaiken, S (1986) Physical appearance and social influence, in Herman, CP, Zanna, MP and Higgins, ET (eds) *Physical Appearance, Stigma, and Social Behavior: The Ontario Symposium* (vol 3, pp143–77). Hillsdale, NJ: Lawrence Erlbaum.

Cialdini, RB (2001a) *Influence, Science and Practice*. 4th edition. Boston: Allyn and Bacon.

Cialdini, RB (2001b) The science of persuasion. *Scientific American*, 284, 76–81.

Clark, E, McCann, TV, Rowe, K and Lazenbatt, A (2004) Cognitive dissonance and undergraduate nursing students' knowledge of, and attitudes about, smoking. *Journal of Advanced Nursing,* 46(6), 586–93.

Clark, KB and Clark, MP (1947) Racial identification and preference in Negro children, in Newcomb, TM and Hartley, EL (eds) *Reading in Social Psychology*. New York: Holt, Rinehart and Winston.

Clark, RD and Maass, A (1990) The effects of majority size on minority influence. *European Journal of Social Psychology*, 20, 99–117.

Claxton, A and Perry-Jenkins, M (2008) No fun anymore: leisure and marital quality across the transition to parenthood. *Journal of Marriage and Family,* 70(1), 28–43.

Clement, RW and Krueger, J (2002) Social categorization moderates social projection. *Journal of Experimental Social Psychology*, 38, 219–31.

Cocking, C, Drury, J and Reicher, S (2007) Bystander interventions during the July 7th London bombings: an account of survivors' experiences. *British Psychological Society Social Psychology Section Annual Conference*. University of Kent at Canterbury, September.

Coles, R (1997) *The moral intelligence of children*. New York: Random House.

Collins, K (2010) Two studies show gender discrimination in the workplace continues. *The Diversity Factor*, 18(4), 21–6.

Condry, J and Condry, S (1976) Sex differences: a study of the eye of the beholder. *Child Development,* 47, 812–19.

Connell, RW (1987) *Gender and Power*. Stanford, CA: Stanford University Press.

Connell, RW (1995) *Masculinities*. 2nd edition. Cambridge: Polity Press.

Connell, RW and Messerschmidt, JW (2005) Hegemonic masculinity: rethinking the concept. *Gender and Society*, 19(6), 829–59.

Conner, M and McMillan, B (1999) Interaction effects in the theory of planned behaviour: studying cannabis use. *British Journal of Social Psychology*, 38(2), 195–222.

Conner, M and Sparks, P (2002) Ambivalence and attitudes. *European Review of Social Psychology*, 12, 37–70.

Conrad, P (1987) The experience of illness: recent and new directions. *Research in the Sociology of Health Care*, 6, 1–31.

Correia, H and Broderick, P (2009) Access to reproductive technologies by single women and lesbians: social representations and public debate. *Journal of Community and Applied Social Psychology*, 19, 241–256.

Cottrell, NB (1972) Social facilitation, in McClintock, C (ed) *Experimental Social Psychology* (pp185–236). New York: Holt, Rinehart and Winston.

Cowan, P and Cowan, C (2000) *When Partners Become Parents: The Big Life Change for Couples.* Mahwah, NJ: Erlbaum.

Cowan, P and Cowan, C (2003) Normative family transitions, normal family process, and healthy child development, in Walsh, F (ed) *Normal Family Processes.* 3rd edition. New York: The Guilford Press.

Cowan, P, Cowan, C, Heming, G, Garrett, E, Coysh, W, Curtis-Boles, H and Boles, A (1985) Transition to parenthood: his, hers, and theirs. *Journal of Family Issues*, 6, 451–82.

Cramer, RE, Mcmaster, MR, Bartell, PA and Dragna, M (1988) Subject competence and minimization of the bystander effect. *Journal of Applied Social Psychology*, 18, 1133–48.

Crandall, CS (1988) The social contagion of binge eating. *Journal of Personality and Social Psychology*, 55, 588–98.

Cross, TP and Saxe, L (2001) Polygraph testing and sexual abuse: the lure of the magic lasso. *Child Maltreatment*, 6, 195–206.

Crowne, BP and Liverant, S (1963) Conformity under varying conditions of personal commitment. *Journal of Abnormal and Social Psychology*, 66, 547–55.

Crump, D (2008) The social psychology of evil: can the law prevent groups from making good people go bad? *Brigham Young University Law Review*, 5, 1441–564.

Daly, KJ (1996) *Families and Time: Keeping Pace in a Hurried Culture.* Thousand Oaks, CA: Sage.

Darker, CD and French, DP (2009) What sense do people make of a Theory of Planned Behaviour questionnaire? A think-aloud study. *Journal of Health Psychology*, 14, 861–71.

Darker, CD, French, DP, Eves, FF and Sniehotta, FF (2010) An intervention to promote walking amongst the general population based on an 'extended' Theory of Planned Behaviour: a waiting list randomised controlled trial. *Psychology and Health*, 25(1), 71–88.

David, B and Turner, JC (1999) Studies in self-categorization and minority conversion: the in-group minority in intragroup and intergroup contexts. *British Journal of Social Psychology*, 38, 115–34.

Davies, M (1996) EPQ correlates of love styles. *Personality and Individual Differences*, 20(2), 257–9.

Davison, WP (1983) The third-person effect in communication. *Public Opinion Quarterly*, 47(1), 1–15.

Dawkins, R (1973, 2006) *The Selfish Gene*. New York: Oxford University Press.

De Vos, J (2009) Now that you know, how do you feel? The Milgram Experiment and Psychologization. *Annual Review of Critical Psychology*, 7, 223–46.

Demarest, EJ, Reisner, ER, Anderson, LM, Humphrey, DC, Farquhar, E and Stein, SE (1993) *Review of Research on Achieving the Nation's Readiness Goal*. Washington, DC: Department of Education.

Denzin, NK (2002) Cowboys and Indians. *Symbolic Interaction*, 25, 251–61.

Denzin, NK and Lincoln, YS (2005) *The Sage Handbook of Qualitative Methods*. London: Sage.

Deutsch, M and Gerard, HB (1955) A study of normative and informational social influences upon individual judgment. *Journal of Abnormal and Social Psychology*, 51, 629–36.

Dixon, JA and Durrheim, K (2003) Contact and the ecology of racial division: some varieties of informal segregation. *British Journal of Social Psychology*, 42, 1–24.

Douglas, KM and Sutton, RM (2004) Right about others, wrong about ourselves? Actual and perceived self-other differences in resistance to persuasion. *British Journal of Social Psychology*, 43 (4), 585–603.

Dovidio, J (1984) Helping behaviour and altruism: an empirical and conceptual overview, in Berkowitz, L (ed) *Advances in Experimental Social Psychology* (vol 17, pp361–427). New York: Academic Press.

Dovidio, JF (2006) *The Social Psychology of Prosocial Behaviour*. Mahwah, NJ: Ehrlbaum.

Dovidio, JF, Piliavin, JA, Gaertner, SL, Schroeder, DA and Clark, RD (1991) The arousal cost-reward model and the process of intervention: a review of the evidence, in Clark, MS (ed) *Prosocial Behaviour: Review of Personality and Social Psychology*. London: Sage.

Drury, J, Cocking, C and Reicher, S (2009) Everyone for themselves? A comparative study of crowd solidarity among emergency survivors. *British Journal of Social Psychology*, 48(3), 487–506.

Duckitt, J (1992) *The Social Psychology of Prejudice*. Westport, CT: Praeger.

Duckitt, J (2001) A dual-process cognitive-motivational theory of ideology and prejudice. *Advances in Experimental Social Psychology*, 33, 41–113.

Duckitt, J (2003) Prejudice and intergroup conflict, in Sears, DO, Huddy, L and Jervis, R (eds) *Oxford Handbook of Political Psychology*. New York: Oxford University Press.

Duckitt, J and Mphuthing, T (1998) Group identification and intergroup attitudes: a longitudinal analysis in South Africa. *Journal of Personality and Social Psychology*, 74, 80–5.

Duriez, B and Soenens, B (2009) The intergenerational transmission of racism: the role of right-wing authoritarianism and social dominance orientation. *Journal of Research in Personality,* 43(5), 906–9.

Durrheim, K and Dixon, JA (2005) *Racial Encounter: The Social Psychology of Contact and Desegregation.* London: Psychology Press.

Duxbury, LE and Higgins, CA (1991) Gender differences in work–family conflict. *Journal of Applied Psychology,* 76: 60–74.

Eagly, AH (1987) *Sex Difference in Social Behavior: A Social-Role Interpretation.* Hillsdale, NJ: Erlbaum.

Eagly, AH (2009) The his and hers of prosocial behavior: an examination of the social psychology of gender. *American Psychologist,* 64(8), 644–58.

Eagly, AH and Chaiken, S (1993) *The Psychology of Attitudes.* Fort Worth, TX: Harcourt Brace Jovanovich.

Eagly, AH and Crowley, M (1986) Gender and helping behavior: a meta-analytic review of the social psychological literature. *Psychological Bulletin,* 100(3), 283–308.

Eagly, AH, Wood, W and Chaiken, S (1978) Causal inferences about communicators and their effects on opinion change. *Journal of Personality and Social Psychology,* 36, 424–35.

Edwards, D (2006) Discourse, cognition and social practice: the rich surface of language and social interaction. *Discourse Studies*, 8(1), 41–9.

Eisenberg, N and Mussen, P (1989) *The Roots of Prosocial Behavior in Children.* Cambridge: Cambridge University Press.

Entzinger, H (2003) The rise and fall of multiculturalism: the case of the Netherlands, in Joppke, C and Morawska, E (eds) *Toward Assimilation and Citizenship: Immigrants in Liberal Nation States* (pp59–86). London: Palgrave.

Epstein, D (1997) Keeping them in their place: hetero/sexist harassment, gender and the enforcement of heterosexuality, in Thomas, AM and Kitzinger, C (eds) *Sexual Harassment: Contemporary Feminist Perspectives* (pp115–31). Buckingham: Open University Press.

Everson, ES, Daley, AJ and Ussher, M (2007) Brief report: the theory of planned behaviour applied to physical activity in young people who smoke. *Journal of Adolescence,* 30, 347–51.

Every, D and Augustinos, M (2008) Taking advantage or fleeing persecution?: opposing accounts of asylum seeking. *Journal of Sociolinguistics*, 12(5): 648–67.

Fade, S (2004) Using interpretative phenomenological analysis for public health nutrition and dietetic research: a practical guide. *Proceedings of the Nutrition Society*, 63, 647–53.

Fagot, BI (1978) The influences of sex of child on parental reactions to toddler children. *Child Development*, 49, 459–65.

Fagot, BI and Leinbach, MD (1989) The young child's gender schema: environmental input, internal organization. *Child Development*, 60(3), 663–72.

Fairclough, N (1992) Discourse and text: linguistic intertextual analysis within discourse analysis. *Discourse and Society*, 3(2), 193–217.

Fazio, RH (2000) Accessible attitudes as tools for object appraisal: their costs and benefits, in Maio, GR and Olson, JM (eds) *Why We Evaluate: Functions of Attitudes*. Mahwah, NJ: Erlbaum.

Febbraro, AR (2003) Alpha bias and beta bias in research on labour and love: the case of enhancement versus scarcity. *Feminism and Psychology*, 13(2), 201–23.

Fehr, B (1988) Prototype analysis of the concepts of love and commitment. *Journal of Personality and Social Psychology*, 55(4), 557–79.

Fehr, B (2004) Intimacy expectations in same-sex friendships: a prototype interaction-pattern model. *Journal of Personality and Social Psychology*, 86(2), 265–84.

Fehr, B and Russell, JA (1991) The concept of love viewed from a prototype perspective. *Journal of Personality and Social Psychology*, 60(3), 425–38.

Festinger, L (1954) A theory of social comparison processes. *Human Relations*, 7, 117–40.

Festinger, L and Carlsmith, JM (1959) Cognitive consequences of forced compliance. *Journal of Abnormal and Social Psychology*, 58, 203–10.

Fishbein, M and Ajzen, I (1972) Beliefs, attitudes, intentions and behaviour. *Annual Review of Psychology*, 81, 487–544.

Fishbein, M and Ajzen, I (1974) Attitudes towards objects as predictors of single and multiple behavioural criteria. *Psychological Review*, 81(1), 29–74.

Fishbein, M and Ajzen, I (1975) *Belief, Attitude, Intention, and Behavior: An Introduction to Theory and Research*. Reading, MA: Addison-Wesley.

Fiske, ST and Linville, PW (1980) What does the schema concept buy us? *Personality and Social Psychology Bulletin*, 6(4), 543–57.

Fiske, ST and Taylor, SE (1984) *Social Cognition*. Reading, MA: Addison-Wesley.

Fiske, ST and Taylor, SE (1991) *Social Cognition*. 2nd edition. New York: McGraw-Hill.

Fiske, ST, Cuddy, AJ, Glick, P and Xu, J (2002) A model of (often mixed) stereotype content: competence and warmth respectively follow from perceived status and competition. *Journal of Personality and Social Psychology*, 82, 878–902.

Fiske, ST, Gilbert, DT and Lindzey, G (eds) (2010) *Handbook of Social Psychology*. 5th edition. New York: Wiley.

Foucault, M (1972) *The Archaeology of Knowledge*. London: Routledge.

Foucault, M (1975) *Discipline and Punish: The Birth of the Prison*. New York: Vintage Books.

Foucault, M (1976) *The History of Sexuality, Vol. 1: The Will to Knowledge*. London: London.

Fox Keller, E (1985) *Reflections on Gender and Science*. London: Yale University Press.

Fredrickson, GM (1999) Models of American ethnic relations: a historical perspective, in Prentice, DA and Miller, DT (eds) *Cultural Divides: Understanding and Overcoming Group Conflict* (pp23–34). New York: Russell Sage Foundation.

Fussell, E (2006) Leaving New Orleans: social stratification, networks, and hurricane evacuation. *Understanding Katrina: Perspectives from the Social Sciences, the Forum of the Social Science Research Council.*

Gallo, LC and Matthews, KA (2003) Understanding the association between socioeconomic status and physical health: do negative emotions play a role? *Psychological Bulletin*, 129(1), 10–51.

Gannon, TA (2006) Increasing honest responding on cognitive distortions in child molesters: the bogus pipeline procedure. *Journal of Interpersonal Violence*, 21(3), 358–75.

Gannon, TA, Keown, K and Polaschek, DLL (2007) Increasing honest responding on cognitive distortions in child molesters: the bogus pipeline revisited. *Sex Abuse*, 19(1), 5–22.

Gavey, N (2005) *Just Sex? The Cultural Scaffolding of Rape*. London: Routledge.

Gawronski, B (2007) Attitudes can be measured! But what is an attitude? *Social Cognition,* 25, 573–81.

Gibbons, FX and Gerrard, M (1997) Health images and their effects on health behavior: social comparison and social influence, in Buunk, B and Gibbons, FX (eds) *Health, Coping and Well-being: Perspectives from Social Comparison Theory*. Mahwah, NJ: Ehrlbaum.

Gibson, S (2011) Milgram's obedience experiments: a rhetorical analysis. *British Journal of Social Psychology*. (In press)

Gilbert, DT (1998) Speeding with Ned: a personal view of the correspondence bias, in Darley, JM and Cooper, J (eds) *Attribution and Social Interaction: The Legacy of E. E. Jones* (pp5–36). Washington, DC: APA Press.

Gilbert, DT and Jones, EE (1986) Perceiver induced constraint: interpretations of a self-generated reality. *Journal of Personality and Social Psychology*, 50(2), 269–80.

Gilbert, DT and Silvera, DS (1996) Overhelping. *Journal of Personality and Social Psychology*, 70, 678–90.

Giles, JW and Heyman, GD (2005) Young children's beliefs about the relationship between gender and aggression. *Child Development*, 76(10), 107–21.

Gilligan, C (1982) *In a Different Voice: Psychological Theory and Women's Development*. Cambridge, MA: Harvard University Press.

Gillmore, M, Archibald, M, Morrison, D, Wilsdon, A, Wells, A, Hoppe, M, Nahom, D and Murowchick, E (2002) Teen sexual behaviour: applicability of the theory of reasoned action. *Journal of Marriage and Family*, 64(4), 885–97.

Goodley, D and Lawthom, R (2008) Disability studies and psychology: emancipatory opportunities, in Gabel, SL and Danforth, S (2008) *Disability and the Politics of Education: An International Reader*. Witney: Peter Lang.

Goodman, S (2010) 'It's not racist to impose limits on immigration': constructing the boundaries of racism in the asylum and immigration debate. *Critical Approaches to Discourse Analysis Across Disciplines*, 4(1), 1–17.

Goodman, S and Burke, S (2010) Oh you don't want asylum seekers, oh you're just racist: a discursive analysis of discussions about whether it is racist to oppose asylum. *Discourse and Society*, 21(3).

Gramzow, RH, Gaertner, L and Sedikides, C (2001) Memory for ingroup and outgroup information in a minimal group context: the self as an informational base. *Journal of Personality and Social Psychology*, 80, 188–205.

Green, AI (2010) Remembering Foucault: queer theory and disciplinary power. *Sexualities*, 13(3).

Greene, S (2003) *The Psychological Development of Girls and Women: Rethinking Change in Time*. London: Routledge.

Grote, NK and Frieze, IH (1994) The measurement of friendship-based love in intimate relationships. *Personal Relationships*, 1(3), 275–300.

Grote, NK, Frieze, IH and Stone, C (1996) Children, family work traditionalism, and marital satisfaction: 'What's love got to do with it?' *Personal Relationships*, 3, 211–28.

Guba, EG and Lincoln, YS (1994) Competing paradigms in qualitative research, in Denzin, NK and Lincoln, YS (1994) *Handbook of Qualitative Research*. New York: Sage.

Hall, S (1996) The West and the rest: discourse and power, in Hall, S, Held, D, Hubert, D and Thompson, K (eds) *Modernity: An Introduction to Modern Societies*. Malden, MA: Blackwell.

Hamberger, J and Hewstone, M (1997) Inter-ethnic contact as a predictor of blatant and subtle prejudice: Tests of a model in four West European nations. *British Journal of Social Psychology*, 36(2), 173–90.

Hamilton, DL (1998) Dispositional and attributional inferences in person perception, in Darley, JM and Cooper, J (eds) *Attribution and Social Interaction: The Legacy of Edward E. Jones*. Washington, DC: American Psychological Association.

Haney, C, Banks, WC and Zimbardo, PG (1973) A study of prisoners and guards in a simulated prison. *Naval Research Review*, 30, 4–17.

Harrell, WA (1978) Physical attractiveness, self-disclosure, and helping behaviour. *The Journal of Social Psychology*, 104, 15–17.

Harrington, MW and Sawyer, M (1992) L2 working memory capacity and L2 reading skills. *Studies in Second Language Acquisition*, 14(1), 25–38.

Hartstone, M and Augoustinos, M (1995) The minimal group paradigm: categorization into two versus three groups. *European Journal of Social Psychology*, 25, 179–93.

Hatfield, E (1988) Passionate and companionate love, in Sternberg, RJ and Barnes, ML (eds) *The Psychology of Love*. New Haven, CT: Yale University Press.

Hatzfeld, J (ed) (2006) *A Time for Machetes: The Rwandan Genocide, The Killers Speak*. London: Serpent's Tail.

Heaven, PCL (2001) *The Social Psychology of Adolescence*. London: Palgrave.

Heaven, PCL and St Quintin, D (2003) Personality factors predict racial prejudice. *Personality and Individual Differences*, 34, 625–34.

Heaven, PCL, Da Silva, T, Carey, C and Holen, J (2004) Loving styles: relationships with personality and attachment styles. *European Journal of Personality*, 18(2), 103–13.

Heider, F (1958) *The Psychology of Interpersonal Relations*. New York: Wiley.

Heilman, M, Wallen, A, Fuchs, D and Tamkins, M (2004) Penalties for success: reactions to women who succeed at male gender-typed tasks. *Journal of Applied Psychology*, 89(3), 416–27.

Hendrick, C and Hendrick, SS (1990) A relation-specific version of the Love Attitudes Scale. *Journal of Social Behaviour and Personality*, 5, 239–54.

Hendrick, C and Hendrick, SS (2004) Sex and romantic love: connects and disconnects, in Harvey, JH, Wenzel, A and Sprecher, S (2004) *The Handbook of Sexuality in Close Relationships*. Mahwah, NJ: Ehrlbaum.

Hendrick, SS and Hendrick, C (1986) A theory and method of love. *Journal of Personality and Social Psychology*, 50, 392–402.

Hendrick, SS and Hendrick, C (1993) Lovers as friends. *Journal of Social and Personal Relationships*, 10(3), 459–66.

Hendrick, SS and Hendrick, C (eds) (2000) *Close Relationships: A Sourcebook*. Thousand Oaks, CA: Sage.

Henriques, J with Hollway, W, Urwin, C, Venn, C and Walkerdine, V (1998) *Changing the Subject: Psychology, Social Regulation and Subjectivity*. 2nd edition. London: Routledge.

Hesketh, B (1984) Attribution theory and unemployment: Kelley's covariation model, self-esteem and locus of control. *Journal of Vocational Behaviour*, 24(1), 94–109.

Hewstone, M (ed) (1983) *Attribution Theory: Social and Functional Extensions*. Oxford: Basil Blackwell.

Hewstone, M and Jaspars, JMF (2010) Intergroup relations and attribution processes, in Tajfel, H (ed) *Social Identity and Intergroup Relations*. Cambridge: Cambridge University Press.

Hey, V (2003) Joining the club: academia and working class femininities. *Gender and Education*, 15(2), 319–35.

Hibbert, S, Smith, A, Davies, A and Ireland, F (2007) Guilt appeals: persuasion knowledge and charitable giving. *Psychology and Marketing*, 24(8), 723–42.

Hochschild, AR (1997) *The Time Bind: When Work Becomes Home and Home Becomes Work*. New York: Henry Holt.

Hodgkins, SL and Baility, S (2009) The discursive construction and invalidation of disability, in Marshall, CA, Kendall, E, Banks, M and Glover, RMS (eds) *Disabilities: Insights from Across Fields and Around the World* (pp213–29). Westport, CT: Praeger Press.

Hogg, MA (1992) *The Social Psychology of Group Cohesiveness*. New York: New York University Press.

Hogg, MA (2006) Social identity theory, in Burke, PJ (ed) *Contemporary Social Psychological Theory*. Palo Alto, CA: Stanford University Press.

Hogg, MA and Vaughan, GM (1998) *Social Psychology*. 2nd edition. Glasgow: Prentice Hall.

Hogg, MA and Vaughan, GM (2002) *Social Psychology*. 3rd edition. London: Prentice Hall.

Hogg, MA and Vaughan, GM (2008) *Social Psychology*. 5th edition. London: Pearson.

Hollway, W (1989) Gender difference and the production of subjectivity, in Henriques, J, Hollway, W, Urwin, C, Venn, C and Walkerdine, V (eds) *Changing the Subject*. Cambridge: Cambridge University Press.

Hollway, W (1998) Gender difference and the production of subjectivity, in Henriques, J, Hollway, W, Urwin, C, Venn, C and Walkerdine, V (eds) *Changing the Subject: Psychology, Social Regulation and Subjectivity,* 2nd edition. London: Routledge.

Hollway, W, Urwin, C, Venn, C and Walkerdine, V (eds) (1989) *Changing the Subject* (pp227–63). Cambridge: Cambridge University Press.

Honeycutt, HM (1981) Altruism and social exchange theory: the vicarious rewards of the altruist. *Mid-American Review of Sociology*, 6(1), 93–9.

Hook, D (2001) Discourse, knowledge, materiality, history: Foucault and discourse analysis. *Theory and Psychology*, 11(4), 521–47.

Horkheimer, M (1995) *Between Philosophy and Social Science*. Boston, MA: MIT Press.

Horner, MS (1972) Toward an understanding of achievement-related conflicts in women. *Journal of Social Issues*, 28, 157–75.

Hovland, CI, Janis, IL and Kelley, HH (1953) *Communications and Persuasion: Psychological Studies in Opinion Change*. New Haven, CT: Yale University Press.

Hovland, CI and Weiss, W (1951) The influence of source credibility on communication effectiveness. *Public Opinion Quarterly*, 15, 635–50.

Howitt, D, Billig, M, Cramer, D, Edwards, D, Kniveton, B, Potter, J and Radley, A (1989) *Social Psychology: Conflicts and Continuities*. Milton Keynes and Philadelphia, PA: Open University Press.

Hsiung, RO and Bagozzi, RP (2003) Validating the relationship qualities of influence and persuasion with the family social relations model. *Human Communication Research*, 29: 81–110.

Hyde, JS (2005) The gender similarities hypothesis. *American Psychologist,* 60, 581–92.

Hyde, JS (2007) New directions in the study of gender similarities and differences. *Current Directions in Psychological Science,* 16, 259–63.

Ikegami, T (2010) Precursors and consequences of in-group disidentification: status system beliefs and social identity. *Identity: An International Journal of Theory and Research,* 10(4), 233–53.

Ingleby, D (1986) Development in social context, in Richards, M and Light, P (eds) *Children of Social Worlds* (pp297–317). Cambridge: Polity Press.

Irwing, P and Lynn, R (2005) Sex differences in the means and variability on the progressive matrixes of university students. *British Journal of Social Psychology*, 96(4), 505–24.

Isen, AM (1970) Success, failure, attention, and reaction to others: the warm glow of success. *Journal of Personality and Social Psychology*, 15(4), 294–301.

Isen, AM, Horn, N and Rosenhan, DL (1973) Effects of success and failure on children's generosity. *Journal of Personality and Social Psychology*, 27(2), 239–47.

Janis, IL (1972) *Victims of Groupthink*. Boston, MA: Houghton Mifflin.

Jenkins, R (2009) *Social Identity.* London: Routledge.

Jetten, J, Hornsey, MJ and Adarves-Yorno, I (2006) When group members admit to being conformist: the role of relative intragroup status in conformity self-reports. *Personality and Social Psychology Bulletin*, 32, 162–773.

Johnson, R and Downing, L (1979) Deindividuation and valence of cues: effects on prosocial and antisocial behaviour. *Journal of Personality and Social Psychology*, 37, 1532–38.

Johnston, TC, Clark, MJ, Dingle, GA and FitzGerald, G (2003) Factors influencing Queenslanders' willingness to perform bystander cardiopulmonary resuscitation. *Resuscitation,* 56(1), 67–75.

Jonas, E, Schimel, J, Greenberg, J and Pyszczynski, T (2002) The Scrooge effect: evidence that mortality salience increases prosocial attitudes and behavior. *Personality and Social Psychology Bulletin*, 28, 1342–53.

Jones, E and Sigall, H (1971) The bogus pipeline: a new paradigm for measuring affect and attitude. *Psychological Bulletin*, 76(5), 349–64.

Jones, EE (1979) The rocky road from acts to dispositions. *American Psychologist*, 34, 107–17.

Jones, EE and Davis, KE (1965) From acts to dispositions: the attribution process in person perception, in Berkowitz, L (ed) *Advances in Experimental Social Psychology* (pp 219–66). New York: Academic Press.

Jones, EE and Harris, VA (1967) The attribution of attitudes. *Journal of Experimental Social Psychology,* 3, 1–24.

Jones, EE and Nisbett, RE (1972) The actor and the observer: divergent perceptions of the causes of the behavior, in Jones, EE, Kanouse, DE, Kelley, HH, Nisbett, RE, Valins, S and Weiner, B (eds) *Attribution: Perceiving the Causes of Behavior* (pp79–94). Morristown, NJ: General Learning Press.

Judd, CH, Ryan, CS and Park, B (1991) Accuracy in the judgment of in-group and out-group variability. *Journal of Personality and Social Psychology*, 61, 366–79.

Kahana, E, Midlarsky, E and Kahana, B (1987) Beyond dependency, autonomy and exchange: prosocial behavior in late-life adaptation. *Social Justice Research,* 1(4), 439–59.

Kameda, T, Ohtsubo, Y and Takezawa, M (1997) Centrality in socio-cognitive network and social influence: an illustration in a group decision making context. *Journal of Personality and Social Psychology*, 73, 296–309.

Katz, D (1960) The functional approach to the study of attitudes. *Public Opinion Quarterly, 24,* 163–204.

Kazdin, AE (2003) *Research Design in Clinical Psychology.* 4th edition. Boston: Allyn and Bacon.

Kelley, HH (1967) Attribution theory in social psychology, in Levine, D (ed) *Nebraska symposium on motivation* (pp 192–238). Lincoln, NE: University of Nebraska.

Kenny, DT and Osborne, MS (2006) Music performance anxiety: new insights from young musicians. *Advances in Cognitive Psychology,* 2, 103–112.

Kerr, NL (1983) Motivation losses in small groups: a social dilemma analysis. *Personality and Social Psychology,* 45, 819–28.

Kerr, NL and Bruun, SE (1983) Dispensability of member effort and group motivation losses: free-rider effects. *Journal of Personality and Social Psychology,* 44, 78–94.

Kiesler, S, Zdaniuk, B, Lundmark, V and Kraut, R (2000) Troubles with the Internet: the dynamics of help at home. *Human-Computer Interaction*, 15(4), 323–51.

Kinder, DR and Kam, CD (2009) *Us against Them: Ethnocentric Foundations of American Public Opinion.* Chicago, IL: University of Chicago Press.

Köhler, W (1929) *Gestalt Psychology*. New York: Liveright.

Kokish, R, Levenson, JS and Blasingame, GD (2005) Post conviction sex offender polygraph examination: client-reported perceptions of utility and accuracy. *Sexual Abuse: A Journal of Research and Treatment,* 17(2), 211–21.

Koole, SL, Dijksterhuis, A and van Knippenberg, A (2001) What's in a name: Implicit self-esteem. *Journal of Personality and Social Psychology*, 80, 614–27.

Kravitz, DA and Martin, B (1986) Ringelmann rediscovered. *Journal of Personality and Social Psychology,* 50(5), 936–41.

Krieger, ND, Williams, R and Moss, NE (1997) Measuring social class in US public health research: concepts, methodologies, and guidelines. *Annual Review of Public Health*, 18, 341–78.

Krosnick, JA, Judd, CM and Wittenbrink, B (2005) Attitude measurement, in Albarracín, D, Johnson, BT and Zanna, MP (eds) *Handbook of Attitudes and Attitude Change* (pp21–76). Mahwah, NJ: Erlbaum.

La Piere, RT (1934) Attitudes vs actions. *Social Forces*, 13, 230–7.

Lahmeyer, HW, Miller, M and DeLeon-Jones, F (*1982*) Anxiety and mood fluctuation during the normal menstrual cycle. *Psychosomatic Medicine*, 44, 183–94.

Latané, B and Dabbs, JM (1975) Sex, group size, and helping in three cities. *Sociometry*, 38, 180–94.

Latané, B and Darley, JM (1969; 1970) *The Unresponsive Bystander: Why Doesn't He Help?* New York: Appleton-Century-Crofts.

Latané, B and Darley, JM (1976) Help in a crisis: bystander response to an emergency, in Thibault, JW and Spence, JT (eds) *Contemporary Topics in Social Psychology* (pp309–32). Morristown, NJ: General Learning Press.

Latané, B and Wolf, S (1981) The social impact of majorities and minorities. *Psychological Review*, 88, 438–53.

Latané, B, Williams, KD and Harkins, SG (1979) Many hands make light the work: the causes and consequences of social loafing. *Journal of Personality and Social Psychology*, 37, 823–832.

Laurenceau, JP, Barrett, LF and Pietromonaco, PR (1998) Intimacy as an interpersonal process: the importance of self-disclosure, partner disclosure, and perceived partner responsiveness in interpersonal exchanges. *Journal of Personality and Social Psychology*, 51, 1173–82.

Lazard, L (2009a) *Deconstructing Sexual Harassment*. Unpublished PhD thesis.

Lazard, L (2009b) Moving past powerlessness? An exploration of the heterosexualisation of sexual harassment. *Psychology of Women Section Review,* 11(1), pp3–11, 1466–3724.

Le Bon, G [1895] (2002). *The Crowd*. Mineola, NY: Dover Publications.

Lee, JA (1988) Love-styles, in Sternberg, RJ and Barnes, ML (eds) *The Psychology of Love* (pp38–67). New Haven, CT: Yale University Press.

Levett, A, Kottler, A, Burman, E and Parker, I (eds) (1997) *Culture, Power and Difference: Discourse Analysis in South Africa*. London: Zed Books.

Levine, M (1999) Rethinking bystander non-intervention: social categorisation and the evidence of witnesses at the James Bulger murder trial. *Human Relations*, 52(9), 1133–55.

Levine, M and Kaarbo, J (2001) Minority influence in political decision-making groups, in De Dreu, CKW and De Vries, NK (eds) *Group Consensus and Minority Influence: Implications for Innovation* (pp229–57). Malden, MA: Blackwell Publishers.

Levine, M, Prosser, A, Evans, D and Reicher, S (2005) Identity and emergency intervention: how social group membership and inclusiveness of group boundaries shapes helping behavior. *Personality and Social Psychology Bulletin*, 31, 443–53.

Lewis, I, Watson, B and White, M (2008) An examination of message-relevant affect in road safety messages: should road safety advertisements aim to make us feel good or bad? *Transportation Research*, 11, 403–17.

Linville, PW, Fischer, GW and Yoon, C (1996) Perceived covariation among the features of ingroup and outgroup members: the outgroup covariation effect. *Journal of Personality and Social Psychology*, 70, 421–36.

Lippmann, W (1922) *Public Opinion*. Boston, MA: Little Brown.

Loseke, D (2009) Examining emotion as discourse: emotion codes and presidential speeches justifying war. *The Sociological Quarterly*, 50(3), 497–524.

Lynch, K and O'Neill, C (1994) The colonisation of social class in education. *British Journal of Sociology of Education,* 15(3), 307–24.

Maass, A and Clark, RD (1984) Hidden impact of minorities: fifteen years of minority influence research. *Psychological Bulletin,* 95, 428–50.

MacKinnon, CA (1989) *Towards a Feminist Theory of the State.* Boston, MA: Harvard University Press.

Macpherson, W (1999) *The Stephen Lawrence Inquiry.* London: HM Stationery Office.

Maio, GR and Olson, JM (2000) What is a value-expressive attitude?, in Maio, GR and Olson, JM (eds) *Why We Evaluate: Functions of Attitudes* (pp249–69). Mahwah, NJ: Erlbaum.

Malle, BF (2004) *How the Mind Explains Behaviour: Folk Explanations, Meaning and Social Interaction.* Cambridge, MA: MIT Press.

Manning, R, Levine, M and Collins, A (2007) The Kitty Genovese murder and the social psychology of helping: the parable of the 38 witnesses. *American Psychologist,* 62, 555–62.

Marks, G and Miller, N (1987) Ten years of research on the false consensus effect: an empirical and theoretical review. *Psychological Bulletin,* 102, 72–90.

Marois, R and Ivanoff, J (2005) Capacity limits of information processing in the brain. *Trends in Cognitive Sciences,* 9(6), 296–305.

Marston, PJ, Hecht, ML and Robers, T (1987) 'True love ways': the subjective experience and communication of romantic love. *Journal of Social and Personal Relationships,* 4, 387–407.

Marston, PJ, Hecht, ML, Manke, ML, McDaniel, S and Reeder, H (1998) The subjective experience of intimacy, passion, and commitment in heterosexual loving relationships. *Personal Relationships,* 5, 15–30.

Martin, CL and Halverson, CF (1981) A schematic processing model of sex-typing and stereotyping in children. *Child Development,* 52, 1119–34.

Martin, R and Hewstone, M (2003) Social influence processes of control and change: conformity, obedience to authority, and innovation, in Hogg, MA and Cooper, J (eds) *The Sage Handbook of Social Psychology* (pp347–66). London: Sage.

Martin, R, Martin, PY, Smith, JR and Hewstone, M (2007) Majority versus minority influence and prediction of behavioral intentions and behaviour. *Journal of Experimental Social Psychology,* 43, 763–71.

Maruna, S and Mann, R (2006) Fundamental attribution errors? Re-thinking cognitive distortions. *Legal and Criminological Psychology,* 11, 155–77.

Marx, K (1902) *Capital: A Critique of Political Economy.* London: Swan Sonnenschein, Lowrey and Co.

Marx, DM and Stapel, DA (2006) It's all in the timing: emotional reactions to stereotype threat before and after taking a test. *European Journal of Social Psychology*, 36, 687–98.

Mausbach, BT, Semple, SJ, Strathdee, SA and Patterson, TL (2009) Predictions of safer sex intentions and protected sex among heterosexual HIV-negative methamphetamine users: an expanded model of the theory of planned behavior. *AIDS Care*, 21, 17–24.

McArthur, LA (1972) The how and what of why: some determinants and consequences of causal attribution. *Journal of Personality and Social Psychology*, 2, 171–93.

McFarlane, J, Martin, C and Williams, T (1988) Mood fluctuations: women versus men and menstrual versus other cycles. *Psychology of Women Quarterly*, 12, 201–23.

McGuire, WJ (1985) Attitudes and attitude change, in Lindzey, G and Aronson, E (eds) *Handbook of Social Psychology* (pp233–346). New York: Random House.

Mead, M (1935) Sex *and Temperament in Three Primitive Societies*. New York: Morrow.

Messerschmidt, R (1933) The suggestibility of boys and girls between the ages of six and sixteen years. *Journal of Genetic Psychology*, 43, 422–7.

Milgram, S (1974) *Obedience to Authority: An Experimental View*. New York: HarperCollins.

Miller, A (2009) Reflections on 'Replicating Milgram' (Burger, 2009) *American Psychologist*, 64, 20–7.

Miller, GR and Boster, FJ (1988) Persuasion in personal relationships, in Duck, S (ed) *Handbook of Personal Relationships* (pp275–88). London: Wiley.

Miller, WR (1983) Motivational interviewing with problem drinkers. *Behavioural Psychotherapy*, 11, 147–72.

Moeller, G and Applezweig, MH (1957) A motivational factor in conformity. *Journal of Abnormal and Social Psychology*, 55, 114–20.

Moscovici, S (1976) *Social Influence and Social Change*. London: Academic Press.

Moscovici, S (1980) Towards a theory of conversion behaviour, in Berkowitz, L (ed) *Advances in Experimental Social Psychology*, 13. New York: Academic Press.

Moscovici, S (1981) On social representations, in Forgas, JP (ed) *Social Cognition: Perspectives on Everyday Understanding* (pp181–209). London: Academic Press.

Moscovici, S (1984) The phenomenon of social representations, in Farr, RM and Moscovici, S (eds) *Social Representations*. Cambridge: Cambridge University Press.

Moscovici, S (1985) Social influence and conformity, in Lindzey, G and Aronson, E (eds) *Handbook of Social Psychology* (pp347–412). New York: McGraw-Hill.

Moscovici, S (1988) Notes towards a description of social representations. *European Journal of Social Psychology*, 18, 211–50.

Moscovici, S (1993) *The Invention of Society: Psychological Explanations for Social Phenomena*. Cambridge: Polity Press.

Moscovici, S (1998) The history and actuality of social representations, in Flick, U (ed) *The Psychology of the Social* (pp209–47). Cambridge: Cambridge University Press.

Moscovici, S (2001) *Social Representations: Explorations in Social Psychology*. New York: New York University Press.

Moscovici, S and Faucheux, C (1972) Social influence, conformity bias and the study of active minorities, in Berkowitz, L (ed) *Advances in Experimental Social Psychology*, vol 6. New York: Academic Press.

Mosovici, S and Nemeth, C (1974) Social influence II: minority influence, in Nemeth, C (ed) *Social Psychology: Classic and Contemporary Integrations* (pp217–49). Chicago: Rand McNally.

Mucchi-Faina, A, Pacilli, MG and Pagliaro, S (2010) Minority influence, social change, and social stability. *Social and Personality Psychology Compass*, 4, 1111–23.

Mugny, G and Perez, JA (2009) *The Social Psychology of Minority Influence*. Cambridge: Cambridge University Press.

Mulholland, E and van Wersch, A (2007) Stigma, sexually transmitted infections and attendance at the GUM clinic: an exploratory study with implications for the theory of planned behaviour. *Journal of Health Psychology*, 12, 17–31.

Mulilis, JP and Lippa, R (1990) Behavioral changes in earthquake preparedness due to negative threat appeals: a test of protection motivation theory. *Journal of Applied Social Psychology*, 20(8), 619–38.

Mullainathan, S and Washington, E (2009) Sticking with your vote: cognitive dissonance and political attitudes. *American Economic Journal: Applied Economics*, 1(1), 86–111.

Myers, DG (2008) *Social Psychology*. 9th edition. New York: McGraw-Hill.

Nisbett, RE (1981) Lay arbitration rules of inference. *Behavioural and Brain Sciences*, 4, 349–50.

Nisbett, RE and Ross, LD (1980) *Human Inference: Strategies and Shortcomings of Social Judgment*. Englewood Cliffs, NJ: Prentice-Hall.

Nissani, M (1989) An experimental paradigm for the study of conceptual conservatism and change. *Psychological Reports*, 65, 19–24.

Nissani, M (1990) A cognitive reinterpretation of Stanley Milgram's observations on obedience to authority. *American Psychologist*, 45, 1384–5.

Nissani, M and Hoefler-Nissani, DM (1992) Experimental studies of belief-dependence of observations and of resistance to conceptual change. *Cognition and Instruction*, 9, 97–111.

Noller, P (1996) What is this thing called love? Defining the love that supports marriage and family. *Personal Relationships,* 3, 97–115.

Norman, P, Armitage, CJ and Quigley, C (2007) The theory of planned behavior and binge drinking: assessing the impact of binge drinker prototypes. *Addictive Behaviors,* 32, 1753–68.

Nowak, MA, Szamrej, J and Latané, B (1990) From private attitude to public opinion: a dynamical theory of social impact. *Psychological Review,* 97, 362–76.

Office of National Statistics (2010) Pay gap statistics. Available at www.statistics.gov.uk/cci/nugget.asp?id=167

Orne, MT and Holland, CH (1968) On the ecological validity of laboratory deceptions. *International Journal of Psychiatry,* 6, 282–93.

Parker, I (1989) *The Crisis In Modern Social Psychology – And How To End It.* London: Routledge.

Parker, I (1992) *Discourse Dynamics: Critical Analysis for Social and Individual Psychology.* London: Routledge.

Parker, I (2002) *Critical Discursive Psychology.* London: Palgrave.

Parliament of the United Kingdom (1995) *Disability Discrimination Act.* London: Crown Copyright.

Parliament of the United Kingdom (2010) *Equality Act.* London: Crown Copyright.

Passer, M, Smith, R, Holt, N, Bremner, A, Sutherland, E and Vliek, MLW (2009) *Psychology: The Science of Mind and Behaviour* (European edition). London: McGraw-Hill.

Passini, S and Morselli, D (2009) Authority relationships between obedience and disobedience. *New Ideas in Psychology,* 27 (1), 96–106.

Pendry, L and Carrick, R (2001) Doing what the mob do: priming effect on conformity. *European Journal of Social Psychology,* 31, 83–92.

Perry, K and Bussey, DG (1979) The social learning theory of sex differences: imitation is alive and well. *Journal of Personality and Social Psychology,* 37(10), 1699–712.

Perry-Jenkins, M, Goldberg, AE, Pierce, CP and Sayer, AG (2007), Shift work, role overload, and the transition to parenthood. *Journal of Marriage and Family,* 69: 123–38.

Petty, RE and Briñol, P (2008) Persuasion: from single to multiple to metacognitive processes. *Perspectives on Psychological Science,* 3, 2137–47.

Petty, RE and Cacioppo, JT (1981) *Attitudes and Persuasion: Classic and Contemporary Approaches.* Dubuque, IA: Wm. C. Brown.

Petty, RE and Cacioppo, JT (1986) The elaboration likelihood model of persuasion, in Berkowitz, L (ed) *Advances in Experimental Social Psychology* (vol 19, pp123–205). New York: Academic Press.

Petty, RE, Briñol, P and Priester, JR (2009) Mass media attitude change: implications of the elaborated likelihood model of persuasion, in Bryant, J and Oliver, MB (2009) *Media Effects: Advances in Theory and Research*. New York: Routledge.

Petty, RE, Cacioppo, JT and Goldman, R (1981) Personal involvement as a determinant of argument-based persuasion. *Journal of Personality and Social Psychology*, 41, 847–55.

Petty, RE and Wegener, DT (1998) Attitude change: multiple roles for persuasion variables, in Gilbert, D, Fiske, S and Lindzey, G (eds) *The Handbook of Social Psychology*. 4th edition (pp323–90). New York: McGraw-Hill.

Petty, RE, Wegener, DT and Fabrigar, LR (1997) Attitudes and attitude change. *Annual Review of Psychology*, 48, 609–47.

Philips, L (2006) *Mental Illness and the Body: Beyond Diagnosis*. London: Taylor and Francis.

Piliavin, JA, Dovidio, JF, Gaertner, SL and Clark, RD (1981) *Emergency Intervention*. New York: Academic Press.

Plumm, KM and Terrance, CA (2009) Battered women who kill: the impact of expert testimony and empathy induction in the court room. *Violence Against Women*, 15(2), 186–205.

Potter, J and Wetherell, M (1987) *Discourse and Social Psychology: Beyond Attitudes and Behaviour*. London: Sage.

Quattrone, GA (1985) On the congruity between internal states and action. *Psychological Bulletin*, 98, 3–40.

Rabbie, JM and Horwitz, M (1969) Arousal of ingroup-outgroup bias by a chance win or loss. *Journal of Personality and Social Psychology*, 13, 269–77.

Race Mackey, E and La Greca, AM (2008) Does this make me look fat? Peer crowd and peer contributions to adolescent girls' weight control behaviours. *Journal of Youth Adolescence*, 37, 1097–110.

Reay, D (1998) *Class Work: Mothers' Involvement in Their Primary Schooling*. London: University College Press.

Regan, PC, Kocan, ER and Whitlock, T (1998) Ain't love grand! A prototype analysis of the concept of romantic love. *Journal of Social and Personal Relationships*, 15 (3), 411–20.

Reicher, S (1984) The St. Paul's riot: an explanation of the limits of crowd action in terms of a social identity model. *European Journal of Social Psychology*, 14, 1–21.

Reicher, S (2008) The psychology of crowd dynamics, in Hogg, MA and Tindale, RS (eds) *Blackwell Handbook of Social Psychology: Group processes* (pp182–208). Oxford: Blackwell.

Reis, HT and Shaver, P (1988) Intimacy as an interpersonal process, in Duck, S (ed) *Handbook of Personal Relationships*. Chichester: Wiley.

Renold, E (2005) *Girls, Boys and Junior Sexualities: Exploring Childrens' Gender and Sexual Relations in the Primary School*. London: Routledge Falmer.

Reynolds, J and Wetherell, M (2003) The discursive climate of singleness: the consequences for women's negotiation of a single identity. *Feminism and Psychology*, 13(4), 489–510.

Rise, J, Kovac, V, Kraft, P and Moan, IS (2008) Predicting the intention to quit smoking and quitting behaviour: extending the theory of planned behaviour. *British Journal of Health Psychology*, 13, 291–310.

Robinson, R (2005) Queerying gender: heteronormativity in early childhood education. *Australian Journal of Early Childhood*, 30(2), 19–28.

Robinson-Staveley, K and Cooper, J (1990) Mere presence, gender and reactions to computers: studying human-computer interaction in the social context. *Journal of Experimental Social Psychology*, 26, 168–83.

Rodriguez, H, Trainor, J and Quarantelli, EL (2006) Rising to the challenges of a catastrophe: the emergent and prosocial behavior following Hurricane Katrina. *The Annals of the American Academy of Political and Social Science*, 604, 82–102.

Rodriguez, R, Marchand, E, Ng, Janet and Stice, E (2008) Effects of a cognitive dissonance-based eating disorder prevention program are similar for Asian American, Hispanic, and White participants. *International Journal of Eating Disorders*, 41(7), 618–25.

Rosenberg, M (1965) *Society and the Adolescent Self-image*. Princeton, NJ: Princeton University Press.

Rosenberg, MJ and Hovland, CI (1960) Cognitive, affective and behavioural components of attitude, in Rosenberg, MJ, Hovland, CI, McGuire, WJ, Abelson, RP and Brehm, JW (eds) *Attitude Organisation and Change: An Analysis of Consistency Among Attitude Components*. New Haven, CT: Yale University.

Rosenthal, R and Fode, KL (1963) The effect of experimenter bias on the performance of the albino rat. *Behavioral Science*, 8, 183–9.

Rosenthal, R and Lawson, R (1964) A longitudinal study of the effects of experimenter bias on the operant learning of laboratory rats. *Journal of Psychiatric Research*, 2, 61–72.

Rosnow, RL and Rosenthal, R (1997) *People Studying People: Artifacts and Ethics in Behavioral Research*. New York: Freeman.

Ross, L (1977) The intuitive psychologist and his shortcomings, in Berkowitz, L (ed) *Advances in Experimental Social Psychology* (pp 174–220). New York: Academic Press.

Ross, L, Greene, D and House, P (1977) The false consensus phenomenon: an attributional bias in self-perception and social perception processes. *Journal of Experimental Social Psychology*, 13(3), 279–301.

Rothbart, M and John, OP (1985) Social categorization and behavioral episodes: a cognitive analysis of the effects of intergroup contact. *Journal of Social Issues*, 41(3), 81–104.

Russell, N (2009) *Stanley Milgram's Obedience to Authority Experiments: Towards an Understanding of Their Relevance in Explaining Aspects of the Nazi Holocaust*. Wellington: Victoria University of Wellington.

Samman, E, McAuliffe, E and MacLachlan, M (2009) The role of celebrity in endorsing poverty reduction through international aid. *International Journal of Nonprofit and Voluntary Sector Marketing*, 14, 137–48.

Sayce, L and Boardman, J (2008) Disability rights and mental health in the UK: recent developments of the Disability Discrimination Act. *Advances in Psychiatric Treatment*, 14, 265–75.

Schlenker, BR, Pontari, BA and Christopher, AN (2001) Excuses and character: personal and social implications of excuses. *Personality and Social Psychology Review*, 5, 15–32.

Schmader, T and Johns, M (2003) Convergent evidence that stereotype threat reduces working memory capacity. *Journal of Personality and Social Psychology*, 85, 440–52.

Schneider, DJ (2004) *The Psychology of Stereotyping*. New York: Guilford Press.

Schwarzer, R (1992) Self-efficacy in the adoption and maintenance of health behaviors: theoretical approaches and a new model, in Schwarzer, R (ed) *Self-efficacy: Thought Control of Action* (pp217–43). Washington, DC: Hemisphere.

Scott, J (2005) *Industrialism: A Dictionary of Sociology*. Oxford: Oxford University Press.

Scott, WE (1966) Activation theory and task design. *Organizational Behavior and Human Performance*, 1, 3–30.

Scroggins, D (2005) The Dutch-Muslim culture war. *The Nation*, 21–5.

Semin, GR and Manstead, ASR (1983) *Accountability of Conduct*. London: Academic Press.

Shamir, M and Sagiv-Schifter, T (2006) Conflict, identity and tolerance: Israel and the Al-Aqsa intifada. *Political Psychology*, 27, 569–96.

Sher, PJ and Lee, S (2009) Consumer skepticism and online reviews: an elaboration likelihood model perspective. *Social Behavior and Personality*, 37(1), 137–44.

Sherif, M, Harvey, OJ, White, BJ, Hood, WR and Sherif, CW (1961) *Intergroup Conflict and Cooperation: The Robbers Cave Experiment*. Norman, OK: University of Oklahoma.

Sherif, M and Sherif, CW (1953) *Groups in Harmony and Tension*. New York: Harper and Row.

Sherif, M, White, BJ and Harvey, OJ (1955) Status in experimentally produced groups. *American Journal of Sociology*, 60, 370–79.

Shotter, J (1989) Vygotsky's psychology: joint activity in a developmental zone. *New Ideas in Psychology*, 7, 185–204.

Sidanius, J, Ekehammar, B and Brewer, RM (1986) The political socialization determinants of higher order sociopolitical space: a Swedish example. *Journal of Social Psychology*, 126(1), 7–22.

Simon, B, Loewy, M, Stürmer, S, Weber, U, Freytag, P, Habig, C, Kampmeier, C and Spahlinger, P (1998) Collective identification and social movement participation. *Journal of Personality and Social Psychology*, 74(3), 646–58.

Simon, B, Stürmer, S and Steffens, K (2000) Helping individuals or group members? The role of individual and collective identification in AIDS volunteerism. *Personality and Social Psychology Bulletin*, 26(4), 497–506.

Simpson, JA, Campbell, B and Berscheid, E (1986) The association between romantic love and marriage: Kephart twice revisited. *Personality and Social Psychology Bulletin*, 12, 363–72.

Skinner, BF (1971) *Beyond Freedom and Dignity*. New York: Knopf.

Smith, CM, Tindale, RS and Dugoni, BL (1996) Minority and majority influence in freely interacting groups: qualitative versus quantitative differences. *British Journal of Social Psychology*, 35, 137–49.

Smith, DE (1988) *The Everyday World as Problematic: A Feminist Sociology*. Boston, MA: Northeastern University Press.

Smith, JA (1996) Beyond the divide between cognition and discourse: using interpretative phenomenological analysis in health psychology. *Psychology and Health*, 11, 261–71.

Smith, JA and Eatough, V (2006) Interpretative phenomenological analysis, in Breakwell, G, Fife-Schaw, C, Hammond, S and Smith, JA (eds) *Research Methods in Psychology*. 3rd edition. London: Sage.

Smith, R, Miller, DA, Maitner, AT, Crump, SA, Garcia-Marques, T and Mackie, DM (2006) Familiarity can increase stereotyping. *Journal of Experimental Social Psychology*, 42, 471–78.

Smith, JA and Osborn, M (2003) Interpretative phenomenological analysis, in Smith, JA (ed) *Qualitative Psychology*. London: Sage.

Solnit, R (2009) *A Paradise Built in Hell*. New York: Viking.

Sprecher, S and Regan, PC (1998) Passionate and companionate love in courting and young married couples. *Sociological Inquiry*, 68(2), 163–85.

Stainton Rogers, R, Stenner, P, Gleeson, K and Stainton Rogers, W (1995) *Social Psychology: A Critical Agenda*. Cambridge: Polity Press.

Stayman, DM and Kardes, FR (1992) Spontaneous inference processes in advertising effectiveness. *Journal of Consumer Psychology*, 1(2), 125–42.

Steele, CM and Aronson, J (1995) Stereotype threat and the intellectual test performance of African Americans. *Journal of Personality and Social Psychology*, 69, 797–811.

Steele, CM (1988) The psychology of self-affirmation: sustaining the integrity of the self, in Berkowitz, L (ed) *Advances in Experimental Social Psychology*, vol 21, pp261–302. New York: Academic Press.

Stephens, NM, Markus, HR and Townsend, SSM (2007) Choice as an act of meaning: the case of social class. *Journal of Personality and Social Psychology*, 93, 814–30.

Stephenson, MT, Benoit, WL and Tschida, DA (2001) Testing the mediating role of cognitive responses in the elaboration likelihood model. *Communication Studies*, 52, 324–37.

Sternberg, RJ (1986) A triangular theory of love. *Psychological Review*, 93, 119–35.

Sternberg, RJ (1995) Love as a story. *Journal of Social and Personal Relationships,* 12, 541–6.

Sternberg, RJ (1996) Love stories. *Personal Relationships,* 3, 59–79.

Sternberg, RJ (1998) *Cupid's Arrow: The Course of Love Through Time.* New York, NJ: Cambridge University Press.

Sternberg, RJ and Weiss, K (2006) *The New Psychology of Love.* London/New Haven, NJ: Yale University Press.

Stewart-Knox, BJ, Sittlington, J, Rugkåsa, J, Harrison, S, Treacy, M and Abaunza, P (2005) Smoking and peer groups: results from a longitudinal qualitative study of young people in Northern Ireland. *British Journal of Social Psychology*, 44, 397–414.

Stone, GL (2002) The lexicon and sociolinguistic codes of the working-class Afrikaans-speaking Cape Peninsula coloured community, in Mesthrie, R, *Language in South Africa* (pp394–403). Cambridge: Cambridge University Press.

Stott, C, Adang, O, Livingstone, A and Schreiber, M (2008) Tackling football hooliganism: a quantitative study of public order, policing and crowd psychology. *Psychology, Public Policy, and Law,* 4(2), 115–41.

Stroebe W, Diehl, M and Abakoumkin, G (1992) The illusion of group productivity. *Personality and Social Psychology Bulletin*, 18 (5), 643–50.

Strassen, N (1995) *Defending pornography*, New York: Scribner.

Sutton, J (2010) The battle of the sexes: Jon Sutton interviews Cordelia Fine about neurosexism and more. *The Psychologist,* 23(11), 900–3.

Tajfel, H (1981) *Human Groups and Social Categories.* Cambridge: Cambridge University Press.

Tajfel, H (1982) Social psychology of intergroup relations. *Annual Review of Psychology*, 33, 1–39.

Tajfel, H and Fraser, C (eds) (1978) *Introducing Social Psychology.* Harmondsworth: Penguin.

Tajfel, H and Turner, JC (1979) An integrative theory of intergroup conflict, in Austin, WG and Worchel, S (eds) *The Social Psychology of Intergroup Relations.* Monterey: Brooks-Cole.

Tajfel, H and Turner, JC (1986) The social identity theory of inter-group behaviour, in Worchel, S and Austin, LW (eds) *Psychology of Intergroup Relations.* Chicago: Nelson-Hall.

Tajfel, H, Billig, M, Bundy, RP and Flament, C (1971) Social categorization and intergroup behaviour. *European Journal of Social Psychology*, 1(2), 149–78.

Taylor, SE (1981) A categorization approach to stereotyping, in Hamilton, DL (ed) *Cognitive Processes in Stereotyping and Intergroup Behavior* (pp 88–114). Hillsdale, NJ: Erlbaum.

Tedeschi, JT, Schlenker, BR and Bonoma, TV (1971) Cognitive dissonance: private ratiocination or public spectacle? *American Psychologist*, 26, 685–95.

Terry, G and Braun, V (2009) When I was a bastard: constructions of maturity in men's accounts of masculinity. *Journal of Gender Studies,* 18(2), 165–178.

Tetlock, PE (1985) Accountability: a social check on the fundamental attribution error. *Social Psychology Quarterly,* 48(3), 227–36.

Thibaut, JW and Kelley, HH (1959) *The Social Psychology of Groups.* New York: Wiley.

Thomas, WI and Znaniecki, F (1918) *The Polish Peasant in Europe and America* (vol 1). Boston, MA: Badger.

Thompson, L, Barnett, R and Pearce, J (2009) Scared straight?: fear-appeal anti-smoking campaigns, risk, self-efficacy and addiction. *Health, Risk and Society*, 11, 181–96.

Tormey, S (2004) *Anti-Capitalism.* London: One World Publications.

Tuffin, K (2005) *Understanding Critical Social Psychology.* London: Sage.

Turner, JC, Hogg, MA, Oakes, PJ, Reicher, SD and Wetherell, MS (1987) *Rediscovering the Social Group.* Oxford: Blackwell.

Turner, RH and Killian, L (1987) *Collective Behaviour.* 3rd edition. Englewood Cliffs, NJ: Prentice-Hall.

Twenge, JM, Campbell, WK and Foster, CA (2003) Parenthood and marital satisfaction: a meta-analytic review. *Journal of Marriage and Family*, 65, 574–83.

Ussher, JM (2006) *Managing the Monstrous Feminine: Regulating the Reproductive Body.* London: Routledge.

Valenti, J (2007) *Full Frontal Feminism: A Young Women's Guide to Why Feminism Matters.* Berkeley, CA: Seal Press.

Van Der Stoep, SW and Johnson, DD (2009) *Research Methods for Everyday Life: Blending Qualitative and Quantitative Approaches.* London: Wiley.

van Dijk, TA (2000) New(s) racism: a discourse analytical approach, in Cottle, S (ed) *Ethnic Minorities and the Media* (pp33–49). Milton Keynes: Open University Press.

Van Dyne, L and Saavedra, R (1996) A naturalistic minority influence experiment: effects on divergent thinking, conflict, and originality in work groups. *British Journal of Social Psychology,* 35, 151–67.

Van 't Riet, J, Ruiter, RAC, Werrij, MQ and De Vries, H (2008) The influence of self-efficacy on the effects of framed health messages. *European Journal of Social Psychology*, 38, 800–9.

Verkuyten, M (2008) Multiculturalism and group evaluations among minority and majority groups, in Levy, SR and Killen, M (eds) *Intergroup Attitudes and Relations in Childhood Through Adulthood* (pp157–72). Oxford: Oxford University Press.

Verkuyten, M and Hagendoorn, L (1998) Prejudice and self-categorization: the variable role of authoritarianism and in-group stereotypes. *Personality and Social Psychology Bulletin,* 24, 99–110.

Veroff, J, Young, A and Coon, H (2000) The early years of marriage, in Milardo, R and Duck, S (eds) *Families as Relationships.* Chichester: Wiley.

Vezzali, L, Giovannini, D and Capozza, D (2010), Longitudinal effects of contact on intergroup relations: the role of majority and minority group membership and intergroup emotions. *Journal of Community and Applied Social Psychology,* 20, 462–79.

Walkerdine, V (1990) *Schoolgirl Fictions.* London: Verso.

Walster, E and Festinger, L (1962) The effectiveness of 'overheard' persuasive communications. *Journal of Abnormal and Social Psychology*, 65, 395–402.

Warshaw, P and Davis, FD (1985) Disentangling behavioral intentions and behavioural expectations. *Journal of Experimental Social Psychology,* 21, 213–28.

Watson, JB (1925) *Behaviorism.* New York: People's Institute.

Watts, S and Stenner, P (2005) The subjective experience of partnership love: a Q methodological study. *British Journal of Social Psychology,* 44, 1–26.

Weiner, B, Amirkhan, J, Folkes, VS and Verette, JA (1987) An attributional analysis of excuse giving: Studies of a naive theory of emotion. *Journal of Personality and Social Psychology,* 52, 316–24.

Weisstein, N (1993) Power, resistance and science: a call for a revitalized feminist psychology. *Feminism and Psychology*, 3, 239–245.

Wellman, B and Gulia, M (1999) Virtual communities as communities: net surfers don't ride alone, in Smith, M and Kollock, P (eds) *Communities in Cyberspace* (pp163–90). New York: Routledge.

West, SG and Brown, TJ (1975) Physical attractiveness, the severity of the emergency and helping: a field experiment and interpersonal simulation. *Journal of Experimental Social Psychology*, 11, 531–8.

Westland, G (1978) *Current Crises in Psychology*. London: Heinemann.

Wetherell, M and Maybin, J (1996) The distributed self: a social constructionist perspective, in Stevens, R (ed) *Understanding the Self*. London: Sage.

Wetherell, M and Potter, J (1992) *Mapping the Language of Racism: Discourse and the Legitimation of Exploitation*. Hemel Hempstead: Harvester Wheatsheaf.

Whitehead, S (2002) *Men and Masculinities*. Cambridge: Polity Press.

Wilder, DA (1990) Some determinants of the persuasive power of in-group and out-groups: organization of information and attribution of independence. *Journal of Personality and Social Psychology*, 59, 1202–13.

Wilkinson, S (1997) Feminist psychology, in Fox, D and Prilleltensky, I (eds) (1997) *Critical Psychology: An Introduction* (pp247–64). London: Sage.

Willig, C (2001) *Qualitative Research In Psychology: A Practical Guide to Theory and Method*. Buckingham: Open University Press.

Zajonc, RB (1965) Social facilitation. *Science*, 149, 269–74.

Zajonc, RB (1980) Feelings and thinking: preferences need no inferences. *American Psychologist*, 35(2), 151–75.

Zimbardo, PG (2007) *The Lucifer Effect*. New York: Random House.

Zimbardo, PG (2008) The journey from the Bronx to Stanford to Abu Ghraib, in Levine, R (ed) *Journeys in Social Psychology: Looking Back to Inspire the Future* (pp85–104). London: Taylor and Francis.

Zimbardo, PG, Haney, C, Banks, WC and Jaffe, D (1973) The mind is a formidable jailer: a Pirandellian prison. *The New York Times Magazine,* 8 April.

Zimbardo, PG, Weisenberg, M, Firestone, I and Levy, B (1965) Communicator effectiveness in producing public conformity and private attitude change. *Journal of Personality*, 33, 233–55.

Index

W
Walster, Elaine 157
'War of ghosts' study 142
Wetherell, Margaret 17–18, 18–20, 67,
    169–70
women *see* femininity; gender
work–life balance, relationships 167–8

Y
Yale model of persuasive communication
    72–3, 78–9, 217

Z
Zajonc, Robert 99
Zimbardo, Philip 106–8